THE MAKING OF THE POSTMODERN PRESIDENCY

THE MAKING OF THE POSTMODERN PRESIDENCY

FROM RONALD REAGAN TO BARACK OBAMA

JOHN F. FREIE

Paradigm Publishers

Boulder • London

Copyright © 2011 Paradigm Publishers

Published in the United States by Paradigm Publishers, 2845 Wilderness Place, Suite 200, Boulder, CO 80301 USA.

Paradigm Publishers is the trade name of Birkenkamp & Company, LLC, Dean Birkenkamp, President and Publisher.

Library of Congress Cataloging-in-Publication Data

Freie, John F., 1947–
  The making of the postmodern presidency : from Ronald Reagan to Barack Obama / John F. Freie.
     p. cm.
  Includes bibliographical references and index.
  ISBN 978-1-59451-782-2 (hardcover : alk. paper) — ISBN 978-1-59451-783-9 (pbk. : alk. paper)
  1. Presidents—United States—History—20th century. 2. Presidents—United States—History—21st century. 3. Political leadership—United States—History—20th century. 4. Political leadership—United States—History—21st century. 5. United States—Politics and government—20th century. 6. United States—Politics and government—21st century. I. Title.
  JK511.F74 2011
  973.92092'2—dc22

                                                                        2010053084

Printed and bound in the United States of America on acid-free paper that meets the standards of the American National Standard for Permanence of Paper for Printed Library Materials.

Designed and Typeset by Straight Creek Bookmakers.

15 14 13 12 11   1 2 3 4 5

For Sasha

CONTENTS

PREFACE

The argument of this book is straightforward: The dominant model used to explain presidential behavior, the modern presidency, is becoming less convincing at actually explaining what presidents do and, consequently, it should be replaced with an alternative—the postmodern presidency.

Since the 1960s the concept of postmodernism has been used to explain a wide variety of social and cultural changes that have sent tremors through the landscape of American society. It has been used to explain new cultural forms, architectural innovations, film genres, music impulses, and aesthetics; indeed, it has been applied to the very idea of who we are as humans (i.e., identity politics). Spanning a large number of disciplines, it has challenged modern assumptions about universality, rationality, hierarchy, dualistic thinking, unity, order, and, when pushed to its extreme, the ability to generalize about anything. Vaclav Havel describes the postmodern world as a place "where everything is possible and almost nothing is certain" (1994). Yet, if one reads political science literature about contemporary American politics it is as if the postmodern disruptions that have had such a profound impact elsewhere have somehow skipped over our national political system, especially the presidency. This seems quite improbable. Why have political scientists been reluctant to seriously consider the postmodern presidency?

There are several overlapping reasons that political scientists have hung on to the modern presidency model in spite of growing concerns about its explanatory power. First, all explanatory models, once adopted, contain levels of inertia that make those who have used the models hesitant to discard them, even in light of contradictory evidence. In his study of scientific revolutions, historian of science

Thomas Kuhn (1970) noted that evidence that runs counter to the dominant scientific paradigm seldom was the driving force for a revolution in thinking. Even though alternative paradigms were available, scientists operating within the dominant paradigm preferred to consider contrary evidence "anomalies" rather than reconsider their entire approach.

Rather than jettisoning the modern presidency perspective, presidential scholars have attempted to salvage it by modifying aspects of the model to better address what they perceive is a changing reality. Much like the frog who boils to death because he sits in water that slowly warms until it is at the boiling point, the changes that have been added to the model are so significant that they have now altered the model to such an extent that the originators of the model would no longer recognize it. The anomalies associated with the modern presidency model are piling up and we are approaching a crisis in the ability of the modern presidency model to adequately explain presidential behavior.

A second reason that the postmodern presidency model has not been embraced relates more to the nature of the image of postmodernism itself. Pushed to its logical extremes by literary criticism and esoteric philosophical discourses, postmodernism has come to be defined by those who have nihilistically concluded that nothing can really be known about anything, that the trivial is just as significant as the seemingly important, and that, ultimately, there is no reality. Put off by such philosophical excesses, many in political science (and elsewhere) have simply rejected the entire postmodern approach. This is understandable as such arguments seem to lead us nowhere helpful.

But postmodernism need not be taken to those extremes and, in fact, to do so would be detrimental. I embrace postmodernism from a pragmatic viewpoint. Clearly, something is quite different about politics today than the politics of the 1950s. By being sensitive to postmodern sensibilities, we can see how the objectives and conduct of politics have changed—shifting our gaze allows us to reinterpret anomalies, seeing how they actually fit into an alternative presidential model. While the logical extension of postmodern thought may provide us with no firm grounding, the postmodern "urge" challenges our preconceived ideas of behavior and encourages us to reexamine our assumptions.

Finally, replacing the modern presidency model with an alternative, whether postmodernism or another model, is difficult because of the uncomfortable fusion of the empirical and the normative aspects of the perspective. On the one hand, the modern presidency model is used as a series of assumptions and generalizations and an identification of variables that are used to explain presidential behavior.

Over the years variables have been more precisely defined, data have been collected to test hypotheses, and additional generalizations and conclusions have been arrived at. All this is in keeping with the detached orientation of academics whose primary goal is explanation. But presidency scholars tend to go one step further—they also embrace the modern presidency model normatively. In other words, they not only use the model as an explanatory framework, but they also believe that the model provides a basis for describing how the president *should* behave. Presidency scholars have fused the "is" with the "ought," and because of that they have made it all the more difficult to jettison a model that is becoming increasingly problematic, even as an explanatory tool.

I should be clear at the outset that I am not embracing the postmodern presidency model normatively. I am not arguing that presidents should behave in the manner in which they do. Likewise, I do not embrace the modern presidency model normatively, but I do not think that political scientists should remain neutral, either. We need to be clearer about the frameworks we are using to explain political behavior and the standards we are using to normatively judge that behavior. I believe that the postmodern presidency model provides a better explanation of contemporary presidential behavior today than does the modern model. Normatively, I prefer using criteria consistent with a participatory model of democracy and, when I do so, I find some aspects of the postmodern presidency beneficial, but many more developments troubling. In other words, it is important to separate our attempts to explain political behavior from our assessments of what is beneficial for democracy.

The making of this book must be traced to the presidency classes I have taught over the years. As I struggled to explain the American presidency to students, it became increasingly obvious to me that many of the assumptions I had learned no longer seemed adequate. I would like to thank those students for allowing me to share my concerns and test my interpretations on them. Their responses and questions forced me to clarify my thoughts and look outside of the box for explanations.

The Faculty Research and Development Committee at Le Moyne College was an important source of support for this project. The faculty on that committee made it possible for me to carve out concentrated periods of time by awarding me a sabbatical and a research grant. I am also grateful to Eric Gorham for reading several early chapters, giving me honest feedback, and raising provoking questions, and my many conversations about postmodernism with Dan Stead helped me clarify the indefinable. Neil Kraus took time off from working on his own research to provide me with helpful suggestions; he is a good friend, and in his own research he is also challenging assumptions. My numerous conversations with Bennett Grubbs about the postmodern presidency helped me maintain my enthusiasm for the project, and his questions forced me to rethink a number of my premature conclusions. Henry Kariel was instrumental in introducing me to postmodern politics. I only wish I could be as optimistic about postmodernism as he was. This book would not exist without the support of Jennifer Knerr at Paradigm. I hope this book warrants her trust.

I would also like to thank my student aides, Mary Saitta, Justine Devlin, and Jenna Newburg, for their help in running to the library, downloading articles, and checking the manuscript for accuracy. Any errors that remain, however, are mine. Two anonymous reviewers provided valuable comments that were encouraging and challenging. Special thanks go to my production editor at Paradigm, Candace English. Her suggestions significantly improved the manuscript.

Variations of parts of this book have been presented at the Western Political Science Association Conference, the Southwestern Popular Culture Conference, and the Evaluating the George W. Bush Presidency Conference. In particular, comments from participants at the latter conference helped me identify themes that run throughout this book. Thanks to everyone at the conference and especially to Todd Belt, who organized it.

No person deserves more recognition than my wife and colleague, Susan Behuniak. An author in her own right, she understands how important time is for writing, and she always protected it for me, far more than I did. She willingly took on tasks that freed me to work on this book, read what I wrote, and gave me honest, thoughtful, and constructive criticism. Without her support this book would not exist.

CHAPTER 1

THE MODERN AND THE POSTMODERN

... For the human being in the White House choices are the only means in his own hands by which to shield his sources of real power...
Richard Neustadt (1980, 79)

If six out of ten Americans said they were for something, the president had to be for it too.
George Stephanopoulos (1999, 336)

Since the Reagan administration, there has been a wide and varied range of reactions to presidential behavior on the part of political pundits, academics, and average citizens. These reactions fall into one of three categories: (1) charges of hypocrisy, deception, and lying (or at least "double speak") on the part of the presidents and/or their administrations; (2) outrage at corrupt, perhaps illegal, and probably unconstitutional executive actions; and (3) from a more coolly academic perspective, concerns that the assumptions commonly used to explain presidential behavior are no longer adequate.

Hypocrisy and Deception

Recent presidents have had more than their fair share of critics who have charged them with purposeful deception, hypocrisy, or simply lying about their actions.

Criticized from both the ideological left as well as the right, Ronald Reagan was accused of saying one thing publicly and then pursuing contradictory policies. One critic, Cora Bell, was so taken by his hypocrisy that she wrote a book about it entitled *The Reagan Paradox* (1989). Less amusing was Bill Clinton's lying about having sex with White House intern Monica Lewinsky, which, after many agonizing months, emboldened his enemies and eventually resulted in his impeachment. Still, Clinton's deceptions about his many trysts were considered by many to be personal failures rather than political deceptions. Of greater consequence were George W. Bush's false claims that Iraq possessed weapons of mass destruction, that Saddam Hussein had the capability of striking the United States with missiles, and that he and al Qaeda were allied. Some critics, giving Bush the benefit of the doubt, said that it was a case of poor intelligence, while others charged Bush with blatantly lying in order to justify an unjustifiable invasion of another country.

Throughout history politicians have been accused of hypocrisy, of bending the truth to suit their own purposes, and even of lying. Thus, we should not be surprised or shocked at such criticisms. However, what make recent criticisms indicators that something more than "politics as usual" is going on are the perspectives of the presidential advisors and the presidents themselves. Presidents have embraced the view that truth and reality are malleable and can be created, re-created, and blended at will.

In one instance, for example, Reagan told reporter Hugh Sidey of what he described as an important experience in his life. He recalled the time in college when he played the lead role of Captain Stanhope in the play *Journey's End*. "I never was so carried away in the theater in my life," he told Sidey (quoted in Sidey 1983, 16). The trouble with the story was that it was not true—he never even acted in the play, let alone had the starring role. When confronted, he admitted that he was not in the play but was probably in the audience and felt that "in some strange way I was also on stage" (quoted in Cannon 2000, 22).

This malleable orientation toward the truth is characteristic of a postmodern political perspective that, at least for the presidency, originates during the Reagan years and extends to the present. Presidential advisors have adjusted to such deceptions in their own unique fashion. When pushed by reporters about the truthfulness of one particular story, Press Secretary Larry Speakes testily, but revealingly, responded, "If you tell the same story five times, it's true" (quoted in Nelson 1983). Twenty-five years later, George W. Bush's former press secretary Scott McClellan attempted to explain why such deception occurred: "[Bush] and his advisers confused the propaganda campaign with the high level of candor and honesty so fundamentally needed to build and then sustain public support" (2008, 312). Perhaps satirist Stephen Colbert captures the essence of the problem, implying that we no longer require that things be true; rather they must just *seem* to be true—a characteristic he refers to as "truthiness."

In the postmodern world, truth—or at least the meaning of words—is contextual. In what some have argued was a defining moment of the Clinton administration, Bill Clinton rationalized to a grand jury why he was not lying when he told an aide that he was not having an affair with White House intern Monica Lewinsky. In a deposition later broadcast on national television, he said,

> It depends on what the meaning of the word "is" is. If the—if he—if "is" means is and never has been, that is not—that is one thing. If it means there is none, that was a completely true statement.... Now, if someone had asked me on that day, are you having any kind of sexual relations with Ms. Lewinsky, that is, asked me a question in the present tense, I would have said no. And it would have been completely true. (Clinton 1998, 3)

Thus, what many believe is deception or even lying is far from it if we accept a malleable perspective of reality. In the postmodern presidency, truth and reality are merely perspectives that can be altered at any particular time to suit political purposes.

Illegal Actions

It is almost political tradition that partisan and ideological critics have claimed that presidents have acted illegally at one time or another. Consequently, it is no surprise to find a plethora of such criticisms of recent presidents. Typical of such criticism is conservative William Bennett, who, when he looked at the Clinton White House, saw "mounting evidence of deep corruption. We see this in the attempts to delay and derail criminal and congressional investigations. In the avalanche of lies. In the tactics of intimidation. In the misuse of office. And in the abuse of power" (Bennett 1998, 2). Yet such criticisms are often dismissed as illustrative of the extreme political rhetoric that has passed as political dialogue in recent years.

Far more disturbing are the indictments leveled by political scientists. Their concerns are less about whether presidential actions are legal or not (controversial presidential behavior is often of debatable legality) and more about the abuse of constitutional power. From time to time throughout American history, presidents have taken actions that are clearly unconstitutional. Yet the rationales provided have usually been couched in terms of necessity (e.g., Lincoln's mobilization of troops at the onset of the Civil War) or in terms of powers inherent in the role of commander-in-chief (e.g., Truman's sending troops to Korea). While of questionable constitutionality, both types of actions have generally come to be accepted by the academic and political communities.

But recent actions by George W. Bush have extended presidential claims far beyond the doctrine of necessity or inherent powers. "Not only does Bush claim an inherent constitutional right to send troops into combat without congressional approval, but he asserts an even more farfetched and dangerous power: that his actions are nonreviewable" (Genovese and Han 2006, ix). While most presidential scholars are outraged by such claims, for the purpose of this book the significance of these developments is that they have the effect of undermining political consensus. Constitutions consist of agreed-upon rules and norms of how government is to be structured and how authority is to be distributed. However, in a postmodern environment agreed-upon principles, such as those represented by a constitution, cannot be trusted. Inherently, postmodernism erodes final principles. The outrages expressed by usually detached academics lead to a third indicator that something dramatic has changed in the presidency.

Puzzlement

Some observers of the presidency are coming to realize that assumptions and beliefs used to explain presidential behavior are less persuasive than they once were. Reflecting upon recent presidential decision-making failures, Richard Pious (2002) challenges us: "We need to question the fundamental assumptions of existing theories and use the conventional axioms and assumptions, not as givens from which to deduce the probabilities of power, but as assumptions open to question" (742). Focusing specifically on unilateral presidential actions, Mayer and Price (2002) conclude that "students of the American presidency should revise the prevailing view of presidential power to include the brute facts of presidents' important unilateral capacities" (380). One event that should have been easy to understand and predict was the impeachment of the president. But, as Canon and Mayer (2001) point out, most experts got it wrong: "One of the most interesting features of the impeachment episode is that virtually all the predictions about what would happen or what impeachment would mean—from both elected leaders and the 'punditocracy'—were wrong" (47). Commenting on the office in general, Pika and Thomas (1992) contend that a global reevaluation is necessary: "[T]he end-of-the-century presidency can best be described as still functioning but in need of reassessment" (42).

Some have suggested that presidential scholarship has become so narrowly focused on particular aspects of the presidency that we have failed to see the larger changes that have occurred in the office itself, especially as the presidency relates to the broader political system. "But something has also been lost—or perhaps it was never attained: we are not, by and large, scholars who examine the functioning of the system as a whole, who see the presidency as but one dimension of the larger system.... Yet, by exploring alternative approaches to leadership, we might begin to consider the relationships between culture, leadership, and governance in ways that are both more theoretically informed and more empirically grounded" (Stuckey and Morris 1998, 189).

Still, while some presidential scholars have concerns that the present model does not adequately explain the reality of how presidents actually behave, most nonetheless continue to embrace the dominant paradigm—the *modern presidency*. The origin of that model can be traced to the Franklin Roosevelt administration, and it found its clearest and most forceful articulation in Richard Neustadt's classic book *Presidential Power*, written immediately prior to John Kennedy taking office. The modern presidency has become the accepted model and, with some modification over the years, it continues to be used to explain presidential behavior.

In this book, I argue that the modern presidency model no longer has the explanatory force that it once had and that, in effect, a new model, the *postmodern presidency*, more effectively explains present-day behavior. As scholars continue to analyze behavior from within the modern presidency paradigm, they will continue to conclude that presidential behavior is paradoxical, that presidents seem disingenuous, that candidates with the "wrong" personality traits and political skills get elected, and that abuses of power are going unchecked. However, if we change our focus and employ the postmodern presidency paradigm, we can begin to see how and why presidents act the way they do. By doing so, we will see that deeper cultural assumptions have shifted and that these changes have had a profound impact on the political system in general, and the presidency in particular.

Emerging in full force in the Franklin Roosevelt administration and running through the Carter years, the modern presidency model was effectively used by scholars to analyze and explain presidential behavior. Perhaps more significantly, the same assumptions and beliefs in the model were the ones that guided presidents themselves. But, beginning with the Reagan administration and continuing into the Obama administration, presidents, whether conscious of it or not, have operated on the basis of different assumptions. At least one scholar has noted this dramatic change: "*In the years since the coming of the Reagan administration, the United States has undergone a transformation in its political institutions and its philosophy of governance of a magnitude not seen since the 1930s*" [emphasis in original] (Williams 2003, 2). Still, most political scientists have failed to adjust their analytical model to this transformation and, consequently, have not fully understood presidential behavior in what is now the postmodern presidential era.

This chapter first introduces the reader to the modern presidency paradigm. For presidential scholars this description will be a review of a familiar topic; for casual observers of the presidency the summary will make overt assumptions that are often used but seldom stated. Following that discussion, the underlying assumptions and characteristics of postmodernist theory, which challenges that model, are presented. Then, without describing in detail all of the specific aspects of the postmodern presidency, critical areas where postmodern politics has altered the presidency will be identified. As alluded to earlier, the following chapters (2 through 7) will then consider how each president, from Ronald Reagan through Barack Obama, has contributed to the making of the postmodern presidency. As will be shown, each president contributes and emphasizes specific components of the postmodern presidency, and each builds upon predecessors. Chapter 7 develops a preliminary assessment of the Obama presidency, while the concluding chapter broadens the discussion to raise questions about the implications and ramifications of the postmodern presidency for the health of American democracy itself.

The Modern Presidency Paradigm

The modern presidency model emerged from, and is an extension of, a broader cultural paradigm—modernism—which includes assumptions and beliefs deeply embedded in society, so deeply that we are seldom conscious of them. Modernism includes a belief in the use of rationality to organize society and solve problems, a positive orientation toward progress and growth (particularly viewed as economic growth), a commitment to the rule of law, and a belief that change is linear and slowly progresses toward desired ends. Modern social and political institutions are organized bureaucratically and often hierarchically in order to improve efficiency. Abstract moral principles are developed to control behavior and are arrived at through reason and analysis; they can be agreed upon by rational people. Modernism assumes that technological developments are desirable and have, over the long run, improved the quality of life.

The dominant paradigm used to explain and evaluate presidential behavior, the modern presidency (sometimes referred to as the strong presidency), is an extension of cultural modernism into politics. Although its roots can be traced to the presidencies of Theodore Roosevelt and Woodrow Wilson, it is commonly believed that the modern presidency was most fully manifest in the presidency of Franklin Roosevelt and most clearly and comprehensively articulated in Richard Neustadt's classic book *Presidential Power,* published first in 1960. Neustadt's book has become arguably the most important book on the presidency in the last 50 years. Over those years, modest changes in the model have been made by others (and, indeed, Neustadt updated his original work), but the basic framework for explaining presidential behavior remains much as it was outlined in that original edition. Writing over 40 years after its publication, distinguished presidential scholar Erwin Hargrove examined the impact of Neustadt's book and concluded, "Richard Neustadt may be bloodied but he is not beaten. His theory of leadership still stands, but some insights have been added to enlarge the scope. And some things that he could not have anticipated have been corrected" (2001, 259).

While understood in different ways, key elements of the modern presidency can be identified. They include the topics covered in the following sections.

Systemic Gridlock

The modern presidency perspective begins with the belief that the constitutional structure and the nature of the political party system that has evolved have produced a political system prone to inaction and gridlock. Every place a president turns, his power is checked by competing powers. As designed by the founding fathers, the courts can review presidential actions to determine their constitutionality, and Congress checks the president with its legislative and oversight powers. But Congress itself is prone to inaction. It is so beset by its own internal checks that the passage of a single piece of legislation often takes years or even decades to achieve.

What's more, even though government bureaucrats in the executive branch are formally responsible to the president, in reality they represent another significant check on presidential action. Composed of over 2.5 million employees located in roughly 400 agencies, departments, government corporations, and commissions, bureaucrats develop loyalties to their organizations rather than to the president. As bureaucrats administer policy, compete with each other for resources, and respond to the demands of elected representatives, their actions are inherently political. While all presidents have attempted to control them, few have been successful at doing so. Thus, even the executive branch itself represents a check on presidential action.

In addition to these substantial checks, a federal system, whereby the national government is given some powers, the states are given other powers, and some powers are shared by both, further functions to constrain the exercise of presidential power. Even more, however, a myriad of local governmental structures exist—some have general governing responsibilities (e.g., towns, cities, counties), while others are responsible for specific functions (e.g., port authorities, water districts, sewer districts). Although there is a complex maze of local government organizations that complicates policy formulation, a belief in the value and importance of local government is widely held by Americans of all ideological persuasions. Thus, even though policies may be adopted (and even funded) by the national government, their implementation is commonly assigned to local governmental officials who may or may not be sympathetic to those policies. Local governments represent yet another check on presidential action.

What the Constitution separates, the political structure does not unite. Although in theory political parties, as national organizations, could function to unite disparate constitutional elements, in reality, American parties reflect and exacerbate the decentralizing tendencies of the separation of powers and federalism. Both the Republican and the Democratic parties have been influenced so much by the federal constitutional structure that they are similarly decentralized institutions composed of activists often at odds with other party members from other parts of the nation. "Federalism ensures that ideological, social, and economic differences are built into the two-party system from the local level up; that is, the two major parties in the United States can look significantly different from state to state" (Maisel and Brewer 2008, 395).

Given the nature of the political system, the danger is not, as some would claim, that government will become too powerful and too oppressive; rather, it is that government will be unable to act decisively to address significant national issues. For example, the health care system has been in need of reform for decades. By strategically using the decentralized political system to construct roadblocks, reform opponents have prevented comprehensive national reform. In a like manner, the government has been unable to respond to the challenges posed by global climate change, poverty, and educational reform, and the United States remains one of the few industrialized countries without a national urban policy. In the modern presidency model, government inaction (or at least the continuation of the status quo) is seen as a greater challenge to democracy than government oppression.

The President Activates the System

Given that the constitutional and political systems create an environment hostile to change, what can be done? An active president is the answer. The modern president should be the initiator of action because he is the only public official who has been elected by the entire nation, he—and he alone—is the only political figure who can legitimately initiate national political action. The president "creates the issues for each new departure in American politics by his actions and by his perceptions of what is right and wrong" (White 1961, 436). Representing the public as a whole, rather than smaller constituencies (e.g. states, congressional districts), the president should use his power on behalf of all Americans. As one scholar put it, "To achieve the unification and coordination of policies, it is essential to place the President in a political environment which constrains him to do more than drift and amiably reflect the current set of victorious interests. He must be given the conditions conducive to the exercise of leadership. He must be not merely enabled but also encouraged to define his goals clearly" (Kariel 1961, 283–284).

But because of the nature of the presidency, institutional changes alone will not assure that a president will act decisively. Ultimately, it is important that the "right" person be elected to the office—a person who wants power and knows how to use it. Much of Neustadt's book is a description of what some of the personal characteristics of an effective president are. Those characteristics are elaborated upon in the following text, but suffice it to say here that the modern president should be an extraordinary politician. "The Presidency ... is not a place for amateurs" (Neustadt 1980, 133). The best presidents are those who are professional politicians but, more importantly, they are politicians who want power and who know how to obtain and use it.

The modern view is that the exercise of presidential power is not a threat to democracy, but rather an expression of it. Presidential action is necessary in order to break through the barriers constructed by narrow interests and act on behalf of the majority of all Americans. Early formulations of the modern presidency model even went so far as to fuse presidential power with protection of the national interest. As Neustadt put it, "[W]hat is good for the country is good for the President, and *vice versa*" (1980, 136). Although most scholars of the presidency hesitate to go that far, there is broad consensus that the president is, and should be, the primary engine of change in the American national system.

The President as Legislative Leader

Scholar Roger Davidson (1999) captures the essence of Congress in this way: "[T]he path of legislation through the House and Senate—always subject to twists and turns—has become even more convoluted and nearly impossible to describe" (68). With almost 200 different working groups in two different branches of Congress, the creation of legislation is slow and methodical. Its Byzantine structure and complex array of rules appear designed more to frustrate than to facilitate the passage of legislation. Consequently, the modern president is expected to take an active role in legislative policy formation and setting the congressional agenda (Neustadt 1955). "The president has become a driving force within the legislative system.... This force works to produce policy output, which is why Congress looks to the president for new initiatives and why it tolerates his influence" (Wayne 1978, 23).

Following the lead of Franklin Roosevelt's New Deal, modern presidents often develop a package of policies connected by a broad theme that summarizes the legislative vision of the president. For example, Truman's legislative proposals were presented as the Fair Deal, Kennedy sketched out what he hoped would be the New Frontier, and Lyndon Johnson ambitiously attempted to create a Great Society. But to be successful with Congress a president must be a skilled politician: "A president's job is to get congressmen and other influential members of the government to think his requests are in their own best interests" (Cronin 1979, 383). The modern president must be a person who is willing and able to bargain and persuade legislators to support him. Whether it is leading through partisan appeals, bipartisanship pleas, twisting arms, making personal appeals, offering pork to obtain votes, or even going over the heads of legislators to appeal to the public to pressure legislators, a modern president should be an active participant in the legislative process.

Although early versions of the modern presidency saw the president operating primarily behind closed doors to influence legislators, revisions of the modern model have added a plebiscitary character to congressional bargaining. Kernell (2007) documents how recent presidents have developed strategies of "going public" whereby "a president promotes himself and his policies in Washington by appealing directly to the American public for support" (1–2), thus putting pressure on members of Congress to cooperate with presidential initiatives. Increasingly, modern presidents have used the modern mass media to forge direct links with the public to build legitimacy and political capital (Rimmerman 1993).

According to the modern presidency model, it is the president, not members of Congress, who is the primary initiator of legislation. But even more, the president is seen as a representative of all the people; he has a national constituency. Members of Congress represent districts and states and, thus, are inherently more responsive to minority (i.e., states and districts) than majority interests. By constitutional design, then, the president is in a better position to articulate a comprehensive legislative vision for the country than are members of Congress.

The President as Master Politician

In American political culture there is a suspicion about professional politicians and, at the same time, a glorification of the amateur. However, those beliefs are in opposition to the requirements of the modern presidency. Presidents must be masters at the craft of politics; they should be professionals. To be successful a president must be able to persuade: "Presidential *power* is the power to persuade" [emphasis in original] (Neustadt 1980, 10). The formal powers of the president to command assure only that a president will be a clerk, but to govern effectively a president must reject command in favor of bargaining. A modern president must accurately assess his resources and vantage points within the political system and, relying upon his political skills, his temperament, and his political experience, convince other Washington politicians that they should do what he wants them to do. In fact, when a president resorts to command it is considered a failure of presidential action. While it is impossible to identify exactly what kind of political experience is appropriate for the development of the skills needed to be a good president, some kind of political experience that develops skills of persuasion is needed. That can only be accomplished by holding prior political offices.

Once in office, presidents possess a considerable number of resources, but few of the most important resources are found in the formal powers of the presidency. What a president does gain from the office is a unique political position—he has access to a professional staff of experts, he has a high level of public visibility, and he is a person with whom other politicians must deal if they wish to be successful. A skillful politician can use these resources to persuade others. But, ultimately, the success of a president hinges upon his interior resources and skills.

One of his most important advantages is his ability to make decisions. The pattern of decisions he makes will establish a reputation which can lead to future influence. Politicians in the "Washington community" keep a keen eye on the president to examine his judgment as he goes about making decisions. "A President who values power need not be concerned with every flaw in his performance day by day, but he has every reason for concern with the residual impressions of tenacity and skill accumulating in the minds of Washingtonians-at-large. His bargaining advantages in seeking what he wants are heightened or diminished by what others think of him" (Neustadt 1980, 48). His professional reputation alone will not persuade, but it makes persuasion easier.

The Rhetorical President

The president must not only be effective at persuading other political actors to support him, he also must educate the American people about the major issues of the day. Most citizens are not attentive to politics on a regular basis; it is only when politics directly impinges on their everyday lives that they pay close attention. The modern president must teach realism to the American people primarily through his actions in addressing issues. If he does an effective job of teaching realism to the American people, he also builds support with other political actors. "A President concerned for leeway inside government must try to shape the thoughts of men outside. If he would be effective as a guardian of public standing, he must be effective as a teacher to the public" (Neustadt 1980, 73–74).

Because of the personal nature of the presidency, a president is in a superior position to control the public dialogue. Furthermore, since the media tends to personalize politics, a president is in an excellent position to dominate the news and, hence, the public dialogue. Using modern electronic communication techniques, he can set the political agenda through his use of rhetoric. Symbolizing the nation as a whole, the president can inspire and unify the citizenry and build support for common endeavors.

The modern president does not attempt to manipulate public opinion through the use of communication technologies; rather he attempts to explain events and decisions. His link with the American people is based upon rational explanation rather than emotional manipulation, and if he does that effectively, the American people will support him.

The rhetorical dimension of the presidency is a recent development and represents a modest revision of the modern presidency model. While all modern presidents communicate with the American people in some fashion, the development of modern electronic communication technologies has enhanced this aspect of the modern presidency.

Presidential Character

Character is associated with a group of traits that have significant social and moral qualities. It involves both a mastery and development of the self as well as the extension of the self into society to shape culture. Warren Susman (1984) comments about character: "[I]ts kind of self-control was the way to fullest development of the moral significance of self. But it also provided a method of presenting the self to society, offering a standard of conduct that assured interrelationships between the 'social' and the 'moral'" (273).

A person with good character is a person who is oriented toward hard work and productivity; is flexible and pragmatic; is adaptive, rational, and courageous; and possesses high self-esteem. Above all, he or she is a person of integrity. The modern president should be a skilled politician, but his desire to engage in the give and take of politics stems from his inner being—he must enjoy the rough and tumble of politics. Confident in knowing who he is, he seeks power not to satisfy some deeply hidden need to compensate for his own insecurities, but because the exercise of power makes it possible for him to improve the nation and the world. With a sense of satisfaction and self-confidence, he now wants to help others.

The presidency, more than any other national office, is affected by the character of its occupants. White House staffers, politicians themselves, quickly assess the best ways of approaching a president by observing his likes and dislikes, his work habits, and the manner in which he approaches his job. Whether a president encourages disagreements among aides or insists on consensus, whether he seeks out problems or avoids them, and whether he is active or passive are all orientations that stem from character and deeply affect the operation of an administration.

The Executive Branch

Constitutionally, the president is responsible for implementing the law of the land. Since FDR, two developments within the executive branch of government have occurred to help him accomplish this task. First, the bureaucracy has expanded exponentially, and second, a White House staff has grown to assist him in controlling that bureaucracy.

In 1932, when FDR took office, the federal government had eight cabinet departments and a budget of approximately $4 billion. By 2009, the number of departments had doubled to sixteen and the size of the federal budget was over $3 trillion. Although little has changed in terms of the responsibility of the president to manage the bureaucracy since the creation of the Constitution, its size and complexity have made the president's job far more difficult. The modern president attempts to manage the bureaucracy by adopting a traditional approach to administration—objectives are defined, analyses are undertaken, rules are developed, offices with clearly defined roles are created, assessments of the performance of bureaucrats are conducted, and adjustments are made based upon feedback. The modern approach to government is rational and hierarchical, with the president overseeing policy.

But the president cannot do the job himself. Over the years the White House staff has expanded to assist him both in policy formulation as well as in the management of the bureaucracy. Unlike the bureaucracy, which is often beholden to outside constituency interests, and his own Cabinet heads, who are often appointed for a host of political reasons, the White House staff is accountable solely to the president, and aides are chosen on the basis of expertise and loyalty. It is the role of the staff to provide information, assist in defining priorities, and developing strategy, but ultimately it is the president who must make decisions. Neustadt is emphatic on this point: "*[N]obody and nothing helps a President to see, save as he helps himself*" [emphasis in original] (Neustadt 1980, 111). It is only the president who should make presidential decisions and, no matter how he organizes his staff, he must remain in charge. Ironically, although the bureaucracy and the White House staff are dependent upon other bureaucrats or other staff to accomplish their tasks, they are ultimately responsible to a single individual whose personality and "gut instincts" can override even the most thorough policy analysis. The modern presidency, in effect, is a model of leadership highly dependent on the personal motivations and skills of the incumbent.

The Electoral Process Is Rational

Although the nomination and election processes appear to be haphazard, messy, and lacking an internal logic, they actually emphasize and reward the skills and talents candidates need to be successful presidents. As presidential candidates collect delegate votes in caucuses and primaries, the less-qualified candidates and the ones who fail to engage voters fall by the wayside until only two, one Democrat and one Republican, remain standing. The partisan contest between the Democratic and Republican nominees is the final struggle between two visions of what America should be like at that particular moment in history. Although the campaigns often fail to emphasize issues and produce electoral mandates, they nonetheless involve significant portions of the electorate in such a manner that they legitimize the person who is eventually elected while still providing citizens with a means to express their interests (Pomper 1975).

According to this model, the average voter is not, and does not have to be, highly informed about politics. Only during critical times (critical elections) will issues be decisive in determining votes. At other times people use shortcuts to make voting decisions. Relying upon the opinions of others, using the track records of candidates and parties, and evaluating and assessing the personal characteristics of candidates may be techniques that fall short of the way the ideal democratic voter is supposed to make decisions, but they represent a form of voting that is reasonable, if not entirely rational (Popkin 1991).

In sum, the modern presidency model places the president at the center of the national political system by placing the expectation of action on his shoulders. Still working within the constitutional structure devised by the founding fathers, the president is expected to persuade other political actors to his point of view by bargaining and negotiating. While a considerable amount of presidential bargaining goes on behind closed doors, the modern president has increasingly reached out to the public to secure popular and legislative support for policy initiatives and to educate Americans about the major issues of the day.

This model has been used to explain, predict, and even justify presidential behavior. Yet its ability to adequately account for presidential behavior is increasingly falling short of providing satisfactory explanations. The model no longer seems to accurately describe presidential behavior in (1) the electoral arena; (2) the political arena; and (3) governance. Further, the modern presidency model, while emphasizing the importance of presidential action, ironically fails to fully appreciate how such actions alter and reshape the political environment itself. In other words, it fails to recognize the importance of precedent and how presidents, regardless of their partisan or ideological orientations, build on the behavior of prior presidents.

Alternative Perspectives

Although scholarship and teaching approach the presidency primarily from a modern presidency framework, alternatives have nevertheless been presented. Recognizing the limitations of the dominant model, two such alternatives have gained traction. Without attempting to debunk the modern presidency model, Stephen Skowronek, in his book *The Politics Presidents Make* (1997), offers an alternative explanation of presidential behavior. Casting a broad net over presidential history, Skowronek argues that the American presidency is marked by cycles of presidential behavior related to the political coalitions that exist when they enter office. Some presidents take office when the dominant regime has been discredited and when resistance to new initiatives is weak. In that environment they can reformulate the nation's political agenda and set a new direction. These are the presidents of reconstruction.

More common are the presidents who enter office during times "when established commitments of ideology and interest are relatively resilient, providing solutions, or legitimate guides to solutions to the governing problems of the day" (Skowronek 1997, 41). These presidents mobilize political support to accomplish the promises and objectives of the established regime. Occasionally, leaders opposed to the accepted system get elected. These opposition leaders attempt to preempt the established agenda and exploit divisions in the dominant political alignments. They try to reconstruct politics, but usually fail in doing so.

The final recurring leadership structure occurs at the end of the cycle and immediately precedes presidents of reconstruction. These presidents find themselves in difficult leadership positions. Although they are affiliated with the established commitments of the previous era, they are confronted with issues and events that defy solutions based upon old assumptions and political coalitions. They preside over the disruption of the prior regime and are often viewed as incompetent.

Skowronek's interpretation of presidential behavior is significant for two reasons that bear upon this analysis. First, the cyclical character of what he refers to as "political time" means that the opportunities for presidential leadership vary and that variation is largely dependent on the effects of prior presidential action: "Presidential leadership in political time ... refer[s] to the various relationships incumbents project between previously established commitments of ideology and interest and their own actions in the moment at hand" (30). In addition, Skowronek recognizes that leadership opportunities are circumscribed by deeper political assumptions and arrangements, what he refers to as "secular time." On this he says, "Presidential leadership in secular time will refer to the progressive development of the institutional resources and governing responsibilities of the executive office and thus to the repertoire of powers the presidents of a particular period have at their disposal to realize their preferences in action" (30).

His general point holds true for postmodern presidents. The shifting paradigm—from the modern to the postmodern—presents both constraints as well as new opportunities for political action. Presidents who embrace this change enhance their ability to successfully act, while those who fail to do so will flounder. This will be shown in the analysis that follows.

Second, Skowronek's analysis makes a strong case for the conclusion that presidential action matters. Not only do presidents respond to the time in which they find themselves, but through their own actions they "disrupt systems, reshape political landscapes, and pass to successors leadership challenges that are different from the ones just faced" (Skowronek 1997, 6). Through their actions presidents can transform both the nature of the presidency as well as the particular political alignments of the time. This is very much the case for the postmodern presidency. True, American politics has been altered through osmosis as our postmodern popular culture has seeped into the political realm. But through specific actions of their own, presidents have also accelerated and reshaped the postmodern political transformation.

While Skowronek's perspective may be seen as complementing rather than replacing the modern presidency model, a second alternative which has emerged represents a more direct challenge. Relying heavily on statistical analysis and employing rigorous "scientific" methods is a body of literature that may be referred to as the rational choice approach. These studies assume that "the president is a rational political actor who has policy goals" (Canes-Wrone 2001, 315) derived from his ideology, his sense of his place in history, or his desire for reelection. Operating in a political environment in which other politicians and even voters "are rational, forward-looking, and policy-motivated" (Canes-Wrone et al. 2001, 534), the president develops and implements strategies to accomplish his policy objectives.

This rational choice approach uses the entire history of the presidency as a database and empirically tests hypotheses about presidential behavior. The goal is not to explain particular presidencies, but rather to develop generalizations and ultimately theories about executive behavior. As one proponent puts it, "What I want is manageable bits of theory—models—one can take to real data and gain powerful leverage. Particularly exciting are crisp ideas that transport across presidential systems, and possibly across history, in form if not detail" (Cameron 2002, 660).

Space does not allow for a thorough critique of the rational choice approach and, indeed, such an endeavor would prove to be exceedingly boring. Suffice it to say that the rational choice approach differs significantly from the approach I take both in terms of the assumptions about human behavior as well as the objectives of the research. While postmodernism admits that some behavior is rational, it also recognizes that behavior is often intertwined with emotion and is sometimes irrational. Furthermore, the objective of this book is not to produce models to explain presidential behavior in general; rather, it is to create an analytical framework that will allow us to develop a deeper understanding of contemporary presidential behavior.

The Postmodern Perspective

One of the challenges of labeling this transformation postmodern is that there is considerable disagreement over the meaning of postmodernism itself. That disagreement often occurs because it has different meanings in different academic disciplines. Perhaps an even more significant challenge in identifying any particular period as postmodern may be found in the theory itself. As will be discussed later, postmodernism questions the very meaning of any particular concept, claiming that all concepts only have meaning given the contexts in which they are found. While agreement is not impossible, it requires considerable qualification. A further difficulty in finding clarity is the fact that modern elements continue to exist within postmodernism. Postmodernism does not so much replace modern beliefs and behaviors as it places them into a different perspective. Given that, it is difficult to identify a particular "threshold point" at which the patterns of presidential behavior have shifted so dramatically as to constitute a paradigmatic change.[1]

Nonetheless, there are some assumptions and beliefs that are common to a postmodern worldview. But unlike postmodernism in most disciplines, the postmodern presidency is not merely an academic exercise; instead, the postmodern presidency emerges out of the everyday operation of presidential politics. Further, it is, to a large extent, a reflection of changes that have occurred in our political culture over the last three decades. The aspects of postmodern culture that bear most significantly upon politics, and particularly the presidency, are briefly identified in the following text. The discussion is far from complete; instead, it represents a slice of postmodern tendencies which are of greatest significance to the theory of the postmodern presidency.

As will be shown in later chapters, presidents beginning with Ronald Reagan and continuing to Barack Obama have added or emphasized particular aspects of postmodernism that, taken together, constitute a shift in paradigms from the modern to the postmodern presidency. No president fits the model perfectly, yet each operates within the postmodern environment. While accepting many of the postmodern assumptions, each president emphasizes particular aspects of that model while deemphasizing other aspects. At the same time, there is an irregular progression toward a more complete postmodern paradigm as presidents, regardless of their political or ideological affiliations, have accepted and built upon many of the behaviors of prior presidents. I will argue that so many of the behaviors of postmodernism are present today, and that so many of the fundamental assumptions of the model have been accepted, that a paradigm shift has taken place. Before delving into the elements of the postmodern presidency, a discussion of some of the fundamental assumptions of postmodernism which are of greatest significance to the postmodern presidency is in order.

Rationality

One of the hallmarks of the modern world is rationality, only one way of relating to and understanding the world from a postmodern perspective. It is commonly accepted in Western industrialized nations that rationality is a preferred way of making sense of the world. By employing it to solve problems, develop theories of how things work, and establish and apply ethical principles, rationality is critical for the creation and maintenance of culture. While it is not the only approach to making sense of the world in the United States, it is widely accepted as superior to alternatives. The postmodern perspective does not reject rationality; rather, it recognizes its advantages but also suggests that it is limited. Postmodernism embraces alternatives—particularly emotion—as legitimate ways of understanding and relating to the world.

In the modern presidency model, voters adhere to at least crude forms of rationality in making voting decisions. In contrast, postmodern politics expands candidate selection to move beyond the rational analysis of issues to include appeals to emotion and symbolism. A postmodern candidate does not ignore issues, but instead uses issues in a symbolic fashion: "[W]hen a candidate takes an issue position in the thick of controversy, voters feel that is the most reliable indicator they have of his true essence. Voters know he has chosen sides. . . . The issue position becomes a form of symbolic speech, telling us what the candidate is all about" (Morris 1999, 33).

In office, a modern president should rely upon the "best and the brightest" for advice, carefully and realistically identifying and analyzing problems and advocating solutions that have been thoroughly examined. Pragmatism in approaching problems is valued. But the postmodern president also realizes that many do not respond to politics in a totally rational fashion. Politics elicits emotion, often veiled, but nonetheless present. As one political strategist puts it, *"The political brain is an emotional brain. It is not a dispassionate calculating machine, objectively searching for the right facts, figures, and policies to make a reasoned decision"* [emphasis in the original] (Westen 2007, xv). Postmodern presidents are not afraid to use emotional appeals to advance policies. Herein lies a potential problem for democratic politics, however. By relying heavily on emotional appeals, the citizen becomes a passive member of an audience. While issues can activate citizens as they argue and debate the merits of various positions, emotional appeals do not lead to deliberative action—merely to feeling. It is problematic that democratic deliberation can be created in this fashion.

Reality

Postmodernism denies the existence of any fixed reality. Instead, meaning and significance are based on the context in which anything appears and is interpreted. Because meaning is derived through interpretation, it is not possible to arrive at a single meaning for any particular event. While some criticize this aspect of postmodernism as being relativistic, a more reasonable interpretation is that it leads to a multiplicity of meanings—a characteristic of postmodernism. Rather than searching for any universal standard by which to judge things, the postmodernist makes assessments on the basis of functionality. At best, one may merely determine that one reality is more *useful* than another in a particular circumstance. Reality is not universally agreed upon and, therefore, it is fragmented and partial depending on context and the position of the observer. "Reason in this sense is a series of rules of thought that any ideal, rational person might adopt if his/her purpose was to achieve propositions of universal validity. Postmodern thought, on the contrary, is bound to discourse literally, narratives about the world that are admittedly partial" (Aronowitz 1988, 5).

This altered perspective about reality is known in the postmodern world as hyperreality—the idea that the modern distinction between reality and representation can no longer be made because "the distinctions between reality and representation collapse so as to make them meaningless" (Parry-Giles and Parry-Giles 2002, 1). In many instances images no longer possess referents in the real world and, therefore, the ability to assess their accuracy and legitimacy is impossible. For example, presidential debates are no longer about reasoned arguments. Instead, they are battles of competing images of the candidates. What provides them with a hyperreal quality, however, is the fact that they are presented not as theater or entertainment, but as serious political debates. With no anchoring in the real world, the only way to analyze images is by the application of aesthetic criteria. Is the spectacle entertaining? Does the image capture our interest? Who looks presidential?

The political implications of this are substantial. The significance of any event is not found in the event itself, but is found instead in the interpretation of the event: "[N]o narrative can be a natural 'master' narrative; there are no natural hierarchies, only those we construct" [emphasis in original] (Hutcheon 1993, 253). Given that, attempts to construct those meanings, and to get others to accept those constructions, are inherently political. Political pundits begin to touch, if ever so superficially, upon this when they criticize politicians for attempting to "spin" interpretations of particular events (e.g., who won a debate). But "spin" is only the tip of the postmodern iceberg. A significant portion of the postmodern presidency is concerned with altering the culture in such a way that assumptions about reality work to one's advantage and to the disadvantage of one's opponent. This would suggest that the postmodern presidency is much more about image manipulation than policy creation and implementation.

The malleable nature of reality has implications in other areas as well. As previously discussed, the modern president should be a master politician—a person skilled at bargaining and negotiating. And while recent adjustments to the model have accurately noted that presidents are increasingly going public, the assumption about the politically malleable nature of reality means that presidents will "go public" in ways not anticipated by the modern presidency model. For example, with the goal of creating new realities by which the people assess them, postmodern presidents are less inclined to employ the modern political tactics of logical persuasion and more inclined to use dramaturgical techniques. Thus, a president is skilled in the artifice of presentation; he is concerned about staging, performance, creating distance and mystery, and presenting the appearance of a consistent image that enhances his authority. In this view, presidential leadership has less to do with the actual power that he may possess than it has to do with eliciting a prescribed response from his audience.

Given this new orientation of relating to the citizenry, skills other than those identified as important for the modern president are valued. Thus, an effective postmodern president must be a skilled actor. He must be aware of when he is "on stage" and when he is "off stage," he must convincingly portray the image of a leader, and he must understand the importance of television to relate to the American people. Television has become the dominant medium by which presidents communicate, and the consequences of that cannot be overemphasized. Not only does the sense of "what is" shift from what is read and heard to what is seen, but the criteria used to judge presidents have also changed. Instead of assessing presidential performance on the basis of decisions made (as the modern model suggests should be done), television emphasizes the private, personal character of the president (Meyrowitz 1995). Because of this, citizens often support a president because they "personally like" him while, at the same time, they may disagree with him on the issues (Clymer 1982).

In a world where reality is malleable, citizens are often at a loss about how to assess political behavior and political events. In an ideal postmodern world, average citizens would be empowered to participate with their own postmodern performances. And, as we will see later in this book, some such performances did emerge in the 2008 presidential campaign, but for the most part the construction of reality is controlled by presidential-communications experts.

The Self

Modernism is concerned with the nurturing of one's genuine self and developing his or her character. Indeed, the idea of "knowing oneself" or knowing "who you are" is valued. Postmodernism, on the other hand, questions the existence of—sometimes even the possibility of—a true self. In fact, some postmodern writers refer to a person as "the subject" rather than the self (Butler 2002). Rather than possessing a true self, the postmodern perspective asserts that there are multiple selves that, under ideal conditions, are malleable. What prevents the expression of these multiple selves is the application of power. Without constraints a person is free to alter one's self in whatever direction one wants. But such environments rarely exist. More common are situations that are structured by power arrangements. When that occurs, some presentations of self are acceptable while others are unacceptable. Thus, the self is defined more by a person's public presentation than by any inner traits he or she may possess. Much as truth and reality are contingent and dependent upon context, so too is the self.

As noted, one of the important factors emphasized in the modern presidency is character. A modern president should have high self-esteem, should possess integrity, and should have a solid sense of himself. In this respect, character is a crucial part of leadership. Examining the early childhood of the quintessential modern president, Franklin Roosevelt, James David Barber (1992) concludes the following: "By accident or design, James and Sara had infused a deep confidence in Franklin Roosevelt, a self-esteem so strong it could overcome the apparent end of his career when he was toppled by polio. And the quality of accretion in his early life, the stage-by-stage building and elaboration of his orientations, give evidence of a sense of the self as developing. FDR grew, sloughing off what he did not need, but mainly adding to his repertoire, deepening his confidence in his stance toward life" (287).

Postmodernism challenges the significance of character and replaces it with personality. Because of the emphasis on public performance, different personality characteristics are likely to be considered of greater importance. However, just as there are different approaches to acting that emphasize different personalities and acting skills to be successful, so too does the successful postmodern president require different personality characteristics. Rather than being static and uniformly applied, these characteristics vary considerably. Thus, a postmodern presidential personality might be closer to what Robert Jay Lifton has called a "protean personality"—that is, a person who conducts a "series of experiments and explorations, some shallow, some profound, each of which can readily be abandoned in favor of still new psychological quests" (Lifton 1968, 17).

Yet politicians with strong self-identity can also be effective postmodern presidents. Individuals who possess the ability to distance themselves from emotional situations, who can segment their lives to the point of being able to adjust quickly to different environments, who can project emotion, and who are open to advice and direction can also excel in the new postmodern political atmosphere. Dramaturgical discipline is a necessity. "[W]hile the performer is ostensibly immersed and given over to the activity he is performing, and is apparently engrossed in his actions in a spontaneous, uncalculating way, he must none the less be affectively dissociated from his presentation in a way that leaves him free to cope with dramaturgical contingencies as they arise" (Goffman 1959, 216). More important than whether or not a president possesses a firm sense of self is whether he has mastered the ability to "act presidential."

At this point the critical distinction between the modern and the postmodern is the distinction between character and personality. Character carries with it a set of internalized moral principles and a commitment to social and political action. Personality, on the other hand, involves an entertaining public presentation of oneself. To accomplish that requires an element of detachment so that a person can gauge the effectiveness of the presentation (i.e., "read the audience") of aspects of his or her personality that are being revealed.

Fragmentation

According to the modern perspective, Americans are bound together by their agreement on a wide range of assumptions about politics and democracy. Regardless of their race, class, ethnicity, gender, or age, citizens are in agreement about the value of basic rights, the meaning of democracy, and the rules of political conflict. Embracing the value of expertise, the modern perspective envisions a citizenry that allows experts flexibility in making decisions with only occasional interference. The primary role of the citizenry is to select its leaders. "The voter's involvement is sporadic—in the nature of meddling rather than continuing participation. Meddling is not a constant process. The electorate intervenes periodically, and only when the occasion is of considerable importance. The voter becomes involved in direct relation to his personal concerns" (Pomper 1975, 92).

Postmodernism paints a much different picture of the citizenry. It envisions a politics of difference or, as some would put it, "identity politics." People identify not as humans, or even Americans, but as members of a particular race, ethnicity, religion, gender, or sexual orientation. Definitions of the self are now derived on the basis of social representations. Thus, one is no longer merely an American, but rather an African-American, European-American, Asian-American, and the like.

Those representations form the basis for groups that can be mobilized to exert political influence. Mobilization occurs on the basis of perceived identity rather than the modern motivation of self-interest. What's more, voters today are far less likely to defer to elected officials and far more likely to participate in politics on a regular basis. "The fundamental paradigm that dominates our politics is the shift from representational (Madisonian) to direct (Jeffersonian) democracy. Voters want to run the show directly and are impatient with all forms of intermediaries between their opinions and public policy" (Morris 1999, 23).

The political implication of fragmentation means that presidents today find it increasingly difficult to present broad national programs that are dependent upon political consensus for support. Instead of developing such sweeping visions as the New Deal or the Great Society, postmodern presidents are more likely to appeal to niche voters by addressing small-bore issues. "The traditional idea of laying out broad platforms has gone away in favor of issues of the moment" (Gronbeck 2009, 237). Yet, ultimately, the fragmentation that characterizes postmodern society means that social problems have become so complex and require such a huge output of coordinated resources that their solutions are beyond the scope of modern government to solve. Problems such as poverty, urban decay, global warming, health care, racism, sexism, inequality, and similar problems are so complex that they not only elude logical solutions, but it is difficult to even define exactly what the problems are in the first place. In the language of administrative postmodernism, they constitute a class of problems called "wicked problems." To deal with such problems requires a new postmodern approach to management—one that is horizontal rather than vertical, uses government to coordinate all relevant actors rather than issuing rules and regulations, and one that views government bureaucrats as facilitators rather than problem-solvers. Such a change would require a radical revision in the operation of the government bureaucracy, but, as we will see, presidents, even postmodern presidents, have at best paid merely lip service to such an idea.

Toward a Postmodern Presidency

While a few scholars have attempted to argue that the postmodern presidency has already emerged (see Barilleaux 1988; Rose 1991; Cammarano 2009), presidential scholars have, for the most part, been reluctant to embrace such claims. This reluctance stems, in part, from a lack of clarity about what constitutes the postmodern presidency (Rimmerman 1993), but also because of a failure of advocates to ground the concept in "theoretical and empirical evidence" (Combs 1989). Is the postmodern presidency merely composed of those presidents who held office after the modern presidents, or are there attitudinal and behavioral changes that constitute postmodern behavior? If the postmodern presidency represents a new theoretical orientation, what are its characteristics? Is there a specific presidency that marks the starting point of the postmodern presidency? How many postmodern characteristics must a presidency possess before being classified as postmodern? Because answers to questions such as these have not been satisfactorily provided, "the idea of a postmodern presidency serves, at best, as a mere footnote" (Fontaine 2003, 63) in research and teaching about the presidency. Nonetheless, if these issues can be addressed there is considerable potential for changing the way the presidency is taught and understood.

Although the remainder of this book will show in greater detail how presidents Reagan, Bush I, Clinton, Bush II, and Obama have been influenced by, and have themselves influenced, the postmodern presidency, it is helpful at this point to briefly preview what is emerging as the postmodern presidency. Box 1.1 provides in summary form a comparison between the modern presidency and the postmodern presidency. A few general points of explanation are in order.

First, over the last three decades postmodern politics have seeped into virtually all aspects of the presidency—albeit sporadically and unequally. While it is easiest to see the application of postmodern strategies in the areas where the president interacts with the public, in fact postmodern assumptions and behaviors have permeated all aspects of the executive branch. How this has come about, how recent presidents have been influenced by the postmodern environment, how they have acted to shape it, or how they have tried to live with the uneasy tensions the modern and the postmodern create will be shown in the chapters that follow.

Second, although I claim that so many of the most critical aspects of presidential behavior have changed that we may conclude that a paradigm shift has occurred, modern presidential characteristics persist (although sometimes in altered forms). For example, both the modern as well as the postmodern models agree that the president must be the primary political agent to activate the political system. At the same time, differences exist about how such actions can be initiated, with the modern model emphasizing bargaining and persuasion while the postmodern model, while not opposed to those techniques, is more open to the use of unilateral action. Similar types of agreements and disagreements exist throughout the comparison of the two models.

Third, while Box 1.1 presents a comprehensive picture of the postmodern presidency, as will be seen, no president examined has fully embraced the approach. Presidents vary in the degree and extent to which they adopt postmodern behaviors. While some enthusiastically embrace the new approach, others actively resist it, while even others try to live within its uneasy tensions and contradictions. In fact, the area where presidential actions are least compatible with the analytical model lie in the area which is probably the most challenging in which to adopt postmodern strategies and also the area that offers the fewest political benefits—governance.

Finally, as can be seen, Box 1.1 groups the characteristics of both models into three general areas: the electoral process, presidential politics, and presidential governance. In a general sense, these three areas will be used in the remaining chapters on each of the presidents as a framework to organize the analysis. At the same time, the analysis must be open to and respond to the unique aspects of each presidency as they relate to the making of the postmodern presidency.

Outline of This Book

The change, then, from the modern to postmodern presidency is a gradual, if uneven, process in which the precedents set by one president are sometimes used and built upon by presidents who follow. Presidential action, while intentionally designed to shape a particular president's agenda, also has the effect of reinforcing, disrupting, or re-creating the political dynamics for subsequent presidents. While presidents remain independent political actors, their ability to act is circumscribed by the political dynamics they inherit. Thus, the political assumptions and power arrangements of the modern presidency create different opportunities for action from those of the postmodern presidency.

Although threads of the postmodern presidency can be traced as far back as the Nixon presidency, my analysis of the postmodern presidency starts with Ronald Reagan because it is Reagan, more than any of his predecessors, who embraced many of the fundamental core elements of postmodernism. Beginning there and continuing to the present, presidents have increasingly accepted the postmodern elements their predecessors used, layering upon them and adding to them, so that what emerges today is a fairly coherent, though still incomplete,

Box 1.1
The Modern and Postmodern Presidency Models

The Modern Presidency	*The Postmodern Presidency*

Electoral Politics

Although appearing chaotic and confusing, the nomination and election processes are rational. They function as a "winnowing process" in which the candidate who is able to present the best vision of the future wins.

Elections are spectacles. They are ritualistic opportunities for voters to emotionally link themselves to the president and the political system.

Voters are minimally interested in politics. During campaigns they watch the candidates and make "reasonable" decisions when they vote. A small number of activists are recruited and work in campaigns. The typical voter does not stay involved in politics between elections.

Some voters are minimally interested and are easily influenced by emotion, while others are intensely interested. The ideal postmodern citizen playfully participates in the campaign.

Presidential Politics

The president must be a master politician who will bargain, negotiate, and compromise. He must use the resources at his disposal to persuade people to do what he wants them to do.

The president must master the art of opinion leadership. Opinion leadership is fully integrated into the decision-making process. He must not be afraid to act unilaterally to achieve his objectives.

The president is the primary legislative leader. He should identify the major problems in society and submit major packages of legislation for action. He must be skilled at behind-the-scenes negotiating to pass legislation.

Broad-themed legislative packages (e.g., New Deal, Great Society) are things of the past. The president should identify "small-bore" issues which appeal to niche audiences. Issues are symbols of the values that he believes in; it is more important that issues be identified and discussed than it is to pass legislation.

Presidential Governance

For a president to be effective, he must manage the White House staff and the bureaucracy. The staff should be organized on the basis of expertise, and the bureaucracy should be run efficiently. While the president needs good advisors, ultimately he is the only person who can make presidential decisions.

The high degree of fragmentation in society makes it difficult to use rules and regulations to design and implement policy in the executive branch. Government action alone cannot solve problems; it can only facilitate solutions by bringing non-governmental organizations, civic groups, and private business organizations together to facilitate action.

vision of the postmodern presidency. The next six chapters of this book will explore the postmodern dimensions of the presidencies from Ronald Reagan to Barack Obama.

We begin in Chapter 2 with Ronald Reagan. Possessing the skills of a Hollywood actor and directed by a skilled group of public relations, media, communications, and political consultants, the Reagan administration mastered the art of image creation and manipulation. Through the use of pseudo-events and controlled media exposure, favorable images were constructed that often contradicted policies the administration was actually pursuing. But it was the manner in which the new electronic technologies (particularly television) were employed to create new realities that represents one of the significant advances toward the making of the postmodern presidency and establishes a sharp break with the modern presidency. Image creation and manipulation were used not just in campaigning, but more significantly, in the day-to-day functioning of the White House.

Less publicized was Reagan's attempt to redefine the role of the federal government. Although overly committed to a conservative ideology to be truly postmodern, Reagan nonetheless challenged the idea that government should be the primary agent to solve social and economic problems. This idea—that government should facilitate problem-solving rather than create programs to solve problems—will be developed more fully (at least in theory if not in practice) by later presidents and will add yet another element to the making of the postmodern presidency.

Chapter 3 shows how Reagan's vice president, George H. W. Bush, employed postmodern campaign techniques in order to get elected but then abandoned them once in office and, consequently, became only the second elected sitting president since Herbert Hoover to fail to obtain reelection. Arguing that he would continue the "Reagan Revolution," his 1988 campaign adopted many of the same techniques Reagan had created, strategically employing them in his assault on the Democratic nominee, Michael Dukakis. During that campaign, Bush added little to the media manipulation approach innovated by Reagan; yet, simply by being elected, he demonstrated that even a candidate whose personality and political skills are not well-suited to postmodern approaches can win if he allows himself to be managed by expert consultants. However, once in office Bush was unable or unwilling to use image manipulation as his approach to governing. In many respects he behaved more like a modern president—preferring to bargain and negotiate behind closed doors with other political elites and foreign leaders. He proved unable to create and market his own reality as Reagan had been so successful at doing and instead became captured by the Washington political elites. Without a sympathetic context to explain his behavior, he appeared insincere when his governance actions contradicted his campaign commitments. Consequently, his presidency is characterized by fragmentation.

Although Bush failed to build upon Reagan's image manipulation and strategy of governing through public actions, he contributed to the making of the postmodern presidency by rationalizing a new vision of the role of government in solving difficult social and economic problems (i.e., wicked problems). Driven less by ideology than Reagan, and guided by a desire to reward those interests which supported him and with whom he was comfortable, Bush lowered the expectations of government's purpose and initiated an administrative orientation that would shift governmental responsibilities to the private and nongovernmental sectors. This approach, dubbed the neoadministrative state, adds a new layer to the postmodern presidency. Still, at this early stage the idea of the neoadministrative state becomes confused with conservative, anti-governmental ideology and, as a result, the postmodern revision of the role of government cannot be realized.

Bush's legacy is found not so much in what he contributed to the postmodern presidency paradigm as it is a demonstration of the power of postmodern techniques. Even presidents whose personal predilections are in the modern direction can be successful if they defer to their advisors. At the same time, when they embrace modern assumptions and employ modern behaviors they do so at their own peril. Bush's presidency was fragmented—partly modern and partly postmodern—but in crucial areas he opted for modern responses, and his use of postmodern techniques was not compelling enough to mask his "behind the scenes" negotiations with what his core constituency called "the enemy." He paid the price with electoral defeat.

The focus of Chapter 4 is on the presidency of Bill Clinton. Clinton not only built upon the postmodern structural changes that had been established by Reagan and Bush, but he also mastered the politics of the postmodern presidency due in large part to his personality—a personality well-suited to a postmodern political world. Derided by his critics as a liar and tagged with the moniker "Slick Willie," Clinton's personality can more accurately be characterized as that of a shape-shifter.

Clinton helped make the postmodern presidency in several ways. First, his personality highlights the importance of possessing the psychological ability to be comfortable shifting positions and presenting a variety of fronts in response to different conditions. Second, as a close observer of Reagan's use of rhetoric and symbols to connect with the American people, Clinton expanded the approach. Where Reagan's symbols were almost entirely visual, Clinton, while also utilizing visuals, further demonstrated how metaphors and issues could be used in a postmodern fashion. Third, Clinton embraced the governance perspectives of his two immediate predecessors and added to that a communications campaign—the permanent campaign—that was designed to provide him the leeway to act unilaterally.

Clinton enthusiastically embraced the Reagan media manipulation strategy. However, where Reagan obediently accepted direction from his media handlers, Clinton actively participated in the entire production, from its conception to its scripting to its directing and finally as the lead performer. His behavior in being able to successfully change positions to suit changing environments highlights the importance of personality in the postmodern presidency. Lacking a firm attachment to either ideology or partisanship, Clinton nimbly jumped from one position to another as political circumstances dictated. In the process of doing so he also demonstrated the symbolic importance of issues in connecting with the American people. However, while Clinton's personality fits well into the postmodern political environment that was evolving, it is not correct to assume that his de-centered personality is the only type of personality that can function in the postmodern atmosphere. Just as actors can approach the same role with different theatrical approaches, so too it is possible for presidents to approach the presidency possessing different personality types.

Breaking with previous Democratic presidents, Clinton embraced the new, scaled-down vision of the role of the federal government and complemented it by "going public" as a strategy to encourage the development of non-governmental solutions to problems. Instead of advocating large, comprehensive government programs (e.g., the New Deal, the Great Society, the New Frontier), he became a proponent of "small bore" issues which appealed to niche voters.

Chapter 5 focuses on George W. Bush, who entered the presidency promising that his administration would not be like Clinton's—that he would make tough decisions based not upon opinion polls, but based upon what was the right thing to do. But only eight months into his presidency America was attacked by al Qaeda and Bush's presidency took on a radical new look. For some critics of postmodernism, the 9/11 attacks signaled the end of postmodern politics, and they embraced Bush's forceful reconceptualization of the world as being divided into the forces of good versus the forces of evil. Instead, however, that forceful, if simplistic, dualistic conception of world politics proved to be merely a postmodern frame designed to provide angry and scared Americans with what they psychologically yearned for at that particular moment in history.

George W. Bush advanced the use of public opinion and image manipulation even further than Clinton had by institutionally embedding it into virtually all aspects of the White House decision-making process. In fact, the postmodern orientation so dominated the Bush administration that they arrogantly and publicly declared that they could create their own reality. Because Bush had little interest in and understood little about policy, he did not use issues in the same manner as Clinton did. Instead, his approach was more in line with Reagan's—using visuals to emotionally connect with the citizenry. But Bush went even further than Reagan had done by creating images that appealed to people's fantasies—in effect, conjuring up hyperreal images.

Yet many would argue that the most significant legacy of the Bush presidency was the expansion of the unilateral powers of the presidency to unprecedented levels. Projecting an image asserting democratic values and respect for law, the actual operation of the Bush administration often undermined the rule of law and subverted key provisions of the Constitution. For the Bush administration the Constitution was seen as merely another potential power base, privileged neither any more nor any less than any other source of power. In fact, this adds an important new element to the postmodern presidency. Postmodernism does not privilege one set of rules over another—they are evaluated on the basis of functionality. Thus, the Constitution must be reevaluated in the light of new circumstances, most particularly for Bush, during a time of war. An important characteristic that Bush contributes to the making of the postmodern presidency is a reinterpretation of the powers of the presidency and, ultimately, a new vision of what is meant by a constitution in the first place.

The 2008 presidential election represents one of the most significant watersheds in American political history and is the focus of Chapter 6. Both the McCain and Obama campaigns employed postmodern strategies as well as a wide variety of postmodern techniques and tactics, but both did so while operating campaigns based on modern top-down control. With the economy in shambles (a traditional Democratic issue), an unpopular war in Iraq, and a Republican president whose approval ratings were comparable to Nixon's when he was forced to resign, McCain ignored and blurred issues, aggressively attacked Obama with questionable accusations, and emphasized his war hero biography while ignoring his extensive political background. These were techniques that had been successfully used by Reagan, George H. W. Bush, and George W. Bush at one time or another.

Obama, while also accepting modern assumptions, broke new ground in the sophisticated use of new digital technologies, technologies that have helped produce our postmodern culture. Through the use of the Internet, cell phones, BlackBerrys, and Twitter, as well as the exploitation of social networking websites, he horizontally linked volunteers and mobilized a massive nationwide army of campaign workers, many of whom had never before been involved in politics. But even more, the 2008 campaign saw an increase in spontaneous citizen participation attached to neither campaign. This was possible because of new viral technologies that facilitated communication and represent yet another new dimension of the postmodern presidency, albeit one not controlled by presidents or presidential candidates themselves.

The Barack Obama presidency (examined in Chapter 7) provides us with a way of gauging the extent to which the postmodern presidency has become an enduring feature of our political culture. All the early indicators suggest that Obama is an awkwardly juxtaposed modern president who finds himself in a postmodern environment. If, as some might suggest, the postmodern presidency is more a characteristic of particular presidents than a paradigmatic change, we should expect Obama's modern orientation to predominate. But if the argument of this book is valid, the Obama administration can be used instead to assess the extent to which even a modern president must resort to postmodern practices in order to govern.

Finally, this book concludes with a brief afterword that normatively questions the democratic nature of the postmodern presidency. Is it a danger to democratic governance or is it a continuation of the democratizing trends that the nation has undergone since its inception?

With this all too cursory introduction to the postmodern presidency, I will return to its origins—the Reagan presidency. Reagan, more than any president in the second half of the twentieth century, rejected the old way of practicing politics (the modern presidency) and attempted to institute a new approach that would eventually transform the national political environment into the foreseeable future. Coming into office declaring that "government is the problem," he set out to create a wholesale change.

Note

1. This problem is not unique to postmodernism. All attempts to classify, even in the hard sciences, suffer from imprecision at the boundaries of concepts (Davis 2005).

CHAPTER 2

RE-IMAGING THE PRESIDENCY

RONALD REAGAN

I did not have cancer. I had something in me that had cancer in it and it was removed.

Ronald Reagan

Lesley Stahl often tells audiences of the time in the fall of 1984 when *60 Minutes* decided to challenge the Reagan administration on the disjunction between its policy actions and the claims being made in the campaign. In an unusually long (almost eight minutes) and critical report, Stahl narrated an exposé which showed pictures of Reagan visiting homeless shelters, glad-handing African-Americans, passing the torch at the Special Olympics, cutting the ribbon at the opening ceremonies of a nursing home, and interacting with school children. While these images were being presented, a voice-over criticized Reagan for reducing funding to homeless shelters, opposing affirmative action, attempting to reduce funding for the disabled, opposing funding for federally subsidized nursing homes, and making massive cuts in school funding. This report was unusual not only in its length, but in its biting criticism of a sitting president. She suspected that the Reagan administration would retaliate—that her press pass would be revoked and that she would never be allowed to set foot in the White House again.

As anticipated, the Monday following the Sunday evening broadcast, she received several phone calls from White House staffers. To her surprise, however, they called not to criticize her, but to thank her. "What!" she exclaimed. "I spent eight minutes on prime time television attacking you. Why are you thanking me?" She quickly learned a lesson in image manipulation. One staffer told her that people don't *listen* to the news, they *watch* it—and she had provided the White House with "golden images" which they couldn't have produced better had they done it themselves. In a later interview with television journalist Bill Moyers, Michael Deaver, a Reagan aide who was responsible for creating and "selling" favorable images of Reagan, explained that even though some people watching the *60 Minutes* piece might initially respond negatively, in the long run it was the visual images that would last, and the images were quite favorable: "[T]he visual outlasts the spoken word," he explained with a sly grin on his face.

While all presidents have been concerned about presenting favorable images, this chapter will argue that Reagan's preoccupation with image manipulation permanently altered the presidency—he re-imaged the presidency. For modern presidents, the campaign to get elected and governance were two largely separate realms of activity that involved different dispositions and different skills. Electoral campaigns were concerned with presenting alternative visions of America, partisan conflict, and image manipulation, while governance concerned the present and bringing people of different partisan persuasions together using pragmatic arguments, bargaining, and negotiating. While some presidents merged the two realms (especially incumbent presidents during reelection years), for the most part elections were seen as activities that resolved conflict (at least temporarily) and reset politics. Reagan broke down the wall separating the two arenas and employed the tactics used in the electoral campaign to govern. As one theater critic looking at the Reagan administration put it, "What Reagan has done is conflate two separate realms, the sociopolitical and the aesthetic, replacing politics with theatre" (Dasgupta 1988, 79). This is the first radical departure from the modern presidency and represents a significant break from prior presidencies. Once the precedent was set, future presidents then followed: "Long after Ronald Reagan has left the White House, the model of news management introduced during his tenure will remain behind, shaping press coverage and therefore public perception" (Hertsgaard 1989, 7).

In addition to the use of images, the Reagan administration was responsible for introducing a second element of the postmodern presidency. While initially cloaked in conservative ideological anti-government rhetoric (and not fully developed because of that), Reagan's argument that government cannot and should not solve all problems marked the beginning of a new vision of what the role of the national government should be in addressing social and economic problems. In asking Congress to adopt his economic plan, he stated his belief this way: "The taxing power of Government must be used to provide revenues for legitimate Government purposes. It must not be used to regulate the economy or bring about social change. We've tried that and surely must be able to see it doesn't work" (Weisman 1981, A1).

As part of this belief, the Reagan administration pursued a policy of deregulation and privatization of functions previously reserved for government. Ideologically wedded to a belief in the superiority of the free market, Reagan sought to eliminate government regulations by using across-the-board cuts and sought to shift government services and activities to "third-party" providers. Although the comprehensive deregulation and privatization driven by his conservative ideology failed to produce the benefits hoped for (the across-the-board approach actually led to a deregulation backlash), the effort represents a first step in the direction of a postmodern administrative approach to management—shifting government functions to non-governmental organizations, a development which will be referred to as the "neoadministrative state."

The final contribution of the Reagan administration to the making of the postmodern presidency came in the area of Reagan's expansion of the use of unilateral actions. In this area the Reagan administration did two things that set precedents for future presidents to unilaterally expand presidential power. First, Reagan used unilateral actions (e.g., signing statements, executive orders, presidential memoranda) as a policy tool. Second, Reagan's attorney general, Ed Meese, got the courts to accept (or at least not strike down) signing statements as a legitimate presidential power. These precedents laid the foundation for the expansion of unilateral presidential power which, when built upon by future presidents, would become one of the defining features of the postmodern presidency.

This chapter examines the origins of these postmodern developments as they were given birth by the Reagan administration. While they would change shape somewhat as future presidents applied them to their own administrations, the new assumptions about what constitutes presidential politics, what the proper role of government is, and what powers a president can and should unilaterally exercise became radically "re-imaged" during the Reagan years.

Reality Is Appearance

The postmodern world is a world of surface images with ambiguous connections to reality. Lacking a referent, images are evaluated not on their ability to represent reality, but on their success at evoking responses and engaging the audience. As Lesley Stahl learned, images override the spoken (as well as the written) word. There are a number of reasons this occurs, but one compelling reason is found in the nature of television itself: "[P]ictures arouse viewers' interest and attention to a greater extent because they give the viewer a sense of participation in an event or, at least, witnessing it personally" (Graber 1996, 87). By drawing people into the event, they become emotionally engaged to such an extent that they discount even dissonant verbal messages. Knowing this, Reagan's image advisors not only were not upset but were, in fact, quite pleased with the *60 Minutes* story.

According to the modern presidency model, a president should not only possess a solid sense of reality, but in relating to the American people he should also "teach realism" (Neustadt 1980). He is not in control of most events, but he can use events to educate—not by speaking, but through his own actions: "[H]e teaches less by telling than by doing (or not doing)" (Neustadt 1980, 74). The Reagan administration turned this principle on its head and, because of that, broke with the modern past. As Reagan biographer Lou Cannon says, "[T]he aides had adopted Reagan's own standard of judging stories by their impact rather than their accuracy" (Cannon 2000, 40). Contrary to Neustadt's claim that the modern president is "not in control of most events," the Reagan administration created their own events or, more accurately, created "pseudo-events"—staged events which appeared to be real.

Pseudo-events are planned rather than spontaneous and are staged primarily (if not exclusively) so that they will be reported and, hence, reproduced. "They are spectacles created for the sole purpose of creating an image" (Waterman et al. 1999, 15). Their relationship to reality is ambiguous, which is what creates their interest; they, in effect, create their own reality merely because they occur (Boorstin 1962). While pseudo-events are nothing new in the history of American politics, the Reagan administration was the first to realize their full potential through the medium of television. Television is particularly susceptible to pseudo-events because "what you see is what you get." Whatever is on television takes on a life of its own, no matter how disconnected it is from reality. This is true of reality television shows such as *Survivor,* as well as news about politics.

This is more than simply spin, the attempt to shape public opinion by convincing others of one's interpretation of events. It strikes at the heart of what constitutes governance. For the postmodern president, the creation, manipulation, and dissemination of images are crucial elements of governance. Modern presidents make decisions, negotiate with other political actors, attempt to pass legislation, and manage the executive branch. While postmodern presidents also do those things, their more compelling focus is on the presentation of images and symbols. As one book argues, we have created an office where policy and "substance" have taken a back seat to the image-is-everything presidency (Waterman et al. 1999). While images of presidents have been with us throughout history, the use of media consultants—experts on the use of television to project images—has fundamentally challenged one of the basic assumptions of the modern presidency. Television is qualitatively different than other forms of communication and is, today, critically important for governance. Press critic Mark Hertsgaard (1989) writes,

> The men around Reagan saw television as the path to power, the ultimate technical fix, the modern American King Maker. More than most of their peers in the politics business, they appreciated that without a sophisticated knowledge of how to exploit television, any politician's hopes of wielding power on a national scale were doomed. Whether candidate or incumbent, a politician desiring a successful presidency had to be able to communicate to the electorate his goals and vision for the country. (17)

How is it possible that postmodern presidents can be so successful at manipulating public opinion? How do presidential advisors create pseudo-events and what techniques do they use to manipulate presidential images? Why does the press—often the conduit for these images—allow itself to be used in such a fashion? And why do the American people accept such manipulation?

Psychological Linkages

Few citizens ever get to meet a president; fewer yet have an opportunity to personally get to know one. And yet virtually everyone has made judgments about presidents—whether they like or dislike them, whether they can be trusted, whether they are strong or weak, or whether they are average, below average, or great. How are such judgments formed?

The early version of the modern presidency posited that a president's reputation was largely determined by assessments made by close observers of the president—those whom Neustadt referred to as "the Washingtonians." The Washingtonians (public-opinion leaders and politicians who interact with the president) continually watch presidential decision-making as well as his standing in the public, and they make judgments about him. Over a period of time, these judgments create his professional reputation, and that reputation is a crucial power resource. In turn, this reputation is filtered through the media to the American people, who were characterized in the early version of the modern presidency model as fairly passive receptacles of elite opinion.

An updated, more idealized version of the modern presidency model envisions citizens as active, rational actors. Citizens make judgments about the president based upon policies he pursues. Thus, on the one hand, they should support presidents whose policies are judged to be close to their own preferences, and, on the other hand, they should withhold support for presidents whose policies are distant from the policies they prefer. Even a modified version of the modern perspective which places less of a burden of rationality on citizens suggests that citizens use a form of "low-information rationality" that relies upon gut reasoning, information processing shortcuts, and rules of thumb to evaluate presidents (Popkin 1991). In all of these instances, judgments about presidents can ultimately be traced to decisions the president makes or policy positions he advocates. They differ only in the extent to which citizens are involved in actively collecting that information and the degree to which their evaluation processes are rational.

In contrast, the postmodern political world is filled with visual images of presidential action. These images are intended not to provide information for rational analysis; rather, they are designed to appeal to the emotions of citizens by subconsciously linking them to the president. One such linkage process is called "presidential identification" (Thomas and Baas 1982; Thomas and Sigelman 1984), and functions to build support for the president by getting citizens to psychologically identify with him. "[C]onsciously or not, most citizens harbor deep-seated feelings of a personal—possibly even an emotional—nature toward the nation's most visible political leader. These feelings can be compared with parallel representations of how one 'would like to be personally in an ideal sense'"

(Thomas et al. 1984). In most instances such linkages are harmless, but when social anxieties become prevalent, the potential for manipulation arises.

When Reagan came to office, Americans were feeling helpless. They felt that their cities were ungovernable; they saw high inflation linked with high unemployment (stagflation), an energy crisis, rampant crime, schools that were failing, illegal drugs becoming an epidemic among the young, and an erosion of the American standard of living. As if that weren't bad enough, 53 American diplomats were being held hostage by a third-rate power—Iran—while Carter seemed unable to do anything right. Negotiations with Iran went nowhere, and a poorly thought-out military operation to rescue them had to be aborted after our aircraft experienced numerous mechanical failures and crashed into each other in the Iranian desert. America seemed as if it was in a state of decline and decay. Feeling that their government (and particularly Carter) had failed them and was impotent in the face of mounting crises, many Americans turned inward, retreating into their private lives and personal concerns. Reagan appealed to citizens' needs to feel good about themselves and their country "by promoting policies and ideology whose symbolic effect is to suggest that Americans, individually and as a nation, need depend on no one. In promoting such an illusion, Reagan soothes the nation's narcissistic injury, understood as a decline in Americans' confidence in their ability to exercise collective mastery" (Alford 1988, 582). Ronald Reagan presented himself as the John Wayne of American politics. He was independent; stood tall against evil; believed unquestionably in the moral goodness of America; told the plain, simple truth; simplified issues; and united Americans. Reagan made Americans, once again, feel proud to be Americans; he motivated and inspired by appealing through emotion (Klein 2006).

The danger of this type of psychological linkage is that it deflects both citizens as well as policy makers from discussing and debating the compelling issues at hand. Citizens, who understandably want to avoid dealing with the reality of social and political deterioration, are attracted to reassuring images, and politicians, who want to avoid making unpopular choices, find it easier to create images than make difficult decisions. Both benefit by a politics of image. This form of politics, referred to by Benjamin DeMott (2003) as junk politics, "personalizes and moralizes issues and interests rather than clarifying them. It's impatient with articulated conflict, enthusiastic about America's optimism and moral character, and heavily dependent on feel-your-pain language and gesture" (36).

The Image-Making Team

While presidents prior to Reagan had staff responsible for communications, the Reagan staff represented a quantum leap in the level of their sophistication. Most significantly, they operated on the basis of radically new assumptions about the role of image manipulation in governance. Deputy White House Press Secretary Leslie Janka was quoted as saying, "The whole thing was PR. This was a PR outfit that became President and took over the country. And to the degree then to which the Constitution forced them to do things like make a budget, run foreign policy and all that, they sort of did. But their first, last and overarching activity was public relations" (quoted in Hertsgaard 1989, 6). White House communications were headed up by Deputy Chief of Staff Michael Deaver. While Deaver was nominally responsible to Chief of Staff James Baker, in operation he was in charge of the administration's communications apparatus and had direct access to the president. Deaver eschewed policy discussions and focused solely on creating Reagan's image and on media manipulation. He was, to a large extent, responsible for staging some of the classic visuals from the Reagan years—Reagan's "Mr. Gorbachev, tear down this wall" speech at the Brandenburg Gate, Reagan's D-Day memorial service at Pointe du Hoc honoring "the men who took the cliffs," and a rugged Reagan riding his horse on the trails at his home in California, Rancho del Cielo. "Every Deaver decision was based on whether it would show Reagan to best advantage" (Cannon 2000, 34).

One of Deaver's principal assistants was David Gergen, a political advisor who had served in the Nixon and Ford administrations and would go on to work for Bill Clinton when Clinton desperately needed to improve his image. Primarily responsible for dealing in a cordial manner with print reporters, Gergen was also responsible for some of the classic "spontaneous" lines that Reagan was noted for. Reagan also made use of pollster Richard Wirthlin. While it is difficult to document the precise degree to which polls were used in the White House, one study of their use concluded that "the use of opinion polls is both frequent and dynamic in presidential deliberations" (Beal and Hinckley 1984, 84). If money were any gauge, it would seem as if Reagan took a dramatic step forward in the use of polling. It is estimated that he annually spent twice what Carter spent on polling, four times what his successor George H. W. Bush would spend, and well over four times what Gerald Ford spent. Still, the Reagan administration did not actually use polling in the creation of policy. As we will see, polling will come to be integrated more fully into the policy-making process in later administrations. While many others were involved in the creation and selling of the Reagan image—presidential aide Richard Darman, Press Secretary Larry Speakes, Lyn Nofziger, and Chief of Staff James Baker—the staff members primarily responsible for public relations were pragmatists Deaver, Gergen, and Baker, along with Reagan's long-time friend Darman (Hertsgaard 1989).

More than previous presidencies, communications in the Reagan White House were institutionalized. What began as occasional meetings of Reagan's image team evolved into regular weekly meetings of what became known as the "Friday Group," which met every Friday at Blair House to discuss the overall communications strategy. The daily communications tactical meetings followed a consistent pattern. At 8:15 every morning, the senior staff would meet and agree upon the "message of the day." The message of the day was a strategy designed to focus media attention on a single issue, and only that issue, on a particular day. It was a concept drawn from the electoral campaign, but the Reagan administration extended it to governance. At 8:30, Deaver would chair the communications meeting, where the day's events were reviewed and coordinated to emphasize the agreed-upon message. This was a tactical meeting that dealt only with short-term activities. Officials in all departments who dealt with communications in their respective departments would then receive computer messages and phone calls telling them what the message of the day was and sketching out what role their departments would or would not play in staging it. Any activities that any department was planning that were not consistent with that message were banned. At 9:15 there would be an informal briefing (a "gaggle") for the press, who would hear the message of the day for the first time. At the briefing reporters would be told about Reagan's activities for the day and the ground rules that would be in effect for photo opportunities or opportunities for asking questions. That would be followed by a more extensive briefing at noon, but unlike the earlier briefing, videotaping would be allowed at this briefing. The tactic was designed to coordinate the entire executive branch apparatus to emphasize one—and only one—point so no matter where reporters went looking for a story, the only one they would find was the one agreed upon earlier by the communications experts, and the only interpretation they would receive was the one developed by the White House. That story would fit into the overall communications strategy determined by Reagan's senior aides at the Friday Group meetings.

Critical for the success of this approach was Reagan's willingness to take direction. Becoming a modestly successful Hollywood actor prior to the method-acting rage, Reagan's acting style was simple and direct. He did what he was told to do by the director. "Ronald Reagan the actor looked good, moved easily, memorized his lines quickly and thoroughly, and took direction very readily indeed. He came along when routine, low budget movies were being turned out in assembly-line fashion—he made eight in one year—and so his patient, cooperative, tell-me-what-to-do attitude was a significant plus" (Barber 1992, 239). He was a "mechanical" actor.

Reagan brought this same acting orientation with him to the White House. His role had changed—he now played the president—and the objective was now to convince people (some of whom were quite skeptical) that Ronald Reagan was capable of being president. His performance as president was based upon the same acting technique he used in Hollywood. He was the same person regardless of the role he played—he only played variations of himself. Distancing himself from the difficult burdens of the presidency, he unquestioningly took direction from his staff and mechanically performed the role of a lifetime, that of president of the United States.

Strategic Considerations

Communications operations for the presidency became increasingly sophisticated and elaborate in the last half of the twentieth century. This expansion was consistent with technological advances in transportation and mass communications and helped transform the presidency. As Kernell (2007) has convincingly documented, presidents "go public" in order to promote themselves and their policies in Washington. In other words, to a degree, communication tactics become a part of the president's bargaining strategy, albeit one that relies more on force than compromise. David Gergen describes this strategy: "For one of the first times I'm aware of, we molded a communications strategy around a legislative strategy. We very carefully thought through what were the legislative goals we were trying to achieve, and then formulated a communications strategy which supported them" (quoted in Hertsgaard 1989, 108). It marked the beginning of the melding of campaigning and governance, a strategy that contributed to the making of the postmodern presidency.

The postmodern president has not only developed highly sophisticated communications strategies and tactics (trends that, by themselves, could be consistent with the modern presidency), but he now operates on the basis of new assumptions about the purpose of communications, thus helping to push the presidency toward its postmodern orientation. As already discussed, the postmodern president believes that reality is malleable and, as shown, the Reagan administration fully embraced this vision. But less fully developed was Reagan's strategic purpose. While Reagan accepted postmodern assumptions about communications, he still operated within the modern presidency's view of the fundamental purpose of communications—to build popular support for himself and his policies. It would fall to later presidencies (particularly the George H. W. Bush and Bill Clinton administrations) to change this. At this point, however, it is important to examine how sophisticated the Reagan image team actually was.

Television

Television has become the single most important technological advance used to link the president to the public. "Television has become the primary medium and tool of both campaigning and governing" (Denton 1988, xii). The first television reporters (e.g., Edward R. Murrow, Eric Sevareid, Howard K. Smith) came from the print media, and they brought with them ethical and professional norms from their experience and training for that profession. Television news was simply and clearly to present reality: "[T]he nightly newscast ideally should function as a reliable source of politically viable information and argument, a reasoned opinion" (Baym 2010, 64). This role fit nicely with the modern presidency.

But by the 1970s and 1980s, television news began to change as the proportion of visual images doubled from earlier years (Barnhurst and Steele 1997). The dominance of the image has altered both news reporting and the presidency itself. "[T]elevision, as a new type of social setting, has fostered the development of both a new way of *perceiving* our leaders and a new *logic* for how politicians are expected to behave" [emphasis in original] (Meyrowitz 1995, 119).

The Reagan image team recognized early on that the media wanted, indeed needed, attractive visuals. Television reporters who cover the White House are extremely competitive. They want their stories to be aired, and they know that one of the ways that will happen is if they can provide compelling visuals—the television equivalent of "good copy." By satisfying this need, the Reagan image team was able to control the message presented on the news, even when the visuals contradicted the policies the president pursued. Examples of how Reagan used images during his tenure as president abound. A brief look at a few drawn from his tax cut initiatives (a critical part of his economic plan—Reaganomics) will illustrate how images were used to disguise reality.

Reagan's belief in the role of government, referred to by supporters and critics alike as the "Reagan Revolution," was composed of a series of dramatic tax
cuts, a reduction in government regulation of the economy, an elimination of
waste in the federal bureaucracy, a reduction in spending on and an elimination
of a number of social welfare programs, and an increase in military spending
to restore a military balance with the Soviet Union. However, the signature
component of the Reagan Revolution was a series of individual and business
tax cuts. Based on a controversial economic theory called supply-side economics, the argument of the Reagan administration was that by cutting taxes, more
money would be put into the hands of taxpayers, who would, in turn, spend
that money, thus stimulating the economy, leading to economic expansion and,
in turn, increased tax revenues (albeit at lower tax rates) that would then reduce
the federal budget deficit.

But if Reagan's tax cut plan was thoroughly analyzed, it was clear that the
most significant economic benefits were to go to the wealthy and to corporations.
Realizing that this would be difficult to obtain political support for, the Reagan
image team implemented a media strategy to create the impression that tax cuts
would benefit everyone—especially the average worker—and not primarily the
wealthy. In a moment of unprecedented candor, one of the prime architects of
the policy, budget director David Stockman, referred to the tax cut proposal as
a "Trojan horse" designed to bring down the tax rates for the people in the top
income brackets (Greider 1981).

The first part of the economic aspect of the Reagan Revolution occurred
almost immediately after Reagan was sworn into office. The administration
abruptly stopped congressional discussion of the Carter-submitted budget and
submitted their own budget which dramatically froze numerous government
programs, especially programs that Democrats had created over the previous
three decades. That was followed a few months later by the second part of the
Reagan economic plan, a bold proposal for tax cuts. To obtain passage of his bill,
the Reagan image team created a spectacle designed to sway votes in Congress.
In prime time, sitting in front of a gold curtain in the Oval Office in the White
House, armed with colorful charts and graphs, Reagan went on television to
pitch his tax cut plan. His appeal was to average citizens, and he immediately
attempted to alleviate their fears about programs which would be cut. He started
by defusing concerns that people had about cuts in Social Security benefits: "I will
not stand by and see those of you who are dependent on Social Security deprived
of the benefits you've worked so hard to earn. I make that pledge to you as your

president. You have no reason to be frightened. You will continue to receive your checks in the full amount due you." While this statement had the desired effect of removing anxiety about Social Security and putting the president on the side of the elderly, it actually contradicted a proposal to cut Social Security benefits that Reagan himself had made only two months earlier. Further, it implied that Reagan was the defender of the elderly against cuts in the program advocated by the Democrats when, in reality, the opposite was the case.

The camera zoomed in on the president seated behind his desk, finally settling with a close-up picture of Reagan's head that virtually filled the screen. He then made a series of additional appeals to average citizens, claiming that his plan would help married couples, widows, and small businesses. Perhaps most compelling was the image of Reagan using the aura of the White House, telling the American people that they were in control of the government: "You wanted to change one little ... two-letter word.... It doesn't sound like much, but it sure can make a difference changing ... 'control by government' to 'control of government.'" At that point he encouraged citizens to call their congressional representatives and ask them to support the bill: "[R]epresentatives honestly and sincerely want to know your feelings. They get plenty of input from the special-interest groups. They'd like to hear from their homefolks."

This tactic, of going directly to the American people and asking them to contact their representatives, was a relatively new development in 1981. Reagan would use it repeatedly during his tenure as president. Although a new tactic, it was not inconsistent with the modern presidency. While using this tactic, Reagan did not abandon other types of political techniques (e.g., bargaining) to obtain support; it can be seen as merely another modern political tactic used to influence Congress.

The postmodern element of the approach is found in the use of image, particularly the close-up of Reagan. As noted earlier, in the modern presidency model the relationship between the president and the American people is mediated by "Washingtonians" (according to Neustadt) and especially the national press. Reagan altered that relationship by using television to go directly to the American people. While it is true that earlier presidents had also used television to make addresses to the nation, the innovation of Reagan's use of television was his ability to use images in such a way that he could establish an intimate, emotional connection with the audience (i.e., citizens). One element of how that was done was illustrated in his 1981 tax cut appeal—the close-up.

In that speech the camera zooms in for a close-up of Reagan several minutes into the speech, just as he makes his appeal to average Americans—to married couples, widows, constituents in southern states, family farmers, and small businessmen. As Bela Balazs (2004) notes, "Good close-ups are lyrical; it is the heart, not the eye, that has perceived them" (274). Close-ups show subtle facial expressions that reveal a person's humanity and give the impression of honesty—it is easier to lie in words than with the face.

A second example, also involving tax policy, occurred in January 1983 while the country was mired in the depths of a recession. In the morning Reagan announced that his administration was encouraging Congress to abolish the corporate income tax—a highly controversial proposal which would primarily benefit the wealthy. The president was presented in front of a dull gray backdrop—a bland, unappealing visual for television coverage. The more compelling visual occurred later that day. At 2:00 in the afternoon, Reagan was filmed in a Boston working-class bar hoisting a beer with red-nosed Irish chaps, a more compelling visual which sent a far different message. That visual made the news on every major network. While the media also reported the corporate tax story, it was the image of Reagan as a man of the people in the Irish pub, not the tax story, that stuck in the minds of the voters.

Yet while visuals were effective, they had to be used strategically. One rule of thumb was that Reagan should not be seen when there was bad news to report; he would only personally be present when announcing good news. This was known as the "lightning rod effect." Thus, when the unemployment or inflation rate went up, the treasury secretary or the director of the Office of Management and Budget (OMB) would talk to the press. But when housing starts improved, they flew Reagan to Houston, where he donned a hardhat and toured a new home that was under construction.

Personal Images

Reagan's advisors faced a dilemma. Polling revealed that many of the policies his administration pursued were disapproved of by the public. In fact, the Reagan administration's policies were far more conservative than were the majority of Americans. In light of this, how could they build popular support? The solution that was arrived at was to sell Reagan the person, rather than to try to sell policies. Reagan was presented to the American people as a strong, active leader who was in charge and made the tough decisions. Because he talked about family values, he became a symbol of those values and was viewed as a man with a deep spiritual core. He appeared friendly and likeable.

As has been reported in numerous biographies and detailed accounts of the Reagan administration, this image contrasted dramatically with reality. While Reagan promised to get America moving again, in fact he was a passive, detached president who naively believed that people always told him the truth, he seldom asked probing questions, and he often left it to his aides to make decisions for him. Although he touted family values, he was the first divorced president and had, at best, strained relationships with his children. Although he often concluded his speeches with spiritual references, he seldom attended church and, while he was genuinely nice, he maintained a cool social barrier between himself and others.

But personal image manipulation presents a paradox. On the one hand, postmodern presidents feel compelled to construct images that reveal televised intimacy of their lives. On the other hand, when they exhibit their intimate selves they run the risk of undermining the interpersonal distance necessary to make a person appear "presidential" (Parry-Giles and Parry-Giles 1996, 191). Yet citizens have a desire to know the intimate details of another person's life (a psychological phenomenon known as scopophilia). Television has enhanced this desire and focused it on the president, resulting in a desire to know the president "personally" (Meyrowitz 1995). Reagan was able to solve this paradox by implementing "a guarded revelation strategy" that allowed citizens to see the private Reagan, but only as president, not as an individual (Parry-Giles and Parry-Giles 1996). Instead of revealing personal thoughts and feelings about himself, he would reflect on his feelings about being president.

Controlling the Agenda

Similar to a modern president, a postmodern president must control the policy agenda. The modern president attempts to do this by proposing a package of policy initiatives and working with other Washington politicians to obtain support. But the postmodern president attempts to control the agenda by dominating media reporting and sometimes using the public dialogue to disguise the real agenda, which is then pursued through less visible actions. The Reagan image team did this using several different tactics. First, as already mentioned, they consistently articulated the message of the day and did not allow deviations from it. Reporters who wanted to pursue a different story would find it difficult to obtain information, at least from official sources in the executive branch. Second, also commented on earlier, they understood reporters' need for stories that contained good visuals, and they provided them. Third, they strictly controlled reporters' access to Reagan. Reagan held few press conferences (he usually performed poorly at them), and spontaneous interactions between the president and reporters were discouraged (Reagan had a penchant for making untrue off-the-cuff comments). When Reagan did allow interviews, he was provided with 3 x 5–inch index cards which told him what to say in response to questions. These tactics were extremely effective. As Sam Donaldson of ABC News said, "They serve up what they want, and also deny us the opportunity to do anything else. So our options are, do nothing or do it their way" (quoted in Hertsgaard 1989, 27).

Fourth, in order to counteract what they viewed as a cynical Washington media, the Reagan team often went around them to local media markets. This was done in one of two ways. One way was to invite news directors, anchors, and reporters from different parts of the country to the White House, where they were provided with special White House meetings. They would be briefed by a cabinet officer on issues relevant to them and then would have lunch with the president. Local news reports were overwhelmingly positive. A second way to go over the heads of the Washington press was to travel to different parts of the country and, while there, allow local reporters and anchors to interview Reagan. They would often be given fairly extensive 30-minute interviews, and the local stations would run parts of the interview over four or five days. Local reporters were, of course, allowed to ask only questions on designated topics. Reporters were excited about getting exclusive interviews with the president, and Reagan received positive coverage all week long at the cost of a one-stop controlled interview.

The sophisticated public relations activities serve multiple purposes. The most visible consequence is that the president is able to dominate and control the public dialogue. But, largely because the traditional media is so focused on trying to obtain compelling visuals and because reporters who follow the presidency are located in the White House itself, they often fail to see—or at least report—activities that require analytical depth to understand. Analysis seldom comes with an attractive image. The Reagan economic plan—Reaganomics—is a case in point.

The Reagan economic plan—massive tax cuts, reductions in domestic programs, and substantial increases in military spending—made it impossible to balance the budget and actually increased the budget deficit dramatically. With the budget under strain, the Reagan administration made an all-out assault on social service programs that were designed by Democrats to appeal to their political base, arguing that it would be fiscally irresponsible to continue to fund such programs (Ginsberg and Shefter 1999). But this partisan political strategy that drove Reaganomics went largely unreported (and when reported, seldom noticed). Instead, reporters tripped over each other to get the best camera angle on the latest photo op served up by the White House.

Once a president accepts the basic assumption that reality is malleable, a new vision of presidential action becomes possible. The Reagan administration rejected Neustadt's admonition that the president must teach reality and contributed to the making of the postmodern presidency by replacing it with the strategy that the president must create a new imaginary reality that masks the underlying intent of the action.

Images in Action: The 1984 Campaign

In some ways it makes little sense to discuss the 1984 Reagan reelection campaign as an event separate from the ongoing operation of the White House. The strategy employed during the campaign was, in fact, quite similar to that employed in the day-to-day operation of the White House. In the election, he won a second term by the largest electoral landslide in U.S. history—525 electoral votes to 10 for Walter Mondale—and won 59 percent of the popular vote. But for most of the campaign Reagan coasted (as he often did while president), limiting his contact with the media, basking in the glow of an economic recovery, and symbolizing the return of America.

According to the modern presidency model, electoral campaigns should be about issues and, to a lesser extent, the personalities of the candidates. In a sense, elections should be battles over differing visions of what America is and what it should be (White 1961). Candidates should crisscross the nation articulating positions on issues and inspiring the electorate. But while issues are important, their linkage to policy is uncertain. According to the modern model, the election "guides and constrains public officials, who are free to act within fairly broad limits subject to their anticipations of the responses of the voters and—this is important in a separation of powers system—to the desires of other active participants" (Polsby and Wildavsky 2008, 258).

In contrast, the postmodern election is dominated by images. Politicians use subtle images that appeal more to citizens' emotions than to their reasoning abilities. Emotions that are tapped are those which are connected to traditional American values—work, family, strength, the innocence of children, small town communities, and patriotism. More than previous presidents, Reagan in 1984 employed images that touched upon these values and, because of that, he was able to obtain support from voters who liked the man even though they disliked his policies.

Perhaps the quintessential ad that illustrates this is Reagan's "Morning in America" television commercial that ran in his reelection campaign. Virtually all of the traditional values linked to emotions are contained in a single minute. The ad starts with soothing symphonic music and a picture of boats pulling out of the harbor in the morning, followed by pictures of men and women going to work. A boy on his bicycle is seen throwing newspapers as a smiling man is picked up by a friend who is driving him to work. Slightly later in the vignette, a grandmotherly woman with a corsage is seen at the wedding of her granddaughter, who is dressed in white as the voice-over says that 6,500 young men and women will get married that day and they can look forward with confidence to their future. A picture of the White House is then shown, and the voice-over says that our country is prouder, as the ad shows children looking upward reverently; our country is stronger, as it shows a man with a blue shirt with an insignia on his sleeve raising an American flag; and our country is better, as it shows another flag being raised by an elderly man. The ad concludes with a picture of Reagan and the American flag. Thus, in a single 60-second ad, Reagan linked himself to the values of hard work, loyalty, patriotism, security, and optimism. He embraced innocent children, small town America, and the traditional family. The ad was hyperreal in that it conjured up images of an America that existed, at best, for a very few people for a very short period of time in the 1950s or, more accurately, never existed at all for most people (Coontz 1992). The family depicted, and the values conveyed, were more commonly seen on television shows such as *Leave It to Beaver* and *The Adventures of Ozzie and Harriet* than they were seen in real life.

A second ad, the "bear in the woods" ad, which subtly focused on foreign policy, pictured a huge grizzly bear lumbering through a forest. A voice-over, sounding similar to Reagan's voice (though not actually his), says, "There's a bear in the woods. For some people, the bear is easy to see; others don't see it at all. Some people say the bear is tame; others say it's vicious, and dangerous. Since no one can really be sure who's right, isn't it smart to be as strong as the bear? If there is a bear." In the background is a slow drumbeat that imitates a heartbeat that slowly increases in tempo and volume. The ad ends with a picture of Reagan and the words "Prepared for Peace." The bear, of course, symbolizes the Soviet Union, and its message is a justification of Reagan's arms race policy—in particular, the controversial Strategic Defense Initiative ("Star Wars"). But there is something far more sinister happening in the ad.

The commercial is the perfect blend of sight and sound to send a message far different from the explicitly stated one. The voice-over script raises the question of whether the Soviet Union (i.e., the bear) is dangerous or not, and then says that since we cannot be sure of that, we must be prepared by arming ourselves. That is a justification for an arms race. Thus, taken at face value the ad is an issues ad. But the visuals and the ominous sound imitating a heartbeat send a more compelling message. Although the commercial actually admits that we don't know if the Soviet Union is dangerous or not (e.g., "If there is a bear"), the visual of the bear answers that pseudo-question (seeing is believing). What's more, the sound imitating a heartbeat conjures up fear as the drumbeat increases in rhythm and volume until, in the final scene, the bear approaches an unarmed man on a hill. Thus, the combination of the video (the bear) with the sound (the drumbeat) taps into our fears and overrides what might otherwise be described as a moderate message. Even on the face of it, the ad is an oversimplification of a complex policy issue. The relationship between the Soviet Union and the United States was complicated not just by an arms race, but by complex geopolitical strategies, prior alliances, historical conflicts, competing economic systems, a history of distrust, and even times of cooperation. Yet the 30-second ad simplifies the relationship and maximizes the threat.

These campaign ads typify the postmodern approach. There is no real discussion of issues or policies; instead the ads link citizens to the president through the use of images which trigger emotions. Indeed, as Cannon (2000) reports, the Reagan campaign managers decided that they could not run on issues in 1984 because the issues did not favor Reagan. Although he largely attempted to avoid making specific references to issues in public, such a strategy is not necessarily inherent in the postmodern approach. As we will see in later chapters, future presidents will sometimes make use of issues (although in a symbolic manner) in making their appeals to citizens. The key factor that lies at the heart of the postmodern approach is not so much the absence of issues as it is the use of emotion (rather than reason) to link the president to the citizenry and the simplification of complex issues. Citizens "need to *feel* that someone is looking out both for their interests and for the *values* that give their lives meaning" [emphasis in the original] (Westen 2007, 122).

Inching Toward a Neoadministrative State

While the Reagan White House had a clear communications strategy driven by pragmatism, the same could not be said of its management vision. Looking back on their approach to managing the executive branch, one could make the case that Reagan took the first step, however small, toward postmodern management. However, unlike his orientation toward image manipulation, which was sophisticated and pragmatic, his management vision was simplistic, based on an unquestioned ideological commitment, and, as a result, contradictory. Nonetheless, his ability to challenge bureaucratic assumptions would, when expanded upon and rationalized by succeeding presidents, produce a more coherent vision of postmodern management. This new perspective ushers in the first characteristics of the "neoadministrative state," a postmodern view of the role of governance. But even future presidents would be unable or unwilling to fully pursue the new administrative direction. The neoadministrative state will be discussed in greater detail in Chapter 3 (George H. W. Bush); Chapter 4 (Bill Clinton), where it emerges as a coherent management philosophy; and Chapter 5 (George W. Bush). It should be noted, however, that all the presidents examined here fail to fully understand the postmodern challenges to administration.

The neoadministrative state found its origins in Reagan's simplistic vision of government bureaucracy but, in reality, go far beyond his knee-jerk rhetoric. Driven by conservative ideology, Reagan's view was based upon two assumptions. First, he believed that private, non-governmental organizations were better at addressing economic and social problems than were government programs. Second, he assumed that government was fraught with waste and inefficiencies and must be trimmed and controlled. The first of these beliefs—a shift in the role of government—represents a break with the modern presidency; it symbolizes the beginning of a postmodern "governance-as-facilitation" model. But Reagan's belief that government bureaucracy was inefficient and had to be controlled was an idea that came from a modern "governance-as-control" model and stands in contradiction to the neoadministrative state.

For the modern president to accomplish many of his goals, he must have the cooperation of the bureaucracy. Decisions that a president makes and policies that he adopts are not self-executing. To obtain compliance, even from those who are legally his subordinates, he must bargain, negotiate, and be willing to compromise (Neustadt 1980). Moreover, a president must organize the bureaucracy in a hierarchical, linear fashion according to established management philosophy.

Bureaucracy is seen as a way of rationally organizing people into offices to address problems and implement policies. Presidents exercise some control over the bureaucracy by being able to make political appointments (Executive Schedule, noncareer senior executives, and Schedule C appointments total about 3,000 officials), trimming or enhancing department and agency budgets, consolidating programs, and cutting layers of hierarchy. Rather than develop a new postmodern management strategy to achieve postmodern ends of shifting the role of government to non-governmental organizations, Reagan attempted to accomplish the task by (1) privatizing many government services, and (2) instituting strategies to obtain greater top-down control of the bureaucracy.

Privatization

Since the mid-1970s, postmodern Third Wave (Toffler 1980) transformations have disrupted social, economic, and political systems throughout the world. (First Wave systems were based on agriculture, and industrialization structured Second Wave societies.) Third Wave transformations have been led by the development of global capitalism. In this new environment emphasis has been placed, at least in government, on "decentralization, dispersing, and fragmenting federal responsibilities and authorities" (Durant and Warber 2001, 222). Consequently, a postmodern vision of the role of government, referred to by Durant (1998) as the "neoadministrative state," designed to address these changed positions has been articulated by public administration scholars. The neoadministrative state is "one in which a sizeable and ever-growing proportion of the federal executive branch no longer directly makes or implements policy. Rather these agencies arrange, coordinate, and monitor networks of public, private, and nonprofit organizations that pursue these things with or for them" (Durant and Warber 2001, 222).

But the drive to reduce government involvement in policy-making and implementation by Reagan came not as a result of a new postmodern vision of administration; instead, it originated in Reagan's blind faith in the benefits of the free market. He believed that the unregulated private sector would stimulate the economy and protect the public—government was seen as a problem, not a solution. Freed of government restrictions, individuals could act solely upon their self-interests and become self-reliant (Williams 2003). To accomplish this task, the Reagan administration wanted to place greater reliance on contracting out government responsibilities to the private sector and make use of user fees for services previously paid for by the government (Levine 1986).

To develop plans to pursue that strategy, Reagan created the President's Private Sector Survey on Cost Control (Grace Commission) in 1982, which produced a 21,000-page report with 2,478 recommendations pushing in the direction of privatization and the reduction of government inefficiencies. It estimated that if its recommendations were followed, it would save $424 billion in three years (a figure which proved to be significantly exaggerated). In addition to the report, the OMB issued two rules, Circular A-76 and Circular A-25. Circular A-76 mandated that whenever the private sector could perform a task at a cost lower than the government, it should be given that task. Circular A-25 said that when the government provided goods or services to private parties, it should charge user fees.

However, for the most part the Reagan administration's efforts at privatization came to naught. There were many reasons for the failure, but perhaps the most significant was Reagan's failure to develop a political strategy to implement the recommendations (Smith 1987). Instead of developing recommendations about how privatization could be implemented in specific policy areas, the administration took the position that after stating the objective, government bureaucrats would simply "make it happen." Thus, as is true of most of what could be said about the Reagan administration, the image, in this case of privatization, was more significant than the reality. Even though very little privatization actually occurred during his eight years in office, by articulating the privatization approach Reagan symbolically altered the public's view of the role of government.

Controlling the Bureaucracy: A Contradiction

As noted, a second prong of the Reagan administration's approach to management was to more tightly control the government bureaucracy. Reagan subjected the bureaucracy to cost-benefit analysis within the modern framework of hierarchical accountability (Tiefer 1994). This approach displayed a distrust of the bureaucracy and was inconsistent with the postmodern concept of the neoadministrative state. Instead, it represented a continuation and distortion of the modern president's approach to administrative governance, albeit with a conservative spin.

Consistent with Reagan's anti-government rhetoric was his belief that government bureaucracy—*any* government bureaucracy—was inefficient, wasteful, and unaccountable. Consequently, Reagan wanted bureaucrats excluded from policy-making roles, tightly controlled by those loyal to him who would be the policy makers, and wanted agencies downsized as much as possible (Rector and Sanera 1987). "Elements of the Reagan strategy included increasing the number of political appointees, screening those appointees for ideological consistency with the president, and targeting appointees to key agencies" (Ingraham et al. 1995, 265). For example, during the first six years of the Reagan administration the number of noncareer Senior Executive Service bureaucrats (i.e., political appointees) increased by 13 percent. This was over three times as large an increase in political appointees as other administrations experienced during this era. By politicizing departments, Reagan could pursue his attack on "big government" through surrogate loyalists located in key administrative departments.

Care was taken to expand the number of political appointees in targeted agencies. A larger number of appointees went to the OMB, the General Services Administration (GSA), the Justice Department, the Environmental Protection Agency (EPA), the Department of Housing and Urban Development (HUD), and the Departments of Education and Agriculture. These departments and agencies became the focus of tighter political control because they were important to Reagan's ideological beliefs or their constituencies were important for his political base (Rockman 1988).

Unilateral Actions: Laying the Foundation

Modern presidents rely on bargaining and persuasion to get other political actors to do what they want them to do. Postmodern presidents also bargain, but they are far more likely to also use command to accomplish their objectives. This is accomplished not by directly ordering people to obey them, but by institutionalizing changes (e.g., changing rules, regulations, and responsibilities, or abolishing or creating agencies) which change how bureaucrats and other political actors interact.

Although presidents before Reagan made use of unilateral executive actions, they were seldom used as policy-making devices—the common interpretation was that they were useful only for routine and minor administrative tasks (Burke 1992; Cooper 1997; Mayer 1999; Kelley 2002, 2003; Howell 2005; Krutz and Peake 2006; Black et al. 2007; Halstead 2007). But the Reagan administration, wanting to obtain greater control over the executive branch and facing partisan opposition in Congress, turned to the use of a variety of unilateral actions to shape policy. These included an array of tactics, including executive orders, presidential memoranda, parallel unilateral policy declarations, proclamations, regulations, administrative directives, executive agreements, bureaucratic appointments, presidential signing statements, and even recess appointments. The overall political strategy is described by Mayer and Price (2002):

> By using their formal powers, presidents structure the institutions that surround them to standardize their interactions with other actors. To convert the bargains that would otherwise require skill and scarce political capital into manageable leadership opportunities, presidents seek routines that encourage compliance from other actors. By creating institutions and processes that make these once-expensive bargains part of the political landscape, presidents alter default outcomes, leaving it to *other* actors to expend resources to undo what the president has done [emphasis in original]. (371)

Thus, the postmodern president sees an increasingly fragmented and partisan political culture where it is extremely difficult to create change. Feeling the pressure to respond to, in many instances, his own lofty campaign promises, he resorts to the use of unilateral actions. By doing so he becomes "the first mover" and resets the policy agenda. Other political actors (e.g., Congress), facing the same hostile political environment but lacking such unilateral powers, are at a disadvantage and often end up accepting what sometimes are presidential actions of questionable constitutionality.

The Reagan administration was particularly aggressive in using many of these powers and, once again, set a precedent for the making of the postmodern presidency—a presidency marked by unilateral executive action. For example, Reagan issued Executive Orders 12291 and 12498, which called for all federal agencies to perform cost-benefit analyses for all regulations and to establish a regulatory agenda that would detail all proposed regulations. The stated goal was to improve federal productivity by 20 percent by the year 1992, but the unstated objective was to shed government of much of its regulatory activity. These orders, noted by few reporters, and objected to by even fewer Washington politicians, had significant implications for the operation of the executive branch. In implementing policy the first priority of bureaucrats would no longer be long-established rules and regulations originating in democratic principles (e.g., transparency, fairness), but they were now to be primarily responsible for applying private market principles of costs and benefits.

Perhaps even more illustrative of Reagan's expansion of unilateral executive action was his use of presidential signing statements. Signing statements are statements of the president, made and signed when he signs congressional legislation, that represent his interpretation of the law. They derive their constitutional authority from the president's oath of office (Article II, Section 1) where the president swears to "preserve, protect, and defend" the Constitution, and the Take Care clause (Article II, Section 3) where the president is charged to "take care that the laws be faithfully executed." Signing statements can be traced back to the Monroe administration, but it was the Reagan administration that got the courts to recognize their legal legitimacy, and it was the Reagan administration that began to expand their use to policy-making and policy control, and to use them to expand the constitutional power of the presidency (Kelley 2003; Berry 2009). Over his eight years in office, Reagan issued 276 signing statements, 26 percent of which questioned the constitutionality of provisions of the law he actually signed.

Until the Reagan administration, the signing statement, although used by previous presidents, was of questionable legality. One of the major obstacles of Reagan's Office of Legal Counsel was "to establish the signing statement as part of the legislative history of an enactment, and, concordantly, to persuade courts to take the statements into consideration in judicial rulings" (Halstead 2007, 3). Attorney General Ed Meese helped make this possible by convincing West Publishing Company to include them in the legislative history of laws. Although the courts have not taken signing statements into consideration when ruling on the constitutionality of laws, neither have they ruled their use unconstitutional. Following Reagan, future presidents made even more expansive use of them.

Efforts to create policy through prerogative powers marks the failure of modern approaches, which relied upon influence, persuasion, electoral mandates, public opinion, and appeals to partisanship to solve problems (Pious 1979). The national political landscape has changed and made such tactics difficult, if not impossible, to use. But presidents, still mindful of the demands the public places on them, feel compelled to act in some fashion to address problems. Consequently, presidents are increasingly relying on unilateral actions to activate the political system. The Reagan administration marked the beginning of the use of unilateral action for policy purposes.

At the same time, Reagan's approach to government management represented a contradiction—a contradiction which will grow with future presidents. On the one hand, presidents recognize that government cannot solve many social and economic problems and that, instead, it should facilitate rather than control. At the same time, presidents who are frustrated by trying to bargain, negotiate, and compromise to develop solutions turn increasingly to unilateral actions. As we will see, presidents after Reagan would come to rely even more heavily on unilateral actions, not so much as an attack on the bureaucracy as Reagan used them, but to make public policy when their own public support was waning (Mayer and Price 2002). Used in this fashion, unilateral actions would become a major element of the postmodern presidency.

The Reagan Postmodern Legacy

It is risky to attempt to define any particular period of time as an "era." What distinguishes one era from another, what patterns of behavior and shared beliefs are central to a particular era, and where one era ends and another begins are issues subject to debate. Attempting to characterize a postmodern era is even more difficult as there is considerable disagreement over the meaning of postmodernism in the first place. Presenting even more difficulty is the fact that postmodernism itself contains modern elements. Consequently, those objecting to a postmodern classification will point to those elements to argue that we are not, in fact, in a postmodern era.

One must start somewhere, however. Some scholars who have written about the postmodern presidency have, perhaps wisely, avoided addressing the issue of exactly when the postmodern presidency began and instead merely focused on analyzing it (Miroff 2000; Parry-Giles and Parry-Giles 2002; Rubenstein 2008). At least one scholar has claimed that it became fully developed beginning with the Carter administration (Rose 1991), but another has argued that the Ford and Carter administrations represent an interregnum between the modern and postmodern eras (Barilleaux 1988). While these earlier attempts at uncovering the roots of the postmodern presidency are not without merit, they fall short of making the case convincingly because their analyses are not firmly linked to postmodern theory (Combs 1989).

The story of the making of the postmodern presidency begins with Ronald Reagan because he was the first to embrace postmodern assumptions and use new technologies, especially television, to fundamentally alter the relationship of the president to the public. In effect, he re-imagined what the role of the president could be in the American political culture. Reagan relied upon spectacle, theatrics, and simulated political events to such an extent that it influenced (perhaps dominated) decision-making in the White House. Future presidents would build upon and expand many of these innovations.

Reagan also initiated a more poorly thought-out campaign of privatization that would be expanded and rationalized more convincingly by later presidents. While this approach could lead to a postmodern redefinition of the role of government, Reagan and his advisors had not fully embraced that idea. Still operating on the basis of modern beliefs about the supposed evils of bureaucracy, their desire to control the bureaucracy and improve imagined inefficiencies actually undermined their attempts to address problems. Nevertheless, Reagan began a process that would, when developed more fully, radically alter the nature of representative democracy. About the Reagan years, Skowronek (1997) concludes, "Far from trying to make the system work, Reagan set about forging a wholly new system, and with it a different understanding of constitutional government itself" (416).

CHAPTER **3**

THE FRAGMENTED PRESIDENCY

GEORGE H. W. BUSH

George H. W. Bush's fractured sentences, physical awkwardness, and apparent inability to identify himself with his era contrasted dramatically with the iconic presidents immediately before and after him.

Timothy Naftali (2007)

During the second presidential debate in 1992 between then-president George H. W. Bush and challengers Bill Clinton and Ross Perot, Bush was caught by television cameras sneaking a peek at his wristwatch, hoping, no doubt, that the town hall meeting–style "debate" would soon end. That uncomfortable moment on the stage at the University of Richmond, broadcast to the entire nation, symbolized the tension that existed in, and defined, the Bush presidency. Bush was a president who was comfortable governing in the modern mold, yet he was pragmatic enough to realize that he had to employ postmodern campaign strategies to get elected. Unlike Reagan and presidents who would follow, he refused to integrate campaign techniques with governance—he resisted the permanent campaign. Because of this, George H. W. Bush's presidency was fragmented—he governed as a modern president, but campaigned (at least in 1988) using postmodern tactics. In his reelection bid in 1992, however, he refused to fully embrace the postmodern campaign strategy, apparently thinking that the American people would recognize and reward him for making tough decisions. He lost to his Democratic challenger, Bill Clinton.

George H. W. Bush desperately wanted to be president. His public career had prepared him for the White House, but it was not until 1980 that he was in a position to launch a serious challenge for the Republican nomination. His bid for the presidency fell short when Ronald Reagan, employing a series of ethically questionable ploys, outmaneuvered him for the nomination and went on to beat incumbent president Jimmy Carter. But Bush's presidential ambitions remained alive when Reagan selected him to be his running mate.

For eight years Vice President Bush watched as the Reagan image team ran the White House. In 1988, after dutifully waiting in the wings, Bush put together his own campaign team skilled in the craft of postmodern campaigning. Once elected, however, he was unwilling to utilize the postmodern governing approach Reagan had devised. Not fully understanding the paradigmatic shift that Reagan had initiated, Bush "separated campaigning from governing, not realizing that part of governing is campaigning" (Hargrove 2008, 197). In the modern presidency, elections resolve political conflicts, at least for a period of time, and reset the political coalitions that can govern until the next election cycle. Bush's view of politics would have fit nicely into the modern presidency perspective. Unfortunately for him, he was out of step with his times. At best we may say that by allowing his 1988 campaign to be managed using postmodern strategies and tactics, combined with his failure to effectively use a similar approach in his unsuccessful 1992 reelection campaign, he has illustrated the staying power of postmodern politics, at least in the realm of campaigning.

Although eschewing the use of campaign techniques to govern (i.e., the permanent campaign), Bush nevertheless helped make the postmodern presidency by advancing a view of executive management that recognized the limitations of government to solve difficult problems (i.e., wicked problems). But even then, his approach was fragmented—a confused approach that drew upon modern and postmodern elements without resolving the tension between them. With a view of government emerging from moderate conservatism embedded in the modern presidency paradigm, Bush sought to limit the size and scope of government and, through the White House Council on Competitiveness, limit bureaucratic discretion. At the same time, Bush extended the postmodern presidency by attempting to shift government programs to non-profit groups. However, those initiatives proved half-hearted because they lacked a sound postmodern base.

More significant for the making of the postmodern presidency was Bush's exercise of unilateral power. Facing high expectations (largely of his own making) and the political reality of gridlock, Bush resorted to the use of unilateral action to advance his agenda. This characteristic of the postmodern presidency would become even more commonly used with future presidents.

Bush the Campaigner: 1988

In order for postmodern candidates to be successful, they must have skilled advisors and handlers who can present the candidate in a positive light. In charge of the 1988 Bush effort was a triumvirate of campaign handlers composed of campaign manager Lee Atwater, media consultant Roger Ailes, and pollster Robert Teeter. Together they created and ran a campaign that hinged on two strategies. First, attack your opponent with whatever will work to raise his "negatives," strategically ignore policy issues which do not favor you, and exploit emotionally charged "wedge issues" which divide the opponent's electoral base. Bush's attacks resulted in not only one of the most negative campaigns ever, but also one of the dirtiest. The strategy of the Bush campaign hinged on the effectiveness of this tactic: undermine the opponent in whatever way possible. Truth was considered "collateral damage."

The second strategy was to re-create Bush's image. At the start of the campaign Bush's political image was difficult to clearly define. At various times during his career he was an extreme Goldwater conservative, a responsible conservative, a Reaganite, and a moderate Republican. Even his recognition as a war hero (the youngest World War II pilot) was continually undermined by an alternative reputation of his being a "wimp." His positions and values also seemed in flux. During the 1980 nomination fight with Reagan, he called Reagan's economic proposals "voodoo economics," yet in the role of vice president he dutifully helped implement those policies. These competing and conflicting images can best be explained as a result of political ambition. In essence, Bush was a pragmatic conservative, but mainly he was a politician who would do whatever was necessary to win political office (Naftali 2007). "Willing to detach his political identity from his own personal history for the purposes of a campaign, he reduced identity to nothing more than the role a politician happened to be adopting at a particular moment for purely tactical purposes" (Skowronek 1997, 433).

Going Negative

The day after Memorial Day 1992, public-opinion polls indicated that Democratic presidential candidate Michael Dukakis led Vice President George Bush by 17 percentage points. The polls further indicated that Bush's negatives were high, while Dukakis was viewed favorably. Given that environment, Bush's campaign manager Lee Atwater developed a game plan based, in part, on a 312-page analysis of the opposition called *The Hazards of Duke* that involved the strategy of altering the public's image of Dukakis by attacking him on wedge issues while changing Bush's image from that of a wimp to a hard-charging leader who would not be pushed around. Dukakis was attacked on six "red meat" issues: (1) that he was a Massachusetts liberal; (2) that he was a card-carrying member of the American Civil Liberties Union (ACLU); (3) that he delayed efforts to clean up pollution in Boston Harbor; (4) that he favored gun control; (5) that, while governor of Massachusetts, he had allowed a black convicted murderer named Willie Horton out of jail on a weekend furlough from prison and, while out, Horton raped and murdered a white woman in Maryland; and (6) that he had vetoed a bill that would have made the reciting of the Pledge of Allegiance mandatory in all Massachusetts schools. The issues selected were "simple, impressionistic issues that appealed to attitudes, created a reaction, not a thought" (Brady 1997, 148). Space does not allow for an examination of how each of these issues was used. Instead, I will focus on one that illustrates how they all functioned on an emotional level to alter the electorate's views of Dukakis.

In 1977 the Massachusetts state legislature passed a bill mandating recitation of the Pledge in all public schools in Massachusetts. Before acting on the bill, then-Governor Dukakis asked for advisory opinions from his attorney general and from the state's Supreme Court. The advice from all quarters was consistent—the bill, as written, was unconstitutional according to a U.S. Supreme Court decision in 1943 (*West Virginia v. Barnette*) and also unenforceable. Dukakis vetoed the bill, but was overridden by the state legislature. Neither Dukakis nor any Massachusetts governor since has enforced the law. But the Bush campaign wasn't interested in the subtleties of the issue; they saw it as a way of emotionally connecting with an electoral bloc that they needed to mobilize. Linking the Pledge issue with attacks that Dukakis was a member of the ACLU and then leaking unsubstantiated rumors that his wife Kitty had participated in a flag-burning protest during the Vietnam War raised questions about Dukakis's patriotism. While not everyone bought into these associations, those who saw patriotism symbolically and felt it emotionally (rather than seeing patriotism as a form of engaged activism) were upset with Dukakis (Sullivan et al. 1992). Dukakis dismissed the attack as silly and superficial and certainly nothing that the American people would believe or take seriously, and initially, at least, he refused to respond.

But the more Dukakis ignored the issue, the more Bush attacked. At campaign stops, Bush, with a flag pin on his lapel, would start the rally by reciting the Pledge of Allegiance and then attack Dukakis: "I do not question the family values of Michael Dukakis, I don't question the love of his family one for the other. But I'll never understand, when it came to his desk, why he vetoed a bill that called for the Pledge of Allegiance to be said in the schools of Massachusetts. I'll never understand it. We are one nation under God. Our kids should say the Pledge of Allegiance" (quoted in Naftali 2007, 58). At one point Bush even went to a factory that made flags, almost literally wrapping himself in the American flag. The Bush team, many of whom had worked in the Reagan White House, recognized the importance of spectacle to link the electorate to the candidate by tapping deeply felt emotions. The strategy (which worked) was to define Dukakis in the minds of the voters before he could do so himself, and to ground that characterization in emotion which resisted rational persuasion.

Attacking on all six issues, Bush sent the clear message: Dukakis "was an eastern elitist who disdained public demonstrations of patriotism ... Even more, the Bush staff ... define[d] Dukakis as a social liberal: overly concerned with the rights of criminals, unconcerned with other people's fears of crime, happy to defend any group or belief, no matter how objectionable to the majority" (Hershey 1989, 81–82). By mid-August Bush had not only erased Dukakis' lead, but had actually surged ahead of his opponent.

The Pledge issue, like the other red meat issues, represented a postmodern approach to campaigning. Like Reagan, Bush appealed to people's emotions rather than their rationality. Atwater exploited people's fears of crime (and possibly racism) with his use of the Willie Horton ads, their feelings of patriotism with the flag issue, their love of God with the school prayer controversy, and their antipathy toward liberals whom, many believed, were undermining the moral and ethical fiber of America by charging that Dukakis was an eastern "liberal" and a "card-carrying member" of the ACLU.[1] Although it was too late and they used the wrong approach, the Dukakis campaign finally responded. Westen (2007) explains how the Dukakis team miscalculated their response to the Willie Horton attack: "As was characteristic of the Dukakis campaign, the response to an emotional attack was a combination of appeals to reason (explanations of the furlough program) and a deafening, seemingly insouciant silence, as Willie Horton's stab wounds to the candidate's heart increasingly infected popular sentiment. Dukakis largely proceeded with business as usual, pressing ahead with themes of 'good jobs and good wages,' as if he had not just been the victim of a brutal political mugging himself" (67–68).

On each of the issues, truth was the real victim. The furlough program was actually developed by a Republican governor, Dukakis was advised by everyone he asked that he should veto the Pledge legislation, and one of the major reasons Boston Harbor could not be cleaned up was because the Reagan administration cut funding to the Environmental Protection Agency. But in a postmodern environment, emotion rules the day. When attacked using emotional appeals, the only effective response is with your own emotional appeals. The Bush campaign understood that; the Dukakis campaign, adhering to modern notions of rationality and truth, did not.

The New Bush

The second prong of the strategy was to remake voters' image of Bush, to give them something to vote *for*. Together, Atwater and Ailes devised a strategy to present Bush as a tough fighter who would pursue a conservative agenda and would vehemently oppose a liberal Democratic Congress. To accomplish this, a number of tactics were employed. Perhaps the most dramatic event in this re-creation (what Atwater called the most important event of the campaign) occurred early in the nomination season, immediately prior to the Iowa caucuses—the Bush interview with CBS News anchor Dan Rather.

Agreeing only to a live satellite interview (CBS wanted to tape it), the Bush team prepared their candidate to aggressively attack Rather (viewed by conservatives as an icon of the "liberal media") if he brought up the controversial topic of Bush's involvement in the Iran-Contra affair, something they fully anticipated would happen. When, as expected, Rather asked Bush about his involvement in the illegal affair, Bush pushed back, attacking Rather for unfairly bringing up what he referred to as a dead issue and attempting to distort his record. "You've impugned my integrity by suggesting with one of your little boards [visuals] here that I didn't tell the truth.... You didn't accuse me of it, but you made that suggestion.... I find this to be a rehash, and a little bit, if you'll excuse me, a misrepresentation on the part of CBS" (CBS Evening News 1988). Rather, sensing what Bush was up to, challenged him: "Mr. Vice President, you've set the rules for this talk here. You insisted that this be live, and you know that we have a limited amount of time" (CBS Evening News 1988). Bush responded with another attack: "Exactly, that's why I want to get my share in here on something other than what you want to talk about. . . . I want to talk about why I want to be president. Why those 41 percent of the people are supporting me. And I don't think it's fair to judge a whole career, it's not fair to judge my whole career by a rehash on Iran . . . I don't have respect for what you're doing here tonight" (CBS Evening News 1988). Running out of time, Rather abruptly, uncomfortably, and sarcastically ended the interview, "Mr. Vice President, I appreciate you joining us tonight and I appreciate the straightforward way in which you engaged in this exchange. There are clearly some unanswered questions remaining" (CBS Evening News 1988). Although Bush lost the opening Iowa caucuses, he established himself as a fighter.

Still, the Republican conservative base never entirely trusted Bush. Even though he took positions against abortion, in favor of prayer and recitation of the Pledge of Allegiance in schools, in favor of the death penalty, and in favor of gun ownership, he was nonetheless viewed as an eastern elite. To change this image, Bush embarked on a series of photo-ops illustrating his "everyman" touch. He was seen pitching horseshoes, listening to country music, eating taco salads and pork rinds, driving an 18-wheel semi around a truck stop parking lot, on his hands and knees using markers to draw his own campaign posters, and taking a boat ride around polluted Boston Harbor. With few press conferences and even fewer substantive speeches, the Bush campaign was composed of images and spectacles. But to capture the conservative base something more dramatic was in order. Such an opportunity arose at the 1988 Republican Convention.

In mid-August the Republicans met in New Orleans to anoint George Bush as their standard-bearer. In his acceptance speech written by Peggy Noonan, Bush belligerently pledged to not raise taxes, modifying a line from a Dirty Harry film. "The Congress will push me to raise taxes, and I'll say no, they'll push, and I'll say no, and they'll push again. And all I can say to them is, Read my lips: no new taxes" (Bush 1988, A28). This phrase brought the convention audience to its feet and solidified Bush with his conservative base. It re-created Bush as a fighter who would take on the "tax-and-spend liberal Democrats." It was, of course, irresponsible to make such a commitment when Reagan deficits loomed and, ultimately, it contributed to his downfall when he agreed to a tax increase as president. But, for the moment, it served its purpose and helped elect him president.

The George Bush of 1988 ran a postmodern campaign. He emphasized symbols over substance, his handlers staged compelling spectacles, he emotionally appealed to voters by touching upon fundamental American values, and he created an attractive image of himself. This could be done because of the use of television and the management of information. "[T]he major reason for Bush's victory was the ability of his handlers to understand that a new form of political campaigning—one based on quickly identifiable symbols and sound bites—was the way to get an electorate that had stopped reading and started watching music videos on television" (Greene 2000, 42).

But the George Bush who ran for reelection in 1992 seemed to have forgotten how he originally got elected. Without Atwater (who died in 1991) and Ailes (who quit in disgust), Bush's reelection campaign took on the characteristics of a traditional, modern campaign. Because of what he considered his success at correcting the problems that Reagan had left him, because of his overseeing the international chaos that the fall of the Soviet Union produced, and because of the success of the first Gulf War, he trusted that the American people would reward him with a second term. But he underestimated Bill Clinton's campaign skills, failed to understand the underlying reasons for Ross Perot's popularity, and failed to employ the kinds of postmodern techniques that brought him victory in 1988. "Bush hurt his reelection chances by conducting a traditional-style campaign that failed to take advantage of new communications technologies. His preference for the status quo led him in part to reject advice that he make use of the emerging forms of communications that the Clinton camp used so effectively" (Barilleaux and Rozell 2004, 44). The Bush experience raises the question of whether a candidate can win election without skillfully employing postmodern campaign tactics and leads to the conclusion that Bush contributed to the making of the postmodern presidency by losing his reelection in 1992.

Governance

To some extent all postmodern presidencies are fragmented—containing modern as well as postmodern elements; there is no clear wall separating the modern from the postmodern. The politics of the postmodern presidency contains diverse elements of both paradigms that are in dynamic flux, sometimes in conflict, sometimes folding into each other, sometimes creating new forms, and sometimes merely dissolve, never to be seen again. But for most postmodern presidencies, the underlying assumptions about campaigning and governing are drawn from postmodern theory. The George H. W. Bush administration was unusual in this regard. Reluctantly, he allowed himself to be controlled by campaign handlers adept at running a postmodern campaign, but Bush's natural dispositions were classically modern and, once in office, he governed as a modern president. As president, he preferred behind-the-scenes negotiating with other politicians and heads of state to public appearances. Even stalwart conservatives were critical of his failure to engage the American people. "He discounts rhetoric because he discounts persuasion of the public. He is governing less by continuous acts of pubic consent than by a small elite's entitlement, the right of the political class to take care of business cozily" (Will 1990, A21).

Raised during the height of the modern presidency in a patrician family where his mother discouraged the use of the word "I," Bush possessed a sense of noblesse oblige. In 1979 he articulated this vision to a ninth grade graduating class at the Greenwich Country Day School, a school he had attended as a young boy: "Those who go to fine private schools like this have a disproportionate obligation to put something back into the system" (quoted in Perry 1979, 1). Consequently, Bush's style of leadership was low-key, incremental, prudent, and cautious. But this low-key, behind-the-scenes approach to governance no longer fit the times. He campaigned on the Reagan legacy; however, he did not fully understand that Reagan had not only changed many of the policies of previous presidents, but that he had also changed the fundamental assumptions about how a president should govern.

"The Vision Thing"

To build support, a postmodern president must engage the public by creating an emotionally appealing vision for America and, while doing so, build personal support. Public support is critical for presidents because it provides them with flexibility (i.e., political leverage) to enable them to govern through persuasion and, perhaps more importantly, through the use of unilateral actions (Cammarano 2009). Without the political buffer that public opinion provides, presidents find it difficult to govern as opponents feel free to criticize presidential actions. Bush failed to provide such a vision.

Because of Bush's failure to engage the public, he was often criticized as either lacking a vision or being unable to clearly articulate it, or both. Even Bush himself admitted as much in a David Frost interview: "I'm not good at expressing the concerns of a nation—I'm just not very good at it" (quoted in Apple 1989, 5). Although he tried to lower expectations and present himself and his presidency as "practical," the press continued to criticize him about what he derisively referred to as "the vision thing."

At the same time, Bush did not totally ignore "the vision thing"—it was more that he approached it indirectly. Instead of going directly to the American people (usually through television) as Reagan had done, Bush attempted to address the issue by cultivating personal relationships with Washington reporters. He seldom resorted to the use of spectacle and pseudo-events, preferring instead to have informal conversations ("chats") with reporters. In this way, he hoped to demonstrate his knowledge of policy and obtain favorable press coverage. This tactic was based on an elite "code of honor" that if you treat people decently they will return the favor (Barilleaux and Rozell 2004). But it was also a tactic taken from the modern presidency playbook, and it proved ineffective.

As noted in the previous chapter, the Reagan White House tightly controlled the information that the press would receive by orchestrating a "message of the day" and providing reporters with compelling photo-ops that assured that their story would make the evening news broadcasts. In contrast, the Bush White House Office of Communications had no message of the day and instead provided reporters with a list of all the day's activities, allowing reporters to make their own decisions about what stories to highlight. The Bush administration expanded the range and increased the number of press conferences, thus providing unprecedented access to help reporters obtain the information they needed. The result was not what they hoped for, however. Instead of sympathetic stories, there was a lack of focus in the stories that came out and confusion in the media about what events were important to cover. In a strange irony, the press, which cynically criticized the Reagan White House for image manipulation, in turn criticized the Bush White House for incompetence because of its failure to manipulate them (Ignatius 1989).

More fundamentally, however, Bush's inability to articulate a vision in the postmodern mold was a result of his ambiguous relationship with Ronald Reagan. Running against Reagan for the Republican presidential nomination in 1980, Bush had criticized Reagan's economic plan as "voodoo economics." But as vice president, Bush faithfully supported and defended Reaganomics and in 1988 ran as a candidate who would continue the Reagan legacy. When, as president, he had to break a pledge he made not to raise taxes (a key element of Reaganomics), he ended up fragmenting the conservative coalition that had elected him and contributed to his electoral defeat in 1992.

The Challenge of Wicked Problems

In the modern age, presidents focused on creating programs designed to address problems that need public attention—racial discrimination, unemployment, inflation, construction of an infrastructure, agricultural crises, inner-city housing decay, energy dependence, etc. To address these problems, presidents worked with Congress to forge legislation to regulate business and create bureaucratic departments and agencies that would implement policies designed to solve the problems. For modern presidents, a host of such programs were often tied together under a concept that would define the overall approach. Thus, FDR created the New Deal, Truman the Fair Deal, JFK the New Frontier, and LBJ the Great Society. Together, these programs resulted in an expansion of the bureaucracy into what became known as the administrative state. This was a logical attempt to deal with social and economic problems—identify the problem, analyze possible solutions, decide which solution is best, adopt a program, create organizations that will implement the program, and empower bureaucrats to do their jobs. Bureaucracies were run on the principles of adherence to rules and hierarchy to assure that everyone would be treated fairly (i.e., the same) and that efficiency and responsibility would be built into the system.

However, the postmodern political world is fragmented, and seldom lends itself to logical problem-solving. Problems are complex, contested, and defy not only solutions, but even clear definitions of the problems themselves. They constitute a class of problems referred to by policy analysts as "wicked" (Rittel and Webber 1973; Roberts 2000; Conklin 2005). Wicked problems defy clear definition. They have numerous interested parties (often difficult to identify) and they require complex problem-solving processes, thus making it difficult to identify solutions (Roberts 2000). Every interested party has its own perspective on what the problem is and what the possible solutions might be. None, of course, are wrong because ultimately there are no right or wrong solutions, only those that benefit or disadvantage particular groups. The significance of wicked problems is that it is difficult to address them while working within the modern orientation toward problem-solving. Wicked problems require that government play a different role to address them.

Those who have studied wicked problems contend that government must develop a horizontal, collaborative organizational approach which is broadly inclusive of interested parties. "[C]ollaboration is premised on the principle that by joining forces parties can accomplish more as a collective than they can achieve by acting as independent agents. At the core of collaboration is a 'win-win' view of problem solving" (Roberts 2000, 6). The role of government changes from one of control, direction, rule-making, and regulation to one of creating and facilitating cooperative mechanisms that coordinate public, private, and non-profit groups to work on problems (Durant and Warber 2001). This vision of the role of government is referred to by Durant (1998) as the "neoadministrative state." It is "one in which a sizeable and ever-growing proportion of the federal executive branch no longer directly makes or implements policy. Rather these agencies arrange, coordinate, and monitor networks of public, private, and nonprofit organizations that pursue these things with or for them" (Durant and Warber 2001, 222). It does not mean, however, that government abdicates its responsibility to address problems and merely turns them over to the private sector. Nor does it necessarily imply government deregulation. Instead, it places government in the role of primary facilitator to bring together interested parties for the purpose of coordination and collaboration. To develop and implement this approach requires a sophisticated understanding of administration, political courage to take on entrenched interests both within and outside of government, skilled advisors, a desire to work collaboratively, and a pragmatic seriousness about solving problems. Above all, it requires an appreciation of government and a respect for bureaucrats.

Not fully understanding the challenges of wicked problems, the Bush administration responded in two contradictory ways. One way was to symbolically recognize that some problems are beyond the scope of the federal government to solve. That was summed up in the campaign phrase of "a thousand points of light," Bush's belief in volunteerism to address social ills. But this approach was primarily a tactic designed to satisfy electoral constituencies and would fail to redefine an active role of government to coordinate those constituencies. Still, at least theoretically, the general outline of the approach was consistent with postmodern governance.

The second strategy was taken directly from the conservative interpretation of the modern presidency—control and limit government bureaucracy. After some initial confusion about how to accomplish this task, the job was finally given to Vice President Dan Quayle, who headed up the White House Council on Competitiveness, which was charged with the task of making America more competitive by reviewing and eliminating many government regulations.

"A Thousand Points of Light"

In his speech accepting the Republican nomination for president on August 18, 1988, George H. W. Bush sketched out his vision for addressing social problems. First and foremost, he believed that government alone could not solve them. Lauding the value of community, he recognized a host of private and non-profit groups that were trying to solve local and national problems through volunteer work and described them by drawing on poetic imagery, if not hyperbole: "a brilliant diversity spreads like stars, like a thousand points of light in a broad and peaceful sky. Does government have a place? Yes. Government is part of the nation of communities, not the whole, just a part" (Bush 1988, A28). In a broad sense this statement is consistent with the function of government in a postmodern age.

Yet, Bush's Points of Light movement turned out to be more symbolic than a genuine approach to governing. Shortly after taking office he supported legislation to provide start-up funding for the Points of Light Foundation, an organization that was supposed to coordinate volunteerism throughout the nation. But rather than having the Points of Light Foundation collaborate with government, Bush saw the "points of light" approach as a *substitute* for government action (Duffy and Goodgame 1992). In addition, Bush created the Office of National Service (ONS) and housed it in the White House. The mission of the ONS was even more obviously symbolic. Its primary task was to identify and honor community and volunteer groups, "points of light," that were working on solving local problems. "Six days a week, the ONS would recognize a Daily Point of Light, and Bush often found the time to attend that formal recognition. During his term, he met with representatives of 675 Points of Light and Vice President Quayle met with another 103" (Greene 2000, 150).

George H. W. Bush's recognition of the difficulty of government to deal with social and economic problems was consistent with the postmodern description of wicked problems. But his response of volunteerism as a replacement for government action was simplistic and ineffective at adapting to the fundamental changes that were occurring in American society. Unlike Ronald Reagan's ideological anti-government response, Bush was more appreciative and understanding of the role of federal civil servants. His Points of Light initiatives actually stemmed more from his patrician sense of noblesse oblige. However, the fragmented political and cultural environment in which wicked problems exist requires government action, not government inaction.

The White House Council on Competitiveness

Shortly after taking office, George H. W. Bush addressed members of the Senior Executive Service at Constitution Hall, publicly showing them that he understood how government worked and that he respected their work. Early in the Bush administration—at least the first year or so—the feeling among bureaucrats was that this would be a kinder, gentler administration than the one they had just experienced. However, with the creation and empowering of the White House Council on Competitiveness, that feeling changed.

The Council, headed by Vice President Dan Quayle, was created by executive order in April 1989, but it was not activated until over a year later. Operating largely in secret, six working groups were established and charged with making recommendations to improve competitiveness in their respective areas. Over the next several years the Council instituted changes in regulations concerning the development of wetlands, air pollution, ozone depletion, product liability lawsuits, and drug approval procedures—in each instance eliminating or changing regulations to create a more favorable atmosphere for business. Perhaps most dramatic, however, was Bush's announcement in his State of the Union address in January 1992 that he was instituting a regulatory moratorium for ninety days, during which time the Council would review all proposed regulations. (The ninety-day review period was subsequently extended 120 days beyond that.)

Unlike the Points of Light movement, which was at least symbolically consistent with postmodern administrative theory, the White House Council on Competitiveness operated on assumptions that government was too big and that regulations hurt economic growth. Rather than reform government bureaucracy to mobilize and coordinate non-governmental groups to address wicked problems, the Bush administration adopted the simplistic view that the free market—if only free of government regulation—was the solution to most of our problems.

George H. W. Bush's management approach was not attuned to the postmodern forces that were challenging government. At best, his approach to administration could be described as pragmatism with a conservative bent and, at worst, it harkened back to an almost premodern noblesse oblige era where volunteerism could solve problems. Although Bush came to the presidency with perhaps the most impressive executive experience of any recent president, he failed to have a transcending vision of the role of government. Unlike other presidents who had broad leadership goals, Bush's approach could be described as "fragmented incrementalism." He offered no cohesive, visionary leadership and, at best, he could be described as a president who responded to the few problems that he believed government could address in a prudent and cautious manner.

Unilateral Actions

Because modern presidents exercise power through persuasion, resorting to command is a sign of failure. Neustadt, for example, says that the use of his formal powers represents a painful last resort that often undermines presidential power (1980), and he encourages presidents to bargain, negotiate, and compromise instead. Recent adaptations of the modern presidency model have added a plebiscite dimension to presidential persuasion, arguing that modern presidents must now use public campaigns to mobilize public opinion in support of policy initiatives (Rimmerman 1993; Kernell 2007). However, postmodern presidents find themselves in even more difficult political environments than do modern presidents. Often saddled with unrealistic expectations that stem from inflated campaign promises and, once in office, finding themselves in a fragmented and polarized political environment, presidents have felt compelled to act, and act quickly. With the national political spotlight on them, they resort to unilateral actions. "With executive orders, executive agreements, national security directives, proclamations, and other kinds of directives, presidents can exert power and initiate change to an extent not possible in a strictly legislative setting. And because of this, they stand a considerably better chance of beating back the public claims made on them, while also redirecting the doings of government in ways that better reflect their own priorities" (Howell and Kriner 2008, 106). Bush made extensive use of unilateral powers, building upon what previous presidents had done and developing new powers. In this respect, he contributed to the making of the postmodern presidency.

Although Bush won the presidency in 1988 quite handily in both the popular vote and the Electoral College vote, the Democrats managed to strengthen their majorities in both the House (by five seats) and the Senate (a gain of one). But partisan opposition alone does not fully account for Bush's extensive use of unilateral action. By acting unilaterally, postmodern presidents can set the political agenda and define the parameters of the policy debate: "If they want to shift the status quo by taking unilateral action on their own authority, whether or not that authority is clearly established in law, they can simply do it—quickly, forcefully, and (if they like) with no advance notice. The other branches are then presented with a fait accompli, and it is up to them to respond" (Moe and Howell 1999, 855).

The use of unilateral action is not specifically found in the Constitution. In fact, it is the very ambiguity of the Constitution regarding the powers of the president that has made it possible for him to assert extensive unilateral power (Moe and Howell 1999). For example, without additional explanation, the Constitution merely says, "The executive power shall be vested in a President of the United States of America." Without precise Constitutional definitions of their powers, the only restrictions on postmodern presidents are political—what strategically is possible given the political dynamics of the time. This further emphasizes the personal nature of the office—a characteristic of both the modern and the postmodern presidencies. Because of the weakening of traditional political associations, presidents increasingly must rely upon their own resources, talents, skills, and ideas to produce change. One way they do that is through the use of unilateral action.

Bush's use of unilateral action occurred in both the foreign and domestic arenas. In the area of foreign affairs, for example, the Reagan administration had broken the ice with the use of unilateral action by using national security directives to create policy (national security directives go by different names under different presidencies). National security directives are not necessarily made public, although until the Bush administration, they were reported to Congress. During his eight years as president, Reagan issued more than 300 and, because of his own passivity, he was sometimes even unaware of what they contained (Tiefer 1994). But they were made on an ad hoc basis and followed no particular procedures. Bush contributed to the making of the postmodern presidency by institutionalizing their creation by formalizing the processes through which they were developed. In addition, he tightened the secrecy surrounding them by withholding their content from Congress (Tiefer 1994). At the height of his popularity immediately following the Persian Gulf War, Bush candidly laid out his view of the president's role in foreign policy: "It is the President who is responsible for guiding and directing the Nation's foreign policy. The executive branch alone may conduct international negotiations, appoint ambassadors, and conduct foreign policy. Our founders noted the necessity of performing this duty with secrecy and dispatch, when necessary" (Bush 1992, 497).

Perhaps no unilateral action illustrates Bush's perspective about presidential power as does his use of signing statements. When a president signs a piece of legislation sent to him by Congress, he sometimes attaches a written statement—a signing statement—that describes his interpretation of the meaning of the bill or provisions of the bill. As mentioned in the previous chapter, it was the Reagan administration that breathed new life into signing statements, allowing them to be turned into policy-making instruments (although the Reagan administration seldom used them in that fashion). Advised by C. Boyden Gray, who was in charge of protecting the president's constitutional prerogatives, Bush expanded their use, turning them into powerful de facto ways of legislating without congressional approval. He boldly asserted his right to strike down particular pieces of legislation that he disagreed with without actually vetoing them. "[O]n many occasions during my Presidency, I have stated that statutory provisions that violate the Constitution have no binding legal force" (Bush 1992, 499).

During his four years in office he issued 228 such statements, far more per year that any other recent president.[2] More significantly, 68 percent of them raised serious constitutional interpretations (Halstead 2007). Rather than vetoing legislation, Bush accepted the bill, but used signing statements to interpret specific provisions of the legislation. In justifying his interpretations, he would sometimes cite floor debates in Congress as reported in the *Congressional Record*. This, of course, provided him with considerable flexibility to interpret legislation in the manner he liked, as the congressional debates would include those who supported as well as those who opposed the bill. In at least one instance the Bush administration, anticipating the passage of a bill they opposed, actually planted an alternative account (which they would later include in a signing statement) by getting supporters in Congress to inject the desired interpretation into the floor debate, even though that side lost in the eventual vote (Tiefer 1994). Illustrative of this strategy was Bush's action on civil rights legislation.

After two years of negotiating, Congress passed the Civil Rights Act of 1991, which sought to restore the law concerning affirmative action to its status prior to a series of Supreme Court decisions that, cumulatively, eroded the effectiveness of the principle in the hiring of minorities. In a bipartisan display, Congress wrote legislation that explicitly overruled two Supreme Court decisions on the subject—the *Watson* (1988) and *Wards Cove* (1989) decisions. Debate was wide-ranging, and the bill's opponents effectively placed their alternative views in the *Congressional Record,* the official record of the proceedings of Congress.

Opposed to the bill, but fearing controversy should he veto it, Bush signed the bill, but added a signing statement that said that the bill would be interpreted consistent with the understanding of those who opposed the bill rather than the clearly articulated view of the majority who passed the legislation. The effect was to turn the law upside down on its most central point. It is unknown how frequently this strategy was used, but it demonstrates the expansion of unilateral power that Bush exercised virtually hidden from public view.

The Bush Character

The modern presidency places considerable emphasis on the president's "interior resources," most especially his character. Because the presidency is a one-person office rather than a collective institution, presidential character becomes critically important. But while character is important for the modern presidency model, it is not for the postmodern president; instead, character is replaced by personality. Where character is concerned with things such as citizenship, duty, honor, work, reputation, morality, and integrity, personality is more likely to be associated with more visible traits such as being fascinating, attractive, forceful, creative, magnetic, and charismatic. On this, Bush was, once again, fragmented. He grew up in a home that emphasized the importance of character, but late in life he found himself in a political environment that operated on the basis of shifting presidential images that engaged people.

Bush was raised in a well-to-do, aristocratic East Coast family which emphasized character formation. He was taught to be humble, competitive, respectful of authority, and loyal, as well as to work hard. Because of their position in society, the Bushes thought it was their responsibility to be in charge of things, but in leading, he was taught by his mother not to brag. He said this about his mother: "I spent my whole life learning not to talk about myself from my mother" (quoted in Barber 1992, 462). This humble orientation—a product of an elite culture—was an admirable dimension of character, but it did not serve him well in a postmodern environment where it was important to separate oneself from projecting attractive personality traits. "George Bush looked for ways to avoid overexposure and exaggerated credit taking" (Barilleaux and Rozell 2004, 136). This led to awkwardness in his 1992 reelection campaign. Proud, yet humble, he believed that he had done a good job as president and that, because of that, he would win a second term. "Throughout, Bush remained convinced that the American people would, in the end, reward him for his patriotism, dedication, and spotless leadership" (Parmet 1997, 504).

One such example of presidential leadership that not only went unrewarded but was actually used against him occurred in the 1990 budget negotiations with the Democratic-controlled Congress. Although Bush had campaigned for election in 1988 on the unequivocal "Read my lips: no new taxes" pledge, he faced a difficult decision in 1990 regarding taxes. After two years of holding the line on taxes, Congress wanted to enhance a number of social programs and pay for them with tax increases. To fail to increase taxes would mean an increase in the federal deficit, something the financial markets were uneasy about. Concerned about the deficit, Bush did what he considered the right thing to do—he broke his no-tax pledge. While he viewed this as an act of responsible leadership, many critics, especially conservatives in his own party, considered it a betrayal. His own press secretary, Marlin Fitzwater, after leaving office, called it the single biggest mistake of his presidency (Fitzwater 1995).

Consistent with his character, but inconsistent with the postmodern political environment, he governed by developing personal relationships with people and opted for small incremental changes rather than engaging public spectacles. As president, he surrounded himself with friends and he dealt with foreign leaders by developing personal relationships with them. He preferred closed-door meetings to Reagan's made-for-television spectacles, and was willing to let others take credit for accomplishments when, in fact, he could have done so himself. Lacking the kind of "take-charge" media-sensitive advisors who ran the Reagan administration, the Bush White House (and subsequent reelection campaign) took their cues from Bush himself and, in the process, failed in the most important postmodern function of the president—to be a publicly visible leader.

The George H. W. Bush Postmodern Legacy

George H. W. Bush's presidency illustrates the powerful effects of the emerging postmodern presidency that had been initiated by Ronald Reagan. When he accepted the advice and direction of his campaign handlers in 1988, he won election. Once in office, however, he eschewed media manipulation and preferred a governance strategy that emphasized bargaining and negotiating behind closed doors. This approach, drawn from the modern presidency model, produced some successes, especially in the more secretive world of foreign policy, but failed miserably in the domestic arena where public leadership was called for.

Nonetheless, Bush contributed to the making of the postmodern presidency by dramatically expanding the use of unilateral actions. He was particularly sensitive to maintaining and expanding presidential prerogatives, and he aggressively used such actions to protect and expand presidential power. While Reagan's major contribution to the making of the postmodern presidency was his practice of image manipulation, Bush's legacy would lie in the use of unilateral action, establishing precedents that were inevitably used by successors. Future presidents would look to the presidency of Ronald Reagan to learn about how to communicate with the American people in a postmodern political environment, while they would look to the George H. W. Bush administration to learn about how to employ unilateral actions to reshape the political agenda.

After the experience of the Reagan administration, some political observers believed that a fundamental shift had occurred in the nature of presidential politics. Yet most pundits and academics were reluctant to suggest that a paradigm shift had occurred, instead claiming that the modern presidency model only needed to be updated to include a more plebiscitary dimension. The George H. W. Bush administration, fragmented and confusing as it appeared on the surface, actually revealed that the foundation of the postmodern presidency had indeed been laid. To get elected, presidential candidates would have to employ postmodern strategies and tactics; to govern, presidents would have to create a permanent campaign (i.e., "go public") and use unilateral actions to set the policy agenda.

At the same time, Bush's presidency raises questions. Do postmodern presidential campaigns encourage candidates to make commitments that, once in office, lead them to use unilateral actions? How can presidents reconcile the demand to run a permanent campaign with the creation of sound public policies? What personalities are best suited for the postmodern presidency?

Notes

1. The "card-carrying" phraseology actually came from an announcement Dukakis made while campaigning in Iowa. It was used repeatedly by Bush to subconsciously link Dukakis to the McCarthy-era accusation of being a "card-carrying member of the Communist Party."

2. Bush averaged 57 signing statements per year; Reagan 31, Clinton 47, and George W. Bush only 20.

CHAPTER 4

THE SHAPE-SHIFTER

BILL CLINTON

Bob Dole should drop out and let the Republicans nominate Bill Clinton. The president will co-opt any Republican position that plays well with the electorate no matter how shortsighted or mean-spirited.
Robert Scheer (1996)

In 1979 Bill Clinton, at age 32, was sworn in as governor of Arkansas, at that time the youngest governor in the nation. Ambitious and cocky, he brought in progressive policy experts from across the nation and promoted an idealistic agenda. The "Wonder Boy" (one of his early nicknames) began a series of programs to improve the crumbling Arkansas road system, improve rural health clinics, encourage small business growth, and promote agricultural exports. In order to pay for these projects, he increased the price of auto registration and established a populist image by being publicly critical of the timber, poultry, and utility industries, which, he claimed, were destroying the environment.

After only two years as governor, he was defeated for reelection by a relatively unknown Republican, Frank White, who campaigned on three issues: the "car tax," a riot of Cuban boat refugees who were temporarily housed by the federal government at a resettlement camp at Fort Chaffee, and the fact that Clinton's wife, Hillary Rodham, had refused to change her last name to Clinton. Clinton believed he had given the people of Arkansas things that they needed. He was stunned by the defeat.

Two years later, Clinton shifted his shape. A now repentant Clinton reemerged to beat White (who was given the nickname "Governor Goofy" by a local reporter) and served as governor until his election to the presidency in 1992. His campaign theme against White was simple, direct, and telling: "You can't lead without listening." This idea—listening to what people want—would structure his new approach to politics and to governing as a postmodern president. Clinton would "listen" to what people wanted by sifting through polling data and then give them the policies that they said they wanted, rather than policies he thought they needed. In the process, he would morph into whatever image was needed at any particular moment in order to sell his product—himself.

Managing the Message

The Clinton presidency began in 1993 in disarray. He was slow in selecting his Cabinet and slower yet in organizing his White House staff. Even after the staff had been chosen, he gave little thought about how they would be organized to get his message across to the American people (particularly the communications staff). "In his first year and a half in office, President Clinton focused on whatever was happening at any given time and devoted scant organizational resources on trying to get ahead of events" (Kumar 2007, 34). Through trial and error, and with the addition of some key advisors, the Clinton White House took shape and eventually meshed into a sophisticated machine.

Issue Strategy

As Ronald Reagan emphasized visual images to emotionally connect with the American people, Clinton placed his primary emphasis on issues. In doing so, he did not reject the power of images—quite the contrary. Blending Reagan's use of images with his own interest in policy, one of his most significant contributions to the making of the postmodern presidency was to use issues *as* symbols. As presidential scholar Bruce Miroff (2000) insightfully noted, "Substance, it often seems in the Clinton presidency, is less the alternative to symbolism than it is a cleverer form of symbolic appeal" (107). One of his principal image handlers, Dick Morris (1999), revealed the inside strategy: "Ultimately, it is not the issue itself that is crucial; it is what a candidate's advocacy of a specific cause says about his values and philosophy. Issues become a form of symbolic speech, an opportunity to speak to a candidate's character and attributes" (176–177). Clinton not only pursued policy initiatives that sent these messages cognitively, but he also usually tried to connect them with compelling visual spectacles which appealed to one's emotions.

Clinton's policy initiatives regarding children are a case in point. Throughout his two terms in office, he held a number of forums throughout the country (and even in Russia) referred to as "Kids Town Meetings," where he met with young people in a pseudo–town hall format. He used those opportunities to either promote legislation that had recently been passed or policies that he was propos- ing. At various times he advocated for full dental care, childhood vaccinations, Megan's Law, the Child Support Performance and Incentive Act, and a public school lunch program that would improve nutrition. Few could remember the substance of any of those proposals, but the image of the President of the United States, surrounded by adoring children, was a compelling spectacle that sticks in one's mind. President Bill Clinton was on the side of the children—he cared.

Clinton's political strategy was to use issues in two ways. First, he would "cherry pick" issues that were commonly considered issues "owned" by his op- ponents and claim them as his own. Both parties traditionally are associated in the minds of voters with certain issues—issues where they are advantaged because of their historical performance in those areas. For example, the Democrats are generally thought to do better on economic issues, civil rights issues, education, and health care issues, while the Republicans are perceived by the American public to be stronger on fiscal responsibility, defense, and foreign policy. Much of what happens in campaigns is to try to focus the campaign dialogue on the issues that benefit you the most and work to the disadvantage of your opponent (Petrocik 1996). Clinton's issue strategy as president went one step beyond this: He not only embraced traditional Democratic issues, but he also tried to steal some issues that were considered Republican issues. One such issue was welfare reform.

In the 1994 mid-term elections, the Republicans produced stunning upsets across the country, becoming the majority party in both branches of Congress for the first time in 40 years by picking up 54 seats in the House and 8 in the Senate. The new Republican speaker of the house, Newt Gingrich, helped engineer many of the victories. During the campaign, Gingrich persuaded all but two of the Republican candidates running for seats in the House of Repre- sentatives to sign on to a package of reform proposals, lumped together as the

"Contract with America," promising that if they were elected and became the majority party, they would attempt to enact those proposals in the first 100 days after taking office. One of the important features in the contract was welfare reform—reducing the time period people could collect welfare, denying welfare to mothers younger than 18, and moving people toward jobs. In early 1995 Gingrich aggressively pushed through many parts of the contract and shifted the political momentum to such an extent that the media questioned whether the president was "relevant" anymore.

But Clinton was a different kind of president. Although Republican opponents attempted to label him a typical "tax and spend liberal," they underestimated his postmodern malleability—his shape-shifting ability. By the middle of September 1995 the Republican-dominated Congress had passed a welfare reform bill, the Personal Responsibility Act, and submitted it to the president for his signature or veto. Seeing his opportunity to shift the political momentum, Clinton vetoed the bill, saying it was too harsh, and worked with the Republicans to develop a compromise piece of legislation (the Personal Responsibility and Work Opportunity Reconciliation Act), which he then took credit for creating. In reality, the new bill was quite similar to the one he had vetoed, and the Republicans had to make very few concessions, at least behind closed doors. Although many of his advisors objected, he followed image handler Dick Morris's advice: "Where an opponent has a clear area of superiority, it is best to bypass it by 'hugging' your adversary on that particular issue so there is no distance between your position and his" (Morris 1999, 193). Because Clinton had no strong commitment to any particular values or any specific issues, he was free to shift positions to fit the mood of the times, which, at that point, was hostile to welfare. Liberals were upset with him, but had no one else to support.

The second way that issues tied into Clinton's communications strategy had to do with the initial selection of the issues. Modern presidents have embraced overarching themes for their presidencies, usually composed of numerous, related policy proposals bound together by a theme (e.g., FDR's New Deal, LBJ's Great Society). This packaging of proposals assumes that a political consensus exists on basic values and beliefs (e.g., poverty is unacceptable in the wealthiest nation in the world). But the postmodern political environment is characterized by fragmentation—the only consensus that exists is on the surface (e.g., a belief in democracy). There is no overarching agreement about what should be done to improve society, or even what the major problems are that should be addressed. Voters are not seen as a mass bound together by common values and beliefs; rather, they are seen as thousands of small clumps loosely bound together by particular interests. Further complicating the ability to unite people is the fact that Americans are increasingly distrustful of government itself (Kohut et al. 1998). In response to this new environment Clinton devised a strategy to connect with people by using small-bore issues targeted to niche voters.

To identify issues—and sometimes even positions on those issues—Clinton made extensive use of focus groups and polling. This orientation (or at least the tactical ability to implement it) emerged slowly in the Clinton White House, and only after it was obvious that his presidency was floundering. To focus his presidency, Clinton called on political consultant Dick Morris, who initially talked surreptitiously with Clinton late at night on the phone and developed a strategy that Clinton embraced.[1] Morris not only developed the general strategy to steal Republican issues, but he also helped identify the specific small-bore issues that could be used to appeal to targeted sections of the electorate. To do this, Morris extensively used polling data: "Polling is the key to selecting the right issue. You must ask the voters a specific question and measure the intensity of their reaction to gauge the impact of an issue" (Morris 1999, 179). No president, up until then, invested as much time, effort, and money in gauging and molding public opinion (Edwards 2000). Policy positions were thoroughly pre-tested with focus groups and even the words and phrases used to talk about them were tested to gauge their effectiveness at eliciting the desired responses. In fact, Clinton relied so heavily on polling that one year he even used it to determine what vacation spot he would select and what he would do when on vacation (he wanted to golf but ended up hiking in the mountains) (Van Natta 2008).

Clinton's issue strategy was tailored to a postmodern political culture characterized by social fragmentation. As society becomes increasingly complex, the idea that any kind of integrated view of what it means to be an American becomes problematic. There is no longer an American public; rather, there are thousands of different groupings of Americans identifying with each other on the basis of race, gender, sexual orientation, occupation, lifestyle, age, and hundreds of other particular characteristics. Clinton's strategy involved identifying those groups susceptible to being appealed to and then developing policy initiatives that would be attractive to them.

The issues chosen had to not only resonate with the targeted segment of the population, but Clinton had to be able to articulate them succinctly. Once again, Morris provided the advice Clinton followed: "There is literally no such thing as an idea that cannot be expressed well and articulately to today's voters in thirty seconds" (Morris 1999, 178). Although brief and to the point, the issue nevertheless had to touch the reality of people's lives (most do not) or else they would ignore what was said. The key was to find the one or two issues that touched a targeted group of voters deeply. Once that was done, the voters tended to remember those issues and discount the positions the president took on other issues less salient to them. But the overall strategy was to inundate the electorate with the discussion of issues.

By his second term Clinton had mastered the politics of small-bore issue appeal. In his 1999 and 2000 State of the Union speeches, for example, he identified 59 particular issues both years where he requested congressional action. The issues spanned the interest spectrum—assistance for elderly women, tax credits for student loans, connecting libraries to the Internet, charter schools, tax credits for child care, lawsuits against tobacco companies who market to children, money for adult literacy, farm crop insurance, aid for Israel to defend itself, and 50,000 more police on the streets to fight crime were among the proposals on which he called for action. The small-bore issue strategy was a way of obtaining political leverage by amassing support from particular interests without attempting the more difficult task of reconciling the potential conflicts among them and working to form a majority coalition. As Press Secretary Mike McCurry candidly explained, "You try to find different ways to engage different audiences at different times. But the truth is, most presidential communications are not aimed at the entire country; they're aimed at different segments of the total population" (quoted in Kumar 2007, 40). In this way, the president comes to act less like a representative of a national constituency and more like the leader of a multiplicity of constituencies (Cohen 2008).

While the small-bore issue strategy is most prominently displayed in State of the Union addresses, Clinton's skill at presenting them in front of smaller, more homogenous audiences was masterful. In his flattering biography, Donald Phillips (2007) talks about Clinton's ability to read audiences and develop just the proper approach to make his point: "Clinton was ... adept at tailoring remarks specifically to his audience" (80). In small group settings he exuded compassion, knowing just what to say and when to say it, when to talk about policy, when to listen, when to tell a story to illustrate a point, when to shake someone's hand, and when to hug someone. His shape-shifting skills served him well in establishing emotional bonds with people, but overall the small-bore strategy produced little in terms of policy proposals that actually were enacted into law.

According to one study, less than 19 percent of the proposals in 1999 and less than 12 percent in 2000 were successfully passed by Congress (Hoffman and Howard 2003). Issues were used by Clinton not so much to create public policy as to convey a symbolic message that he cared about and supported the members of the groups and their concerns.

Images

As is the case with many presidencies, the Clinton White House looked to prior administrations for guidance about how to handle anticipated problems. Clinton's image advisors were well aware of the Reagan administration's image manipulation efforts, but rather than placing policy-making and image manipulation in the hands of only a few individuals, the Clinton administration was organized into groups. There were weekly meetings of policy and communications advisors to identify the weekly agenda, smaller groups to focus solely on conveying the message of each day, teams that would concentrate on television ads promoting policies, and scheduling teams that would decide when and where media events would take place. Unlike Reagan, however, Clinton was intensely involved in the discussions, chairing and making the final decisions in virtually all of the group meetings.

What Clinton failed to understand, however, was how significantly the nature of press reporting would change during his administration and how those changes complicated the task of image control. When Reagan entered the White House in 1981, most Americans obtained their news from the three major television networks—ABC, CBS, and NBC. The network newscasts were remarkably similar—obtaining their stories from the same sources, operating with similar assumptions about what constitutes news, airing at the same time in the evening, lasting the same length of time, using the same reporting formats, and even cutting away for commercials at the same times. Given this degree of predictability, it was relatively easy for Reagan's communications specialists to control the flow of news and produce favorable stories and compelling visuals, since the daily rhythms of the reporters were standardized and news cycles were built around predictable deadlines. This meant that the White House had time to produce events they knew would be visually appealing, and the predictability of the daily news cycle gave them the opportunity to strategically provide reporters with just enough information at exactly the right time to control the stories that would be broadcast.

But during the Clinton administration, news coverage began its dramatic postmodern change toward a "new media age" (Davis and Owen 1998; Baum 2003; Hamilton 2003). "[I]nstead of three networks, anchors, and correspondents who constitute the main purveyors of your event, you have a rapidly changing news environment with little center to it" (Kumar 2007, 3). Twenty-four-hour cable news channels, looking for a constant flow of news, sped up the news cycle, and market forces dictated that whatever was the latest story, whether true or not, was reported. Accuracy and truth were victims, and public confidence in the traditional news sources declined precipitously.

This accelerated news cycle changed not only how news was reported, but also how decision-makers behaved. Former press secretary for the State Department Margaret Tutwiler cogently describes what others have referred to as the "CNN effect": "Time for reaction is compressed. Analysis and intelligence-gathering is out" (quoted in Livingston 1997, 3). Fearing they would lose control of the interpretation of events, political decision-makers scrambled to keep up with news that was breaking virtually by the minute from around the globe.

The Clinton administration was especially caught in a bind because they were also continually harassed by scandals. From day one of his administration Clinton was faced with a non-stop parade of scandals and accusations—the Gennifer Flowers affair, the Paula Jones harassment charges, the Kathleen Willey groping charges, the never-ending Whitewater scandal, Vince Foster's suicide, the firing of long-serving employees of the White House Travel Office, and, of course, the Monica Lewinsky affair which led to Clinton lying in a deposition and, ultimately, to his impeachment. These scandals served as lightning rods for the hordes of new media that descended on the White House. Illustrative of this siege was the destruction of the north lawn of the White House, the site used by reporters to file reports so they could get a background visual of the mansion. In the summer during which the Monica Lewinsky scandal broke, Washington experienced one of its wettest and warmest in history. The combination of wet weather with the increased mass of news reporters produced a muddy morass. To try to correct the problem, the White House covered the area with packed gravel, producing what reporters referred to as "pebble beach."[2]

More significant, however, was the effect of the new media on the behavior of the Clinton administration. After an initial period of confusion, the Clinton communications team adapted and, by the beginning of his second term, a disciplined pattern of communications meetings was established, focusing on the production of spectacles and creating an image of Clinton as a protector of basic

American values. Clinton shaped his image primarily through the use of two techniques: speeches and what one aide referred to as the "Arsenio Strategy."

Clinton paid a great deal of attention to speeches, reading each for exactly the correct wording—heavily editing each speech. Presidential aide John Podesta describes how involved he was: "Every time you'd put a text in front of him, he'd make you stand over his chair. He'd struggle over a phrase or a word" (quoted in Kumar 2007, 38). Some speeches were delivered to broad audiences (e.g., State of the Union speeches), but most were delivered to smaller audiences and focused on narrow small-bore policies (e.g., one White House speech was given to television weather forecasters about climate change).

In an attempt to avoid what he considered a hostile Washington media, Clinton often went on the road to give speeches that would be covered by local (usually friendly) media. These minor addresses (at graduation ceremonies, union and professional conferences, trade associations, etc.) allowed Clinton to get his messages across while obtaining favorable media coverage. More than any of his predecessors, Clinton made extensive use of these minor addresses—what, in essence, amounted to almost one every other day while in office (Kernell 2007). These speeches allowed him to demonstrate his expertise while exuding concern about the issues that the groups he was addressing cared about.

The second technique used to shape the president's image was the use of longer, informal, talk-show formats which avoided the national media—the "Arsenio Strategy." Clinton had used similar communication approaches successfully in the 1992 campaign to control his message, target specific audiences, and provide him with better opportunities to shape his image. He hoped he could achieve the same results while governing. This approach involved using several different formats: talk-show appearances, in-depth appearances on "soft" media outlets (e.g., MTV), in-depth interviews by local television anchors throughout the country, and town hall meetings. Employing a variety of verbal and nonverbal techniques—simple acts of courtesy toward interviewers, never arguing while politely disagreeing, asking questions of audience members—Clinton was able to demonstrate empathy while showing mastery of the issues (Denton and Holloway 1996).

However, this ability to emotionally connect can cut in contradictory directions. On the one hand, authority is maintained and enhanced by maintaining distance (Goffman 1959). This is referred to in the popular press as looking and acting "presidential." But by becoming too familiar, too revealing, and too common, a president can actually undermine his own authority. Clinton, always confident in his political skills, believed that he could successfully walk the fine line between appearing presidential and becoming too personal. Staged speeches in front of niche audiences maintained the requisite distance and enhanced Clinton's authority, but the Arsenio Strategy moved him uncomfortably close to the edge of becoming too personal. This line was clearly crossed in the reporting of the Monica Lewinsky scandal.

On the other hand, although people generally gave Clinton poor personal approval ratings throughout his presidency, they nonetheless perceived of him as compassionate, caring, and a person who tried to do what was best for the American people (Harvey 2000). This, once again, is illustrative of the fragmented nature of the electorate, reflected in the complex manner in which presidents are evaluated by the public. Since Reagan, a low correlation exists between presidential job approval ratings and personal approval (McAvoy 2003). For Clinton, the disconnect between job approval and personality also existed, but it was the reverse situation as Americans disapproved of his personal behavior but still thought he did a decent job as president. It is this postmodern fragmentation that befuddled political pundits during the Monica Lewinsky scandal and made it possible for Clinton to remain popular while lying in a deposition and being the first president since Andrew Johnson to be impeached by Congress.

The Clinton Personality

As a result of his study of Japanese atomic bomb survivors, Robert Jay Lifton identified a new personality orientation, one he called "protean man." Protean man is a person whose life "is characterized by an interminable series of experiments and explorations—some shallow, some profound—each of which may be readily abandoned in favor of still new psychological quests" (Lifton 1968, 17). Protean man possesses no inner self and can therefore easily adapt to new environments. He is attracted to the idea of change, including the idea of remaking himself, but he is also drawn to an image of the mythical past. Even more interesting, Lifton concludes that protean man is drawn to a "never-ceasing quest for imagery of rebirth" (1968, 27). Protean man is virtually identical to this description of the postmodern individual: "Postmodernism regards 'the individual' as a sentimental attachment, a fiction to be enclosed within quotation marks. If you're postmodern, you scarcely believe in 'the right clothes' that take on your personality. You don't dress as who you are because, quite simply, you don't believe 'you' are.

Therefore you are indifferent to consistency and continuity" (Blonsky 1992, 50). Protean man is an accurate description of Bill Clinton.

Clinton has been derisively called "Slick Willie" by critics who claimed that he constantly changed positions; embraced the nickname "The Comeback Kid"; was described by reporter Jacob Weisberg (1999) as "someone who habitually played games with the truth" (35); had "a readiness to reinvent the self to match the moment" (Miroff 2000, 113); "seems unaware of the discrepancies between what he says and what he does" (Renshon 1995, 73); possesses "an indiscernible moral core" (Parry-Giles and Parry-Giles 2002, 125); and was a leader who could skillfully set goals and realize them while at the same time behave in a reckless "anything-goes" fashion (Greenstein 1998). One of his closest advisors described Clinton as a person who wanted to be all things to all people (Drew 1994). Exactly who President Bill Clinton was and what he believed in remain a mystery. However, his malleable personality served him well in the postmodern political environment in which he operated.

With little inner turmoil, he easily reversed positions on welfare reform, a balanced budget, and a middle class tax. Seeing an opportunity for political gain, he embraced Dick Morris's plan, referred to as triangulation, to play off liberal Democrats against conservative Republicans and then present himself as a moderating force. He was adept at developing 30-second commercials to promote policies while also immersing himself in and becoming an expert on complex multi-faceted issues. With few fundamental values that could be identified, he was a chameleon-like pragmatist, demonstrating an ability to successfully adapt to almost any political situation and turn it to his advantage. Miroff (2000) concludes that "Clinton has repeatedly demonstrated how poll-tested repositioning on the issues can alter and enhance the president's image" (123). In commenting on an interview of Clinton about the CIA's involvement in Haiti, political psychologist Stanley Renshon (1995) makes the following observation: "The ethical calculus expressed appears very responsive, not to what is right, but to how his action would look in the morning papers" (66).

Richard Neustadt, in developing his theory of presidential power, recognized the importance of character. A successful president had to possess self-confidence, a sense of purpose and a direction, a sharp sense of personal power, and an ability to control decisions. Hemmed in by institutions which make action difficult, it was important to have a president with the strength of character to make the system work. But in the modern era, there were traditional institutional and political allegiances that were relatively predictable. In the postmodern political environment, that is no longer the case. Although merely flirting with the concept of postmodernism, Skowronek (1997) accurately describes the present difficulty faced by presidents: "The politics they make will have to adjust to a world in which warrants for change can no longer simply be assumed and terms for the exercise of power are no longer simply given" (445). In this postmodern environment, the person with "character" and consistency is too rigid. Instead, postmodern politics "demands above all that we constantly adapt and that our personalities, statements, and styles become a reflection for those around us rather than being innate" (Smith 1994, 28). Without a firm commitment to any core values, Clinton deftly shifted positions for political advantage depending on the political situation at hand.

The Permanent Campaign

On December 10, 1976, pollster Pat Caddell submitted a 62-page essay to then–President-Elect Jimmy Carter titled "Initial Working Paper on Political Strategy." Caddell stated, "Essentially, it is my thesis that governing with public approval requires a continuing political campaign" (quoted in Blumenthal 1980, 39). This concept was dubbed "the permanent campaign" by Clinton senior advisor Sidney Blumenthal in his book by the same name. While Carter accepted and acted on some of Caddell's suggestions, he never fully embraced the idea. It remained for Clinton to enthusiastically add this critical element and, by doing so, contribute to the making of the postmodern presidency (Jones 2000).

The permanent campaign requires an extensive use of polling, a strategic use of spectacles, and a commitment to extensive travel. It is based on the postmodern assumption that nothing is ever settled in postmodernism. One of the political consequences of that is that elections no longer settle political disputes as they once did in the modern era. Therefore, for the postmodern president, every day is election day. To govern, he must continually build popular support: "[A] politician needs a permanent campaign to keep a permanent majority" (Morris 1999, 72). While this worked against President George H. W. Bush's weaknesses, it played to Clinton's strengths. In many respects he was a natural campaigner: He was at his best giving speeches, he adored the enthusiasm of crowds, he loved meeting and talking with people from all walks of life, he was adept at ingratiating himself with local media, and he exuded compassion. Yet one consequence of this approach is that it highlights the celebrity nature of the presidency, even beyond its institutional significance. This "celebrity effect" spotlights the personal nature of the presidency and opens presidents up to the media behaving as if they were paparazzi.

While Clinton loved campaigning, his administration did not begin with a permanent campaign strategy. Instead, he adopted it after two years in office where he saw the Democrats lose control of the Congress in the 1994 mid-term elections and watched passively as his popularity plummeted. To bolster his approval ratings and rebuild his political leverage, he took Dick Morris's advice and embraced the permanent campaign, raising huge amounts of money to run television ads in support of his policies and "going public." Morris's role started as an informal advisor, and he was eventually put on the White House staff and often participated in policy discussions. In this respect, Clinton also contributed to the making of the postmodern presidency by moving in the direction of institutionalizing the role of political advisor, placing it in a far more significant policy-making position than it had occupied in previous administrations.

The 1996 Campaign: A Bridge to Nowhere

By the time of his reelection campaign in 1996, Clinton had, because of his use of the permanent campaign, mastered the strategy of the postmodern campaign. In the spring and early summer of 1996, many of the more formidable potential Republican presidential nominees (e.g., Colin Powell, Pete Wilson) for one reason or another either decided not to enter the race or simply dropped out after only a modest run. Although some early primary contests put a scare into the Bob Dole camp, starting with the South Carolina primary, Dole racked up an impressive series of primary and caucus wins and by late March he had established himself as the presumptive nominee of the Republican Party.

Although the Democrats experienced a humiliating electoral defeat and a loss of both houses of Congress in the 1994 mid-term elections, no serious candidates emerged to challenge Bill Clinton for the nomination. In an uncharacteristic show of unity, the Democratic convention nominated incumbent President Clinton by acclamation.

To a large extent the presidential campaign of 1996 was framed by the acceptance speeches of the two candidates. At the Republican convention in San Diego, former senator Bob Dole[3] attempted to tackle head-on what some believed to be his most significant weakness—his age. Although projecting an image of youthfulness, at 73 years of age he was the oldest first-time presidential nominee of a major party (Reagan was slightly older at the time of his second nomination). Attempting to present his age as "experience," in his acceptance speech he appealed to Americans who were concerned about Clinton's ethical shortcomings:

> Let me be the bridge to an America that only the unknowing call myth. Let me be the bridge to a time of tranquility, faith and confidence in action. And to those who say it was never so, that America's not been better, I say you're wrong. And I know because I was there. And I have seen it. And I remember. And our nation, though wounded and scathed, has outlasted revolutions, civil war, world war, racial oppression and economic catastrophe. We have fought and prevailed on almost every continent. And in almost every sea. We have even lost. But we have lasted, and we have always come through. And what enabled us to accomplish this has little to do with the values of the present. (Dole 1996)

Although he used the bridge metaphor only three times in the acceptance speech, he "repeatedly developed the theme of deification of the past" (Benoit 2001, 74), arguing that traditional values are superior to contemporary values.

After the Republican convention, Dole, like most presidential nominees, received a modest boost in his favorability ratings. Clinton, realizing that elections are about the future, not the past, was elated after hearing Dole's speech—his campaign theme had just been handed to him by, of all people, his opponent. Two weeks later, on August 29, Bill Clinton delivered his own acceptance speech at the Democratic convention in Chicago. Traveling to the convention by train, reminiscent of Harry Truman's whistle-stop campaign in 1948, Clinton created a spectacle that the media could not ignore; it would be his only reference to the past. Instead, his speech embraced the metaphor of building a bridge to the future:

> Four days ago, as you were making your way here, I began a train ride to make my way to Chicago through America's heartland. I wanted to see the faces, I wanted to hear the voices of the people for whom I have worked and fought these last four years.... And maybe more important, when we just rolled through little towns, there were always schoolchildren there waving their American flags, all of them believing in America and its future. I would not have missed that trip for all the world, for that trip showed me that hope is back in America. We are on the right track to the twenty-first century.... I love and revere the rich and

proud history of America. And I am determined to take our best traditions into the future. But with all respect, we do not need to build a bridge to the past. We need to build a bridge to the future, and that is what I commit to you to do. So tonight let us resolve to build that bridge to the twenty-first century, to meet our challenges and protect our values. (Clinton 1996)

Throughout the speech (over twenty times) Clinton used the bridge metaphor and, using it to link a host of policy proposals to fundamental American values, a "bridge to the twenty-first century" became his campaign theme. Identifying a host of small-bore issues ranging from installing V-chips in televisions to expanding the military, Clinton employed the metaphor "building a bridge to the twenty-first century," linking those proposals with values such as personal responsibility, community, equal opportunity, and a belief in technological progress.

Clinton's use of the bridge metaphor was a brilliant example of postmodern campaigning for several reasons. Metaphors are important because they frame how people interpret and react to the world. Clinton's "bridge to the twenty-first century" metaphor not only tapped into people's beliefs that elections should be about the future, but it subconsciously developed a contrast with his opponent, whose bridge seemed more about the past. But even more, the use of the metaphor, to some extent, shielded Clinton from one of the criticisms often leveled against him—that he lies. Metaphors, because they are not intended to be taken literally, are neither true nor false. Thus, the power of the metaphor is not found in its verifiability, but rather its significance lies in its ability to resonate with the audience. In this respect, Clinton's bridge to the twenty-first century—although there was little substance to it—was compelling because it functioned to criticize his opponent, appealed to the electorate, and was difficult to discredit.

Yet the use of metaphors alone is not inherently postmodern. Indeed, modern presidents and even traditional presidents have used metaphors extensively. But the use of metaphors by modern presidents functioned to create frames in which they would construct arguments about the efficacy of decisions in addressing problems, in effect to convince people to support policies through the use of logic and argumentation.

Metaphors are seldom used by postmodern presidents in such a fashion. Instead, metaphors are used to establish the legitimacy of policy proposals and decisions by linking them to the prevailing value preferences of the nation (Hahn 1987). Presidential candidates and presidents do not submit information to the citizenry and invite deliberation; instead, they present policies and ask for support merely because they conform to our values. But because the political environment—especially the postmodern political environment—is multilayered and fluid, when postmodern presidents employ metaphors, they, in effect, reconstruct the past in such a fashion that it works to the benefit of the constructor. Reagan had effectively used such metaphors in his 1984 "Morning in America" reelection theme, but Clinton contributed to the making of the postmodern presidency by showing the power of such metaphors. Used effectively, as Clinton had done, they were powerful enough to overcome Clinton's own ethical difficulties, failings that in the past could easily have destroyed other politicians. In the final analysis Clinton emerged as the candidate who was attractive because he best understood and cared about average Americans, while Dole was highly respected for the quality of his character, but was not perceived of as being in step with the nation.

The Reinvention of Government

On September 7, 1993, on the South Lawn of the White House, President Bill Clinton and Vice President Al Gore stood in front of an array of pallets piled high with an estimated ton of notebooks and bound volumes of federal regulations and outlined a new initiative to "reinvent" government. They unveiled a report, the National Performance Review (NPR), which contained more than 800 recommendations that, over a five-year span, would cut 252,000 bureaucrats, improve efficiencies in administration, and save taxpayers $108 billion. The NPR, prepared under the guidance of Vice President Gore, was the product of over six months of interviews and research.

Clinton contended that he was advocating a new way for government to relate to the American people: "This isn't about changing the government, it's about changing the country" (quoted in Taylor 1993, A1). The report recommended what, if adopted, would become a new paradigm for the management of government. Based upon assumptions drawn from the latest practices of successful businesses, the NPR emphasized that bureaucrats should focus on results rather than rules, that they should view citizens as customers, that authority should be decentralized to empower those "on the front lines," and that new ways should be found to make government more efficient (Moe 1994). To illustrate the absurdity of bureaucratic rules, Vice President Gore toured the country (including an appearance on the *Late Show with David Letterman*) with a government-approved ashtray in hand. In order for the government to purchase the ashtray, he explained, bureaucrats had to adhere to ten pages of regulations, including a detailed description of how many pieces it was allowed to break into (no more than 35) if struck with a steel punch on a maple plank 44.5 millimeters thick. When he dramatically smashed the ashtray on the *Late Show with David Letterman* and counted the pieces, the mini-spectacle captured the attention of the public, feeding into their already cynical views about government regulation of virtually anything.

While many of the recommendations in the report were implemented and did result in greater efficiencies, my interest is in how, if at all, the initiatives relate to the making of the postmodern presidency. As was true of George H. W. Bush's Council on Competitiveness, the NPR focused primarily on improving efficiencies and saving money by eliminating or simplifying government regulation. However, it failed to achieve its larger objectives of fundamentally changing the bureaucratic culture to address wicked problems (discussed in detail in Chapter 3). It did not recommend that the bureaucracy coordinate inclusive, horizontally collaborative approaches, nor did it suggest how stakeholders involved in persistent problems could be brought together. Instead, the strategy behind the NPR was designed to (1) build public-opinion support for the administration; (2) deny the Republicans and Ross Perot supporters one of their most popular issues—the anti-government message; and (3) shift political power from the legislative branch to the executive branch, thereby enhancing the unilateral authority of the president.

Americans have always been skeptical of the use of government. But beginning in the mid-1970s and extending into the 1990s and the twenty-first century, the anti-government movement intensified. Public-opinion surveys during this time revealed that Americans believed that the public sector was inherently inefficient (Bahl 1984). Taxpayer revolts emerged in California, New Jersey, Massachusetts, and Michigan, and state legislatures in many states passed tax limitation legislation. Ronald Reagan was elected in 1980, saying that government was the problem, not the solution, and both he and his immediate successor tried to initiate programs to reduce the size of the bureaucracy. With one eye on the polls and the other on a budget he had just submitted to Congress that contained few cuts, Clinton used the NPR as a marketing tool that promised significant savings not for the next year, but over the following five years (Barnes 1993).

While the attack on government regulation played well in middle America, the more specific target was the Perot voters. In 1992 Ross Perot garnered 19 percent of the popular vote, mostly on the basis of anti-government themes. According to Clinton's advisors, the strategy to win over these disaffected voters would be to provide convincing evidence that dramatic downsizing of government was occurring under his administration (Ifill 1993). Thus, much as Clinton shifted positions to steal issues from his opponents, he used the NPR to steal Perot's major theme. By embracing regulatory reform and promising even greater cuts in the future, Clinton was able to significantly undermine Perot's support. Running again in 1996, Perot won less than 9 percent of the vote.

Tactically, Clinton used the reinventing-government initiative to steal one of the major issues that both the Republicans as well as Perot championed—the large size and extensive regulatory scope of government. This was consistent with his overall strategy to steal his opponents' issues by agreeing with them. Yet, while the use of the NPR was part of a postmodern shape-shifting strategy, the underlying vision of the NPR was based on a hyperreal belief about government.

The dominant metaphor of the reinventing-government movement was to view the citizen as a customer. That model restricted the involvement of citizens (only some citizens are served by any government policy) and placed them in a reactive role where they were limited to either liking or disliking services and hoping that bureaucrats, like good business owners, would change if enough customers objected (Frederickson 1994; Schachter 1995). But the purpose of government management has never been to be run like a business. Bureaucracies in democracies must adhere to underlying democratic principles in their operations and, consequently, will never be as efficient as businesses. Government cannot act arbitrarily: It must respect the Bill of Rights, it must treat all citizens with respect and fairness, it must be transparent, and it must provide services that will not discriminate. These are not principles of management that lead to efficiencies. To require government to adopt the business model really represents an attempt to manipulate citizens' feelings about government by using a model of management that never can, and never should, be applied to government management.

At another level, the reinventing government movement failed to recognize the position citizens in the postmodern era should have vis-à-vis government itself. Rather than acting as reactive customers, citizens should be more similar to owners, whereby they play proactive roles and control the agenda. Perhaps even more important, the postmodern approach to administration encourages authentic discourse among bureaucrats and citizens (Fox and Miller 1994). This alternative model was not what the reinventing-government movement advocated.

Finally, the NPR initiative shifted the locus of power between the executive and legislative branches of government. In this respect, it had a similar effect to that of the unilateral actions that postmodern presidents have taken. The report recommended that management responsibility devolve to the lowest practicable bureaucratic level, a level of government bureaucracy that seldom receives oversight from Congress. In fact, congressional oversight was seen as a nuisance because they over-regulated and micromanaged executive agencies: "Congress should simply pass the bill submitted by the President ... and let executive branch officials reinvent their agencies" (Moe 1994). This transfer of power from the Congress to the presidency has been identified as one of the central elements of the NPR (Kettl 1995) and it, in effect, severed a long-standing avenue of accountability and further contributed to the expansion of presidential power.

Unilateral Actions

As noted in the previous chapter, George H. W. Bush was aggressive in his use of unilateral actions. Facing a Democrat-controlled Congress, he employed tactics such as executive orders, proclamations, signing statements, and national security directives to control the political agenda. Just as Clinton looked to Ronald Reagan for clues about how to create and manipulate images, he looked to Bush to develop a go-it-alone governing style. In some instances he was able to combine both approaches. His creation of the Grand Staircase-Escalante National Monument illustrates how he combined the features of spectacle, targeting niche voters, and unilateral action into a single pseudo-event.

On September 18, 1996, Clinton stood next to Vice President Gore and actor Robert Redford and announced the creation of the 1.7-million-acre Grand Staircase-Escalante National Monument—what would become the largest national monument in the nation. To avoid protests which would mar the photo opportunity, the signing took place on the south rim of the Grand Canyon, 70 miles south of the monument itself. Standing in front of El Tovar Lodge, only a few feet from the exact spot where Theodore Roosevelt stood in 1908 when he created Grand Canyon National Park, Clinton signed Proclamation 6920, using the 1906 Antiquities Act, which allows for the federal protection of objects of historic and scientific interest. The creation of the monument had the effect of banning mining and road building, angering many Utahans who wanted the area developed. While many residents of Utah were angry, labeling the action a land grab by the federal government, environmentalists praised the action.

Clinton knew that he would never get the Republican-controlled Congress to support the creation of the national monument through legislation. Instead, he worked around Congress by using a presidential proclamation. At the same time, he knew that the media would not be able to resist the photo opportunity. With the spectacular scenery of the Grand Canyon in the background, the handsome visage of Robert Redford at his side, and the president acting to protect the environment, media coverage was assured. Clinton knew that he would probably lose Utah in the upcoming election (as he had in 1992), but environmental voters elsewhere were the real targets. "The political logic was clear, and his institutional authority allowed President Clinton to pursue political and programmatic gains without incurring significant political costs" (Mayer and Price 2002, 369).

Clinton made early and extensive use of unilateral actions. In the first few weeks of his administration, he issued 25 presidential memoranda and 18 executive orders (Cooper 2001), and by the end of his eight years he ended up with 364 executive orders, 880 presidential proclamations, 381 signing statements, and 148 national security directives. Still, the Clinton administration was not unique in its use of unilateral actions and, in fact, he did not surpass his predecessors. Reagan issued more proclamations and executive orders, and Bush made more signing statements, on average, per year. "Clinton is clearly within the tradition of recent presidents who have used the administrative presidency strategy to achieve their goals" (Aberbach 2000, 129).

Although Clinton may have used unilateral powers more skillfully than his predecessors to control the policy agenda, his contribution in this area to the making of the postmodern presidency was that his actions demonstrated that aggressive unilateral action was part of a structural change, rather than merely a partisan change. Republican presidents Reagan and Bush both encountered Democratic Congresses, and while Clinton faced a Republican Congress in six of his eight years, his use of unilateral actions was consistent regardless of whether Congress was in Democratic or Republican hands. The use of unilateral power is not so much related to whether Congress is controlled by the opposition party as it is by other factors. Presidents strategically use them to try to moderate more sweeping policy shifts they anticipate Congress adopting or to break congressional gridlock (Howell and Kriner 2008).

The Clinton Postmodern Legacy

Bill Clinton contributed significantly to the making of the postmodern presidency in at least three areas. First, Clinton's personality was ideally suited for postmodern politics. With a loosening of political alignments and coalitions in the postmodern political environment, the personality of the president becomes even more important in determining behavior than it was during the modern era. Clinton possessed a self-confidence that grew out of his mastery of political skills rather than any sense of his inner self, and his lack of a central core of beliefs or values provided him with a malleability that allowed him to adapt to a variety of different situations and to take on issue positions that ran counter to his previous positions.

Yet while Clinton's postmodern personality served him well as president, it is not clear whether the kind of protean personality that he possessed is the only personality type that can operate effectively in the postmodern political world. It is true that his personality allowed him to operate in that environment, but so too could other personality types. The personality of the president is significant, but not necessarily determinative.

The second area where Clinton contributed to the making of the postmodern presidency was by demonstrating how issues can be used symbolically to connect emotionally with the American people. As shown in Chapter 2, the Reagan administration demonstrated the power of the visual, and in many instances it was used to override unpopular issue positions the president took. Clinton was able to meld visual images with policy initiatives and, by doing so, target niche voters far more effectively than Reagan had done. Reagan's emphasis on images was based on the modern idea of the existence of a mass public. But Clinton, by targeting through the use of small-bore issues and related images, was able to emotionally connect with members of targeted groups of the electorate.

Third, perhaps Clinton's most significant contribution to the making of the postmodern presidency was his creation of the permanent campaign. He dramatically expanded his travel outside of Washington and, by raising large amounts of money, aired advertisements on television in key states in support of policies, even in non-electoral years. An important element of Clinton's legacy is that he has eliminated the distinction between campaigning and governing—the tactics and strategies of campaigning are now a critical part of postmodern governing.

In other areas Clinton merely employed tactics of previous postmodern presidents. Like Reagan, he used spectacles and visuals to emotionally link himself with the citizenry, and like Reagan and especially Bush, he made extensive use of unilateral powers. Like Reagan, he used events not to educate the American people about the merits and limitations of policy, but to market his own proposals. Although many liberals were disappointed in the Clinton administration because they believed he had wasted his considerable political talent, from a different perspective he contributed significantly to the making of the postmodern presidency.

Notes

1. Initially Morris's contacts with Clinton were kept secret. He was given the code name "Charlie" when communicating with the president.

2. Under the George W. Bush administration, the gravel was replaced by fieldstone. Reporters renamed the area "Stonehenge."

3. Dole resigned from the Senate June 11, 1996, so that he could focus full-time on running for the presidency.

CHAPTER 5

THE HYPERREAL PRESIDENT

GEORGE W. BUSH

Who are you going to believe—me or your own eyes?
Chico Marx, dressed as Groucho, in *Duck Soup*

Originally scheduled to return to their home port in San Diego on January 20, 2003, the 6,000 crew members onboard the nuclear-powered aircraft carrier *USS Abraham Lincoln* received word on New Year's morning that their deployment in the Persian Gulf would be extended. They were playing a major role in the air war over Iraq. With its mission completed three months later, the carrier was approaching San Diego in late April, but suddenly the ship was ordered to stop. On April 26, Scott Sforza, a former ABC producer who now worked for the White House as deputy communications director for television production, arrived to stage a presidential visit. The *Lincoln* was to provide the backdrop for President George W. Bush to proclaim a military triumph in Iraq. The excited crew asked Sforza to construct a large red, white, and blue banner proudly proclaiming "Mission Accomplished," which would be strategically placed behind the president during his speech on the deck of the carrier.

On May 1, the ship turned so that reporters would not photograph land in the background as the small Navy S-3B Viking jet carrying President George W. Bush approached. Piloted by John "Skip" Lussier, the jet, coming in at 150 miles per hour, caught the fourth and final steel arresting cable stretched across the flight deck, abruptly bringing it to a stop. Beneath the canopy where Bush sat, the words "George W. Bush Commander in Chief" were painted. Within minutes Bush hopped out of the plane wearing a gray flight suit, helmet tucked under his arm, and strode across the flight deck, reminiscent of the film *Top Gun*. He was swarmed by cheering members of the crew. "Yes, I flew it," he told reporters. "I miss flying, I can tell you that," he added.

After enjoying a meal below deck, he emerged three hours later in a business suit to give a speech during prime-time television, surrounded by the crew members that guide planes dressed in jackets of vivid red, green, yellow, and blue. In his speech he declared that "major combat operations in Iraq have ended" and linked Saddam Hussein with al Qaeda as he erroneously had done numerous times before. He reminded everyone that we were there to liberate the Iraqi people and eliminate Hussein's weapons of mass destruction.

The *USS Abraham Lincoln* event was a hyperreal spectacle designed to sustain Bush's popularity and maintain public support for the war. Much of what happened that day was the creation of a new reality disconnected from what one White House aide referred to as the "reality-based community" occupied by journalists. Bush had, at best, taken the controls of the jet for a short period of time and was merely a passenger during take-off and landing, but the image projected was that he was the pilot. The ship was only a few miles from shore, but the background image made it appear as if it was in the middle of the ocean. There was no connection between Saddam Hussein and al Qaeda and, in fact, Hussein was our ally only a few years earlier. To the embarrassment of American intelligence experts, Iraq possessed no weapons of mass destruction, but the rationale provided for the war was that those (nonexistent) weapons were an imminent threat to America. And as Americans would painfully discover years later, contrary to the images of joyous Iraqis flooding into the streets of Baghdad welcoming American liberators, military operations were far from over, and in the years to follow, Iraqi citizens would conduct a bloody fight against troops they considered "occupiers." As one critic said, the Bush administration was "now eagerly promoting a brave new world in which it was given that there could be no empirical reality in news, only the reality you wanted to hear (or that they wanted you to hear)" (Rich 2006, 163).

Image Manipulation

Effective White House advisors understand the strengths and weaknesses of the president they work for and try to enhance his strengths and mitigate his weaknesses. Ronald Reagan looked like a president, but had little interest in, and understood little about, the intricacies of policy. His advisors created compelling visuals and kept him away from the probing questions of the press. Alternatively, Clinton was regarded as a "policy wonk" who loved to talk at length about policy, so much so that he often would lose his audience as he explained far more than was necessary. While he could be effective at looking presidential, he had a tendency to be too informal. Thus, his advisors attempted to get him to talk about policy, but briefly, and present such discussions in presidential-looking settings. Nonetheless, advisors found it difficult to control Clinton, as he wanted to take charge of all such decisions.

George W. Bush's advisors understood early on that knowledge of policy was not his forte. While some believed he was not intellectually up to the challenge, people nonetheless viewed him as honest and sincere. Even more, people liked Bush as a person, even though many of them disagreed with his positions on the issues that mattered the most to them (Kumar 2007). With this in mind, his advisors took a Reaganesque approach. They limited press interaction with the president, restricted access to information (at least in the first term), tightly controlled messages, and carefully staged events. The Bush administration began with the objective of presenting an image of "dignified authenticity" (Gregg 2004). As it so happened, this approach served Bush well in the initial aftermath of the 9/11 attacks. He conveyed a sense of outrage at the evilness that was directed toward innocent Americans and reassured people that those responsible would be punished. "A central element in Bush's transformed relationship with the American people after September 11 is how genuinely the public perceived him as sharing their pain, but also sharing their more martial emotions demanding justice" (Gregg 2004, 96). This approach was not spontaneous; it was the product of careful planning—controlling the flow of information and carefully staging events.

Emotions

The Bush administration was masterful at creating spectacles that emotionally linked the president with the American people. Spectacles are symbolic events in which images conjure up broader and deeper meanings. They are narrowly focused to convey particular meanings and draw clear distinctions between the performers (the president) and the audience (citizens) (Miroff 2006). Early in his presidency, spectacles dominated Bush's actions, many of which revolved around the 9/11 attacks. The most effective tapped into people's intensely held emotions about the attacks.

While the facts of the 9/11 attacks became relatively clear shortly after they occurred, their meaning remained to be defined. Were they a hostile response to American foreign policy or did they represent a broader rejection of Western values? Were they attacks on modernization? Were they part of a broader terrorist war against America, or an isolated incident? Through the use of spectacle, Bush symbolically defined the meaning of September 11. One of the most spectacular attempts at doing this occurred on the first anniversary of the attacks.

On a day-long journey on September 11, 2002, Bush traveled from Washington, D.C., to Pennsylvania and to New York City, the sites of each of the crashes, speaking infrequently but, nonetheless, sending a powerful message to the American people. Starting with an early morning service at St. John's Episcopal Church across from LaFayette Park, he was driven across the Potomac River to the Pentagon, where he complimented the military for enduring the loss of 184 people and then immediately focusing on preparing a military response. This somber ceremony ended with perfectly choreographed F-16 fighter jets roaring overhead. The message was clear: Bush was commander-in-chief of the world's most powerful military force and gained his strength from his religion.

The memorial pilgrimage then journeyed to Shanksville, Pennsylvania, where United Airlines Flight 93 crashed. In a field of knee-high grass, the president and his wife, Laura, laid flowers at the site and sang *The Battle Hymn of the Republic*. At one point Bush was so overwhelmed with emotion that he could not complete the song. From there, the caravan ventured on an emotional visit to the dusty 16-acre pit of ground zero in New York City. Arriving at 5:00 P.M. the president and the first lady walked down a 460-foot ramp that led to the base of what used to be the towers of the World Trade Center, seven stories below ground. As they descended, they were flanked by an honor guard of firefighters, police, and other rescue workers who had spent months clearing the site. There he placed a wreath and made his way around a circle of 1,000 family members and friends of the victims, often hugging and reassuring them.

The day concluded with a seven-minute prime-time speech from Ellis Island. Three barges of Musco lights were sent across New York Harbor and tethered in the water around the base of the Statue of Liberty, illuminating the 305-foot symbol of freedom. With the statue over his right shoulder and a large American flag fluttering in the breeze over his left shoulder, the president reassured the nation and reminded citizens of their most cherished values—tolerance, justice, and freedom. At the end of an exhausting day, White House Chief of Staff Andrew Card whispered to Bush, "You're a great president" (Bumiller 2002).

Following the 9/11 tragedy, Americans sought meaning in order to understand what happened and come to grips with it (Pyszczynski et al. 2003). Through the use of a dramatic, symbolic spectacle, Bush provided that meaning. Americans should rely upon their religion for help, and they should take pride in the military strength of the nation; the attacks were attacks on the values and way of life of Americans, and we should respond by committing ourselves to the American dream and pursuing justice for those who attacked us. Yet it is important to grieve for the families of the victims. With few words (none were needed) Bush embodied how Americans felt, and his soaring approval ratings reflected the fact that he had struck a deep emotional chord.

While it could be argued that these types of spectacles were beneficial in uniting a country during a time of crisis, the Bush administration's use of fear is more problematic. Speaking to an audience at St. Anselm College in New Hampshire early in 2003, senior presidential advisor Karl Rove candidly sketched out the strategy for reelection. As unemployment remained at uncomfortable levels, the federal deficit skyrocketed, and the Bush tax cuts failed to stimulate the economy, Bush, explained Rove, would campaign on the issue of terrorism and the fact that "the country has not been hit since 9/11" (Clines 2003). But to make that issue "come alive," to affect people directly, a few terrorist scares were needed.

Only a week prior to the 2004 election, a flurry of polls indicated that the contest between George W. Bush and John Kerry was a statistical dead heat. The election was up for grabs. In late October, Osama bin Laden released an 18-minute video, aired on Al Jazeera, where he once again threatened to attack the United States. As revealed years later in a tell-all book by then–Secretary of Homeland Security Tom Ridge, the assessment by intelligence experts was that there was nothing new in the video. Yet Homeland Security was pressured by unnamed White House advisors to increase the color-coded security alert system. Ridge, aware of the fact that whenever the alert system was increased Bush received a 5 percent boost in approval ratings, initially resisted, but finally agreed to issue the alert increase (Ridge 2009). On October 29, only a week before the election, the color alert was upgraded from yellow to orange. In the election Bush edged Kerry by slightly more than 2 percent of the vote. One psychological study of the electoral effects of reminders of death immediately prior to the election concluded that "George W. Bush's victory in the 2004 presidential election was facilitated by Americans' nonconscious concerns about death" (Cohen et al. 2005, 183).

By presenting his interpretation of 9/11 as an act of war, and responding by declaring a "war against terrorism," Bush emphasized the symbolic importance of the event. Statistically, any single American ran a greater risk of being killed by a lightning strike than being killed in a terrorist attack, but polls indicated that Americans *personally* feared for their lives. Emotion overrode logic. What's more, this fear remained for a majority of Americans years after the attacks themselves (Gardner 2008). This residual, personalized fear was then exploited by the Bush administration in the 2004 election.

In times of crisis people look to strong leaders and are hostile toward those who disagree with the accepted authority. "When danger looms, Americans want a strong figure in charge and so Republicans worked hard to make sure Americans sensed danger looming" (Gardner 2008, 308). For example, Bush's hungry wolves ad has become a classic ad in campaign lore. It was quite different from Reagan's 1984 "Morning in America" ad, and is more similar to, though more explicit than, his bear-in-the-woods ad. In the ad, a pack of hungry wolves is seen in a dark forest, lying in wait. With dark, ominous music playing in the background, a voice-over accuses Kerry of weakening America by voting to reduce the military budget. Suddenly, the wolves rise up and run toward the camera, in hot pursuit of a weakened prey (i.e., Kerry's America).

Once again, the reality of the danger of terrorism for the average American was quite different from the presentation by the Bush administration. This hyperreality became so distorted that members of the administration claimed that the lack of a second terrorist attack actually became the evidence of its existence. In testimony before a congressional committee, FBI Director Robert Mueller, ignoring a report from his own agency that said that al Qaeda did not possess the ability to pull off another attack within the United States, said, "I remain very concerned about what we are not seeing" (quoted in Gardner 2008, 311).

The Bush administration relied heavily on exploiting the fears that the American people had about terrorism. Provided with a powerful emotional event, the 9/11 attacks, Bush provided interpretations of the event which distorted the danger of terrorism and deeply touched Americans' sense of grief. But this hyper-real manipulation was not to last. As the reality of the war in Iraq dragged on, and as the pictures from the effects of Hurricane Katrina came to dominate the media, Bush lost the ability to control images. When this happened, his approval rating plummeted and criticisms of his policies increased, providing a snowball effect that left his presidency disabled.

The Image Team

While images of presidents have been with us throughout history, the use of media consultants—experts on the use of television to project images—has fundamentally challenged one of the basic assumptions of the modern presidency. Television is qualitatively different than other forms of communication and is, today, critically important for the presidency. Communications advisors attempt to control the presentation of messages so that a single, focused communication dominates the news every day. In the early years of the Bush administration, image control was masterful. As Michael Deaver, one of the chief architects who crafted the Reagan image, said about the Bush team, "They understand the visual as well as anybody ever has. They watched what we did, they watched the mistakes of Bush I, they watched how Clinton kind of stumbled into it, and they've taken it to an art form" (quoted in Bumiller 2003, 1).

The two advisors primarily responsible for communications were Karen Hughes and Karl Rove. Counselor to the president, Hughes was in charge of the operations component of communications, overseeing the Press Office, the Office of Communications, the Office of Media Affairs, and the Speechwriting Office. Her job was to make sure that the message designed by others in the White House was effectively and convincingly presented. She planned messages as much as six months in advance. But she was also in charge of making sure that one, and only one, main message would be conveyed each day. Once the decision had been made about what that message was, an operations team would develop the staging event in which the message would be presented. All White House officials and relevant departments and agencies were instructed via email about what to say when dealing with reporters. No deviation was tolerated (Auletta 2004). An anonymous White House staffer defiantly explained the strategy to a reporter: "They're going to have to write what we say, because it's all we're going to give them" (Bai 2002).

One of the strengths of the Bush media team was the creation of visuals. To make them compelling, a team of professionals drawn from the national television networks was hired. Scott Sforza, a former ABC producer, was responsible for creating the "message of the day" backdrops; Bob DeServi, a former cameraman for NBC, directed the technical aspects of the event; and Greg Jenkins, a former Fox News television producer, was in charge of staging. These three media experts worked with Communications Director Dan Bartlett to create events that would send appealing visuals. Bartlett candidly explained the strategy: "Americans are leading busy lives, and sometimes they don't have the opportunity to read a story or listen to an entire broadcast. But if they can have an instant understanding of what the president is talking about by seeing 60 seconds of television, you accomplish your goals as communicators" (quoted in Bumiller 2003, 1). An effective visual was one that would convey the intended message, even with the sound on the television turned off. This was their goal.

Occupying a position with uncharacteristic access to the president was Karl Rove. Technically, Rove was senior advisor to the president in charge of the Office of Strategic Initiatives (OSI), but he had carte blanche to become involved in whatever issues he felt had partisan political implications. Senator Bill Frist of Pennsylvania described Rove in the following way: "Everybody knows that in terms of putting it all together, in terms of the politics, in terms of strategy positions and also policy, that Karl is the hub, the central node of activity that surrounds the presidency" (quoted in Berke and Bruni 2001, 1).

Although Bush liked to claim that he would not make policy decisions on the basis of polling and even had a personal disdain for polling, Rove's omnipresence at policy discussion meetings made such an assertion seem disingenuous. In actual operation, the OSI monitored and analyzed a wide variety of surveys, news organizations, and privately commissioned polls and focus groups—those data were used by Rove when he advised the president. At Rove's urging, with one eye on the polls and the other on political strategy, Bush changed his positions on steel tariffs, farm subsidies, affirmative action, arms sales to Taiwan, the regulation of carbon dioxide emissions from power plants, price controls on natural gas, and the creation of a Department of Homeland Security, among other things. While Bush did not adhere to anything like a "60 percent rule" that would determine a position as had been used in the Clinton administration, he contributed to the making of the postmodern presidency by thoroughly integrating the political implications of decisions into policy discussions more than had been the case for any previous president.

Hyperreality

In a postmodern world truth is contextual; consequently, what many believe is deception or even lying becomes merely an alternative interpretation. In the postmodern presidency truth and reality are merely perspectives—perspectives that can be altered to suit one's purposes. The Bush administration embraced this belief. As one White House aide candidly said, "We're an empire now, and when we act, we create our own reality. And while you're studying that reality—judiciously, as you will—we'll act again, creating other new realities, which you can study too, and that's how things will sort out" (Suskind 2004, 44).

The most innocent behavior that stems from that assumption is spin. Spin is an interpretation of an event designed to persuade others to one's interpretation. Something actually happened or was said, but the meaning of it is subject to interpretation.[1] While all presidents have used spin, it increased and intensified with the use of television. As Reagan demonstrated, the image can be used to overwhelm the written or spoken word. By staging compelling visual spectacles, interpretations which do not even rely on the written or spoken word can be created.

Spin works best when people have little information and few opinions about issues. Sadly, that applies to many Americans. "The hard truth is that on most policy issues, large proportions of the public know or care little about the specifics, and thus have developed no meaningful opinion about them" (Moore 2008, 18). Thus, spin is primarily directed at the American people rather than political elites. While some have claimed that presidents attempt to shape opinions of the public to have them, in turn, pressure their elected representatives (Kernell 2007), research indicates that this is seldom a successful tactic (Edwards 2008). Instead, a president attempts to shape public opinion for at least two other reasons: First, to set the issue agenda, and second, to build personal approval which provides the president with flexibility and space (i.e., political leeway) he needs to act unilaterally (Cammarano 2009). In addition to spin, however, Bush employed even more controversial tactics designed to create alternative realities. Illustrative of that is how the Bush administration went about presenting the war in Iraq.

War is hell. Put bluntly, the strategy of war is to kill people and destroy property until the enemy accepts defeat—a brutal reality often ignored by politicians and glossed over by the media. But since the war in Iraq effort was highly dependent on public opinion, this was not the image of war that the Bush administration wanted the American people to think about when American forces invaded. An alternative had to be presented. To do this, the Bush administration made liberal use of the postmodern technique of hyperreality. In modernity, representation is used to approximate the closest description of reality possible. For example, photographs or drawings of objects in the world are representations of things that actually exist. In such instances we may argue, debate, or discuss how accurate the representations are, how much the representations distort reality, what the representations include or exclude, and the like. In other words, it can stimulate healthy debate and dialogue.

In postmodernity, however, representations are not of real objects, but of objects that never existed in the first place. Disneyland is often cited as the perfect example. With its re-creations of Disney cartoon characters such as Pluto, Mickey Mouse, and Donald Duck (people who walk around in costume greeting children), and robotic presidents who lived in different time periods talking with each other, it creates representations of things which have no referents in the real world. This kind of disconnect with reality is possible to a considerable extent because of the advent of new, mostly visual technologies. This hyperreal orientation was used extensively by the Bush administration to sell and prosecute the war. To illustrate this, a brief look at some of the strategies used to stage the war is helpful. Box 5.1 provides a quick glimpse at some of the hyperreal aspects of the war as produced by the Bush administration. It is not intended to be a comprehensive list, but rather it is a small sample designed to illustrate how the strategy was employed and to suggest the extensive nature of its use.

The Bush representation of the war was not a representation of what was actually happening in Iraq (that would be modernity); rather, it was a representation of America's idealized vision of war as created over the years, primarily in Hollywood films. While there are, admittedly, different interpretations of war in film (the Vietnam War in particular produced more cynical interpretations), the dominant myth emerges primarily as a way to make sense of World War II. Elements of that myth are found in the first column of Box 5.1. The second column identifies the Bush administration's presentation of the war in Iraq, while the third column identifies the reality of war. As can be seen, the Bush presentation is consistently closer to the Hollywood myth of war than what was actually happening on the ground and in the air in Iraq. While space prevents a full elaboration of all aspects presented in the table, discussion of a few points will be illustrative.

Perhaps the most widely publicized gap between the reality of Iraq and the Bush presentation of the war involved the rationale for the war itself. The

Box 5.1
Hyperreality and the Iraq War

Hollywood War Myth	Bush Hyperreality	Reality of War
War is a last resort. We have no choice but to fight. The enemy is evil.	Saddam Hussein supported al Qaeda, possessed weapons of mass destruction, ignored UN resolutions to allow for inspections, and had the desire and capability to strike the United States.	Hussein did not support al Qaeda, did not possess weapons of mass destruction and posed no imminent threat to the United States. UN inspectors were conducting inspections and could not find weapons of mass destruction. Iraq did not possess the capability of striking the United States.
We are not alone; all civilized countries recognize evil, believe our cause is just, and will help us fight.	The United States led a "Coalition of the Willing" against Iraq. It was composed of 49 nations.	Two countries in the "Coalition of the Willing" withdrew before hostilities began, four had no standing armies, and only four countries actually committed troops. Ninety-eight percent of the troops were from either the United States or the United Kingdom.
Fighting should be conducted against armed combatants. The harm caused to civilians and property should be minimized. Civilians are our friends.	The active combat operations, given the name Operation Iraqi Freedom, began with air strikes designed to destroy the infrastructure and key military targets. The "Shock and Awe" bombing was surgically conducted with laser-guided bombs to minimize civilian casualties.	Bombings were designed to destroy the infrastructure of Iraq—water, electricity delivery, communications, transportation, and food delivery systems. Between 6,000 and 7,000 civilians died during the active phase of the war.
Wars are fought to achieve "higher" purposes, such as liberating people or preventing genocide. War solves problems.	Saddam Hussein was an evil dictator who supported terrorism; he was overthrown. A base for democracy in the Middle East will be established. The people of Iraq were liberated and welcomed American troops.	Hussein was a brutal dictator who killed thousands of his own people. Americans became seen as an occupying force and triggered a civil war in Iraq. Over 150,000 Iraqi civilians died in bombings subsequent to the invasion.

Hollywood myth is that America only goes to war as a last resort, particularly if we are subject to a surprise attack. The most famous such attack, of course, was the Japanese attack on Pearl Harbor, mythologized in films such as *From Here to Eternity, In Harm's Way,* and *Tora! Tora! Tora!* In this myth, Americans are a peace-loving people who are ambushed by an evil, deceptive enemy. In response to this heinousness, we reluctantly but bravely go to war to protect ourselves and free the world of oppression. The Bush rationale for war—that Saddam Hussein (who was often likened to Adolf Hitler) possessed weapons of mass destruction, had the capability of attacking the United States, and was allied with al Qaeda—was a justification that tapped into this myth. The narrative that was presented was that we did not want to go to war but that we were forced into it by an evil enemy who could not be trusted, refused to cooperate with the United Nations (UN) inspection teams, and was bent on our destruction. The reality, of course, was that all of Iraq's weapons of mass destruction had been destroyed by UN inspectors years before the 2003 invasion, Iraq had no capability to deliver weapons of destruction to the United States, and Saddam Hussein was not aligned with al Qaeda. But the Bush justification for war connected so effectively with the Hollywood myth that even five and one-half years after the invasion of Iraq, 37 percent of Americans still believed the false claim that Iraq possessed weapons of mass destruction when the war began. Once the Bush administration was able to link the rationale with the myth, the myth became a referent of its own and overrode reality.

Other aspects of the Bush administration's presentation of the war likewise were more similar to the Hollywood war fantasy than to reality. For example, although 98 percent of the troops involved in the invasion were from only two countries (the United States and the United Kingdom), Bush created the "Coalition of the Willing," initially a group of forty-nine countries. But other than the United Kingdom, the coalition included relatively obscure countries such as the Marshall Islands, Micronesia, Palau, the Soloman Islands, and the like, some of which did not even have military forces. In a like fashion, the bombing of Iraq (the Shock and Awe phase), which marked the beginning of the war, was presented as if highly accurate precision-guided bombs virtually eliminated civilian casualties. While 68 percent of the bombs dropped were, in fact, precision guided, not all of those actually hit their targets (the Pentagon estimated that between 7 and 10 percent of the precision-guided bombs went astray) (Schmitt 2003). The organization Iraq Body Count, which relies on western newspaper reports to estimate civilian deaths, estimated that 7,356 Iraqi civilians died as a result of the invasion alone (Sloboda and Dardagan 2004).

Throughout the invasion the media was provided with compelling stories and visuals that supported the idealized war myth. One which dominated the news for some time was the story of Army Private First Class Jessica Lynch. A petite 19-year-old blonde Army clerk, she was turned into a hero when the convoy she was in was ambushed, killing nine of her comrades. She was injured (supposedly stabbed and wounded by enemy gunfire) as she mowed down Iraqi soldiers with her M-16 until finally running out of bullets, was captured, and was taken to a hospital where initial reports were that she was slapped about, strapped to a hospital bed, and interrogated by Iraqi fedayeen. Eight days later she was rescued in a daring midnight raid by Army Rangers and Navy SEALs who, using night-vision goggles and coming under heavy fire, found her and brought her to safety.

While this story captivated the nation and ties into the heroic war myth that the military leaves no (wo)man behind, it turned out to be largely false. In reality, Lynch was neither stabbed nor shot—her wounds came entirely as a result of the crash of the Humvee she was riding in when it ran into another vehicle in the convoy; she never fired a shot at the enemy because her gun jammed, and she got down on her knees and prayed when surrounded by the enemy rather than trying to fight them. While a biographer of her story claims she was raped, she claims that the biographer manipulated her words and says that she does not remember that happening. Doctors at the hospital deny that her wounds were consistent with being raped and said that they took exceptionally good care of her, providing her with treatment that exceeded that given to Iraqis in the hospital. She was given the only specialist bed in the hospital, three bottles of blood (two donated by the hospital staff), and was assigned one of only two nurses on the floor.

When the Rangers and SEALs raided the hospital to rescue her, a military cameraman accompanied them to record footage. A doctor at the hospital described the raid and, in doing so, unknowingly described the hyperreal nature of it: "We heard the noise of helicopters," said Dr. Anmar Uday. "We were surprised. Why do this? There was no military, there were no soldiers in the hospital. It was like a Hollywood film. They cried, 'Go, go, go,' with guns and blanks and the sound of explosions. They made a show—an action movie like Sylvester Stallone or Jackie Chan, with jumping and shouting, breaking down doors" (quoted in Kampfner 2003). Only a few hours after the successful rescue, the military proudly showed the video and, in a briefing for reporters, General Vincent Brooks proudly declared, "Some brave souls put their lives on the line to make this happen, loyal to a creed that they know that they'll never leave a fallen comrade" (quoted in

Kampfner 2003). Months later, after being discharged from the Army, Lynch accused the Bush administration of manipulating and distorting her story for propaganda purposes (Helmore 2003).

According to the modern presidency model, a president should "teach realism" (Neustadt 1980). Admittedly, the president is not in control of many events, but he can use events to educate about things that are difficult to understand. In contrast, the postmodern world is a hyperreal world where images have little or no connection to reality but are more powerful because they are linked to fantasy and illusion. Daniel Boorstin (1962) explains why those illusions are so powerfully held: "We are the most illusioned people on earth. Yet we dare not become disillusioned, because our illusions are the very house in which we live; they are our news, our heroes, our adventure, our forms of art, our very experience" (240). Images are evaluated not on their ability to represent reality, but on their success at evoking emotion and engaging the audience.

In postmodernism the president tries to make events interesting so that they will be reported and reproduced. Since reality tends to be mundane and seldom piques our interest, events must be connected to heroic myths that we use to make life exciting. Hyperreal events and objects are interesting because of their ambiguous relationships to reality and their connections to myths, and once they have been effectively staged they create their own reality merely because they occur (Boorstin 1962). As media critic Michael Wolff said of the Jessica Lynch story, "She can't take back being a star. The fact that she says it's all made up doesn't make a difference. It's been decided she's a star, and that's the only indisputable fact" (quoted in Helmore 2003). By mastering the art of the hyperreal, the Bush administration contributed to the making of the postmodern presidency.

Managing the Bureaucracy

At the beginning of the twenty-first century, both liberals and conservatives recognized that government alone could not solve fundamental social problems (i.e., wicked problems) such as homelessness, drug addiction, poverty, or the failure of public education to adequately prepare students for the future. Bush, embracing the image of the "compassionate conservative," put it this way: "[T]he American people also recognize that there are social problems that are not getting solved by the government and that there is a vital role that we can play, as a compassionate society, to help those who are less fortunate" (quoted in Scully 2001, A1).

At first glance, this approach is consistent with a vision of the postmodern management of the executive branch discussed by Durant (1998) in his analysis of the "neoadministrative state." As mentioned in previous chapters, the neoadministrative state is "one in which a sizeable and ever-growing proportion of the federal executive branch no longer directly makes or implements policy. Rather these [government] agencies arrange, coordinate, and monitor networks of public, private, and nonprofit organizations that pursue these things with or for them" (Durant and Warber 2001, 222). But, as we will see, played out in the George W. Bush administration this became an ideologically tainted, half-hearted approach focused more on building electoral coalitions and creating images than solving real problems. In this respect it was quite similar to what all presidents, modern or postmodern, do when using the bureaucracy to implement policy. Bush's orientation toward the management of government was a combination of his father's belief that volunteer organizations could solve social problems, and Ronald Reagan's belief in the free market as a panacea for virtually any social or economic problem. Overlying each was Bush's belief in God, but more importantly, his desire to reward those who had elected him and to maintain those coalitions in order to get reelected.

Faith-Based Initiatives

In the 2000 presidential campaign, George W. Bush attempted to blunt the common perception of conservatives that they did not care about the disadvantaged of society by advocating what he referred to as a principle of "compassionate conservatism." Conservatives, he claimed, cared about the disadvantaged; they simply didn't believe that government programs were effective at solving problems. Instead, conservatives preferred non-governmental solutions such as those developed by faith-based organizations. Bush's faith-based-initiative program was to be a part of that approach. The program was supposed to mobilize "armies of compassion" that would receive federal money to support programs designed to address poverty, drug abuse, alcoholism, homelessness, crime, literacy, and the like.

Facing what he anticipated to be a skeptical Congress, Bush moved quickly to fulfill his campaign pledge. On January 29, 2001, Bush issued Executive Orders 13198 and 13199, the first of his administration, and created the White House Office of Faith-Based and Community Initiatives and liaison offices in the Departments of Justice, Housing and Urban Development, Labor, Health and Human Services, and Education. The departmental offices were charged with facilitating the processing and evaluation of grants to faith-based organizations, thus encouraging the flow of money to organizations that had difficulty obtaining government funding because of their religious orientations. University of Pennsylvania political science professor John DiIulio, a strong believer in consensus-building, was appointed to head the initiative. DiIulio had helped sketch out Bush's compassionate conservative perspective on the campaign trail and believed that the faith-based initiative could provide the foundation for a new public philosophy that would "promote active benevolence in all sectors of civil society and ... institute results-driven competition within social-welfare bureaucracies, federal, state and local" (DiIulio 1999, 10). Local networks beginning at the level of the family were to be coordinated with, and supplemented by, government and other nonprofit organizations.

This vision of the role of government in addressing social problems was consistent with the postmodern view of the neoadministrative state. It placed government in a horizontal relationship with civic groups; still maintained an important role for government in terms of coordination, financial, and organizational support; and potentially, at least, created an atmosphere of openness for all interested stakeholders to participate.

But the faith-based-initiative program never evolved as DiIulio had hoped. Bogged down with constitutional issues concerning the separation of church and state, freedom of speech, and the issue of employment discrimination practiced by many religious groups, Congress refused to pass legislation that would have funded the program. Furthermore, after the 9/11 attacks, Bush focused on the War on Terror and put all domestic programs, including faith-based initiatives, on the back burner. After only a few months on the job, DiIulio resigned (when taking the job, he agreed to serve only six months), and complained that most senior White House staffers were uninterested in policy and, instead, were more interested in communications and media strategies (Mucciaroni and Quirk 2004). Furthermore, the Bush White House was dominated by advisors who, at bottom, not only did not believe that government should create and direct social programs, but also did not believe government should play any role whatsoever in addressing those problems (Suskind 2003).

David Kuo, a committed Christian and a Special Assistant to the President who worked for DiIulio and stayed on after he left to try to make the program a success, became similarly disillusioned. Karl Rove was impressed by the positive public response the program was receiving, so Kuo was sent across the country to run conferences where groups were encouraged to submit grant applications, even though he knew that the program was inadequately funded and that few, if any, of the groups would be awarded money. The conferences were, in effect, a public relations gimmick. After resigning, Kuo reflected on his experience in the Bush White House: "George W. Bush loves Jesus. He is a good man. But he is a politician; a very smart and shrewd politician. And if the faith-based initiative was teaching me anything, it was about the president's capacity to care about perception more than reality. He wanted it to look good. He cared less about it being good" (Kuo 2006, 229).

The faith-based-initiative program, though having minimal impact on solving any of the social problems at which it was supposedly directed, was effective at accomplishing two objectives. First, it redirected limited resources to groups that supported Bush. Organizations headed by evangelist Pat Robertson, Bishop Harold Ray, noted Republican operatives, and other groups that even had the appearance of being based in Christianity received high ratings in their grant applications and most of the money available, regardless of their effectiveness at solving problems (Kuo 2006). Second, the program proved to be a public relations bonanza. The press dutifully reported Bush's proposed budget announcements of huge expenditures for faith-based programs, but when it actually came to funding the programs, the press often missed the story—the Bush administration often failed to fight for the programs and, even when they were funded, the Bush administration often failed to spend the money. Talking about how the press was manipulated in this regard, Kuo says, "This approach allowed the White House to make grand announcements and then do nothing to implement them with impunity" (2006, 228).

Regulation and Deregulation

The postmodern view of government management is horizontal and envisions the bureaucracy playing the role of facilitator, bringing together all stakeholders in a cooperative manner to solve problems. Bush publicly rejected the modern, regulatory view of government and embraced a conservative, deregulation perspective, derogatively labeled "cowboy capitalism" by critics—a term later embraced by advocates of low taxes, deregulation, and free trade. Inheriting rhetoric from the Reagan administration, he criticized "big government" and lauded the benefits of the free market. For example, in his 2005 State of the Union address, typical of most of his major speeches on the economy, Bush criticized the federal government for spending too much, praised the benefits of tax cuts and new markets abroad, asserted his desire to eliminate regulations imposed on small businesses, and called for a comprehensive review of the federal tax code. In hyperreal fashion, this conjured up images of the myth of capitalism, an economic system free of government regulation, and an economic system that never existed in America.

When the economy began deteriorating in the second half of 2008, the commonly expressed belief was that it was due to Bush's deregulation policies of the financial markets that allowed (and perhaps even encouraged) speculators to behave irresponsibly. Typical is this criticism from Bush's home state of Texas: "The jobless rate rose to 7.2 percent in December, the highest in 16 years. The total number of jobs lost in 2008 was 2.6 million. That's 2.6 million families that are now unsure of how to pay the bills. That is 2.6 million families wondering how to put food on the table and keep a roof over their heads. All of this came about because of Bush's deregulation" (Maxwell 2009). Yet the reality of the role the Bush administration played in deregulating the economy is more complicated.

When speaking publicly Bush was a forceful voice against government regulation. But if we examine the actual behavior of his administration, a mixed bag about regulation emerges. In fact, the Bush administration was not opposed to government regulation; it was only opposed to regulation that hurt its political base. For example, after an analysis of the Bush administration's protectionist trade policies against Vietnamese catfish, Chinese textiles, South Korean computer chips, and foreign drugs, libertarian Llewellyn Rockwell (2003) concluded that the Republican party was so strongly influenced by big business that its free trade policy was empty rhetoric and that it actually pursued a protectionist policy for businesses it favored.

The Bush administration's handling of cattle grazing on public lands illustrates further how regulation was used for partisan political purposes. The federal government owns about 28 percent of the land area of the country, more than 600 million acres, mostly in the west. Much of this land was set aside for national parks, monuments, historical preserves, and cemeteries. Other land not set aside was used by private parties under the regulation of the federal government. One important use was cattle grazing. The Secretary of the Interior is responsible for issuing grazing permits, setting fees, and establishing grazing districts, while also protecting the land from overuse and using scientific analyses to determine appropriate regulations to achieve those objectives. Although controversies occur from time to time over how to best use the land, which type of grazing (e.g., cattle, sheep) should be given priority, and the cost of the permits and fees, over the years only modest changes had been made in those policies—at least until the Bush administration took office.

In 2006 and 2007, over the objections of staff scientists from the U.S. Fish and Wildlife Service, the Bush administration instituted a new series of regulations that lowered grazing fees, limited the definition of "interested public" to exclude many environmental groups from being consulted in making decisions, restricted the scope of what should be considered when developing environmental impact statements, and gave ranchers who made improvements on public lands (e.g., wells, fences) partial ownership in such improvements. These changes did not open up grazing to the free market (to do so would result in increased fees); rather, it maintained regulations that benefited special interests—interests politically aligned with the Bush administration (Wrabley 2008).

But in the area of financial markets, the Bush administration's policies were more in line with deregulation. Although many of the policies that affected the financial markets were the responsibility of independent commissions (e.g., the Federal Reserve, the Securities and Exchange Commission), those in charge were Bush appointees and they followed policies approved of and encouraged by the Bush administration. In other areas, however, the government policies of light regulation of commercial banks, even lighter regulation of investment banks, and virtually no regulation of the "shadow banking system" (i.e., hedge funds, private equity funds, and bank-created investment vehicles) encouraged excessive risk-taking and speculation (Crotty 2009). While the Bush administration was not solely responsible for this, its actions of loosening regulation added to an already dangerous situation.

Of all the postmodern presidents already considered, George W. Bush was the least attuned to the changing reality of the postmodern administrative state. Using hyperreal images of our capitalist myth, he called for deregulation and, attempting to steal Democratic issues, he recast conservative volunteerism through faith-based organizations. Still, these efforts were not designed to develop a new form of executive management. The new postmodern approach to governance is not synonymous with the conservative belief in deregulation. Instead, it advocates a new approach to how government should work with private and civic organizations to address complex social and economic problems. It argues for a form of rule-making and regulation that is horizontal, with government playing the role of faciltator.

Unitary Executive Theory

Postmodern presidents have been quite willing to use unilateral powers to control the political agenda. But until the George W. Bush administration, they had largely done so within the constitutional framework established by the Founding Fathers. Just as the Bush administration had employed hyperreal images to manipulate public opinion, so too it created a hyperreal vision of executive authority to justify a range of extra-constitutional and extra-legal actions—what became known as the unitary executive theory. But as is so often the case, the roots of this theory go back to prior presidencies—in this instance, to the Reagan Justice Department.

During the second term of the Reagan administration, Attorney General Ed Meese, office heads Theodore Olson and Charles Cooper, future Supreme Court Justice Samuel Alito, and other Justice Department attorneys sketched out what would become known as the unitary executive theory. With the intellectual support of legal analysts from the conservative Federalist Society, their goal was to devise a way of controlling the regulatory power of the executive branch while, ironically, expanding the authority of the president. To accomplish this they meticulously parsed language in Article II of the Constitution (the vesting and oath clauses) to argue that the Constitution "deigned to empower the president to exercise sole control over the removal of Executive branch officials, to direct the actions of such officials, and to nullify the decisions or actions of others that are believed to impede the president's full control over the Executive" (Spitzer 2009, 9). In essence, the Bush administration made two bold claims: (1) that the president's power was the ultimate and final authority in the executive branch, and (2) that his powers were unreviewable by either the legislative or the judicial branches (Spitzer 2006). These claims, of course, fly in the face of Supreme Court decisions which have upheld the independence of independent regulatory commissions, and the well-accepted and well-documented principle of checks and balances. In this respect, the Bush administration did not merely attempt to expand the use of unilateral power, but rather it shifted the underlying principle of where presidential authority resided. Commenting on the Bush presidency, one scholar concludes, "It is something entirely different, not because the Bush presidency was the first to expand the powers of the office, but because it was the first to attempt to do so by implementing a wholesale rewriting of the office's constitutional and legal powers under the banner of the unitary executive" (Spitzer 2009, 13).

Scholars have been virtually unanimous in condemning the Bush administration's expansion of presidential power. His actions have been found to be a violation of treaties and international law (Weaver and Pallitto 2006), deceitful (Rich 2006; McClellan 2008), an unlawful attempt to override congressional legislation (Bumgarner 2007), an unjustified extension of executive privilege (Weaver and Pallitto 2005), and an abuse of the authority granted the president by the Constitution (Adler 2006a). President George W. Bush's expansive use of power occurred in virtually all areas of executive authority, from the post office, where he claimed the right to open mail without a warrant; to energy policy, where he claimed the right to keep even the names of people consulted secret, to the unilateral reinterpretation and nullification of treaties; to the right to ignore the Geneva Convention standards regarding torture. Even a cursory examination of the use of some of these unilateral actions illustrates the extent to which Bush asserted presidential control.

Using the long-standing principle of signing statements, Bush became far more aggressive in expanding presidential authority than had any of his predecessors (Berry 2009). Over 85 percent of his signing statements contained constitutional challenges or objections, compared to 65 percent for his father and 27 percent for Bill Clinton. From 2001 to 2008 he used signing statements to void, or refuse to enforce, approximately 1,100 provisions of laws, over twice as many as any other president (Savage 2006, 2007; Spitzer 2009). For example, on at least four different occasions, Congress passed legislation allowing U.S. troops to serve as advisors in Columbia to battle narcotics-funded rebels. In each case Bush signed the law but then indicated in signing statements that as commander-in-chief he did not have to obey any of the restrictions regarding how troops would be used.

A second area where Bush expanded the use of unilateral actions beyond the bounds of the law was in his use of extraordinary renditions. Renditions—surrendering persons to foreign jurisdictions—are commonplace occurrences in international affairs, and the procedures followed are usually specified in treaties. But the Bush administration pursued a policy of "extraordinary renditions," whereby people would be forcibly and illegally removed from a country where they had a legal right to be and handed over to clandestine non-judicial authorities in another country for interrogation (i.e., torture). This process is not recognized as legal in international law, nor is the use of torture to obtain information considered legal.

Since such activities are shrouded in secrecy, it is difficult to document the extent to which the Bush administration used this activity. Nonetheless, some cases have received public attention. One such case involved Maher Arar, who had dual citizenship in Canada and Syria. Returning to Canada from a family vacation in

Tunis, he was detained while changing flights at John F. Kennedy International Airport in New York under suspicion that he had ties to terrorist groups. His body and baggage were searched without a warrant, he was denied access to a lawyer, he was held in solitary confinement for almost two weeks, and finally, against his protests, he was sent to Syria, where he was held in an underground cell the size of a grave and tortured for almost a year. After objections and pressure from the Canadian government, he was released; it was later revealed that he had no ties to any terrorist organizations, and no information linking him to terrorist groups was obtained even with the use of torture. Although Arar sued in American courts, his case was dismissed as the Bush administration successfully argued that to hear the case would force them to reveal state secrets. He remains on a list of people barred from entering the United States.

Extraordinary rendition is a violation of international law, and its implementation, especially when performed within the territory of the United States, violates American law and the constitutional protection of habeas corpus. Although torture violates the widely accepted Geneva Conventions, Bush claimed he had the authority to suspend those provisions because they applied to prisoners of nation states, and terrorists did not represent such states (Adler 2006b). White House Counsel Alberto Gonzales (who went on to become attorney general) argued that the Geneva Conventions were "quaint," but out of date, and in a Justice Department memorandum, it was stated that "general criminal laws must be construed as not applying to interrogations undertaken pursuant to his Commander-in-Chief authority" (Yoo 2003, 13).

In order to use extraordinary rendition, the Bush administration had to resort to the use of the secrecy privilege. Over the course of eight years, Bush used the previously rarely used claim extensively. In fact, in one district-court case, it was invoked 245 times with at least one of the invocations covering a document that had already been made public (Weaver and Pallitto 2005). The state secrets privilege differs from executive privilege, a more commonly reported upon claim. Executive privilege is based in the constitutional doctrine of separation of powers and is a qualified privilege designed to protect the confidentiality of communications within the executive branch by presidential advisors from other branches of government and from the public. In contrast, assertions of the state secrets privilege have no constitutional basis (they are actually traced back to crown privileges in England) and the claims are absolute. "[T]he ultimate reason for upholding its use is on the practical grounds that it was necessary to the survival of the state" (Weaver and Pallitto 2005, 92). Since it is connected to neither the

Constitution nor to legislation, there are no policy guidelines that control its use. Further, because both the Congress and the courts have been reluctant to challenge its use, it "virtually guarantees that its assertion in any particular case will be successful and that the costs for abuse of the privilege will be minimal or nonexistent" (Weaver and Pallitto 2005, 111).

The unitary executive theory is based upon the false belief, often stated by former Vice President Dick Cheney, that the powers of the president had been weakened by congressional meddling in the executive branch (Milbank 2004). As was shown in earlier chapters of this book, the reality is that unilateral presidential powers have grown dramatically over the last three decades. But the George W. Bush administration went even further, expanding the use of unilateral action to such an extent that provisions of the Constitution that limited presidential power were now being ignored. Although claiming that a constitutional basis existed for the unitary executive theory, most scholars agree that no such justification can be persuasively made. Professor Robert Spitzer (2009) captures the essence of the judgment of academics when he sarcastically says, "[T]he Bush unitary executive is an honest reading of the Constitution only if the reader is standing on his or her head at the time" (15).

The creation of the unitary executive theory represents perhaps the most dangerous form of hyperreality in which the George W. Bush administration participated. Based on a far-fetched interpretation of the intent of the founding fathers, the Bush administration created a theoretical and legal justification of executive power that had no grounding in historical reality. Ultimately, the administration's ability to expand presidential power to the extent that it did occurred because neither of the other two branches of government was able or willing to check Bush. But by failing to check this expansive view of presidential power, the Congress and the courts allowed Bush to wage a war on the basis of false premises and effectively suspend part of the Constitution previously thought to be sacrosanct.

The George W. Bush Postmodern Legacy

More than any previous postmodern, president George W. Bush made use of hyperreality to govern. Although previous presidents had actively attempted to create images to manipulate public opinion, none had employed image creation that was as disconnected from reality as the Bush administration's. As a result,

George W. Bush has contributed to the making of the postmodern presidency to the extent that the limitations on power found in the Constitution have been eroded and replaced with limitations found only in the form of elite political support and public opinion. Bush was able to do this because he was successful at cultivating public opinion and Congress lacked the political will to check such abuses. While some recent court decisions have attempted to rein in some presidential actions, for the most part the courts have been reluctant to limit presidential power.

This raises fundamental questions for democracy. Is democracy nothing more than electing a president every four years and then letting him behave like an elected monarch, doing as he pleases? Have we, unconsciously, altered our political system and redefined what we mean by constitutionalism so that it no longer refers solely to a written document, but now refers to accepted norms of political behavior? If the major checks on the abuse of power are located in public opinion, are the American people informed enough to make reasonable judgments and develop responsible opinions?

Note

1. Spin has become so overt that, following presidential candidate debates, campaign staff gather in a room designated by the media as the "spin room" to explain why their candidate won and why the others lost the debate.

CHAPTER 6

HORIZONTAL POLITICS

THE 2008 PRESIDENTIAL ELECTION

It's their campaign now. We're at the point where, if this is going to
work, it's going to be because of them. All we have to do now is have
faith in them.

Joe Trippi (2008, 119)

On Saturday, February 10, 2007, in Springfield, Illinois, Senator Barack
Obama stood before a crowd of 16,000 cheering supporters and announced
that he was running for president. Standing in 16-degree weather, in front of
the Old Capitol Building where Abraham Lincoln had given his famous "house
divided" speech almost 150 years earlier, Obama invoked themes that would
link him with the past and, simultaneously, define his campaign: "Together,
starting today, let us finish the work that needs to be done and usher in a new
birth of freedom.... That is why this campaign can't only be about me. It must
be about us—it must be about what we can do together. This campaign must
be the occasion, the vehicle, of your hopes, and your dreams."

The parallels with Lincoln could not be ignored. Both Lincoln and Obama
were born in other states (Kentucky and Hawaii) but were adopted sons of Illinois,
both were lawyers, both served for short periods in the Illinois legislature (Lincoln
in the Assembly and Obama in the Senate), both had modest national political
experience, both were rhetorically brilliant, both were politically ambitious,

both ran for president during times when the nation was divided (in Lincoln's time between the North and the South, in Obama's time between red and blue states), and both were physically similar—tall and lanky. But perhaps the most dramatic and emotionally charged connection revolved around their most obvious difference—one was black, the other white. As president, Lincoln signed the Emancipation Proclamation freeing the slaves and gave black Americans hope that they could achieve equality; Obama, a black man running for president, would, if elected, symbolize the achievement of that hope.

Perhaps more than most politicians, Obama understood the symbolic significance of elections. They are not only crucial for selecting political leaders, but in many respects, elections constitute the sacred rituals of democracy (Hirschbein 1999). Thus, they are both functionally and symbolically significant. They carry with them strong emotional attachments that are based in fundamental American civic values. Involvement in the electoral process, whether intense or vicarious, offers "transcendent ritualistic gratification" (Hirschbein 1999, 22). Consequently, by participating in the electoral process, citizens attach themselves to the political process by developing attitudes of support for the system.

The symbolic nature of elections, while more obvious in postmodernism, also characterizes at least one of the roles they play in modernity. But precisely because of the overtly symbolic nature of elections in postmodern politics, the possibility that "spaces of appearance" may be created for citizens where they "may express themselves directly over time and initiate collective action" exists (Gorham 2000, 29). Unnoticed by the mainstream media on that chilly February day was the hidden structure of the Obama campaign, a netroots electronic organization that would be fully integrated into the campaign. Only 24 hours after his announcement, over 1,000 Internet groups that had already been organizing for Obama on their own accessed Obama's website and began using the site's online tools to help them organize local groups. Over the duration of the campaign, these groups would grow exponentially, creating new spaces for citizens to express themselves and establish associational relationships with each other—and in the process, politically empowering themselves and each other. But did the opportunities to participate created by the new digital technologies offer the possibility that new postmodern spaces of appearance would be created, or was the Obama campaign merely a more technologically sophisticated version of a modern insurgent campaign?

Senator John McCain's announcement that he was running for president stood in stark contrast to Obama's and illustrated some of the significant differences between the two campaigns. In a 20-minute speech in Portsmouth, New Hampshire, on April 25, 2007, with the Portsmouth Naval Yard serving as a backdrop, McCain kicked off his campaign in front of what newspapers described as an often "listless crowd" of "a few hundred people" who stood in the cold rain. His speech was continually disrupted by a small, vocal group of anti-war protesters. McCain's comments presaged the strategy his campaign would follow: "I'm not the youngest candidate, but I am the most experienced. I know how the world works; I know the good and the evil in it. I know how to fight, and I know how to make peace. I know who I am and what I want to do" (quoted in Helman 2007, A1). He was to run a campaign not on issues, but on his biography.

The Obama team would masterfully use symbolism and spectacle to connect with voters, while the McCain campaign, although understanding their importance, used them poorly. Obama linked himself with a hallowed historical figure that virtually all Americans respected, while McCain highlighted his military experience, obtained during the divisive Vietnam War, while the war in Iraq was similarly dividing the nation. The Obama campaign's use of the Old Capitol Building, not far from Lincoln's modest Springfield home, could not be ignored by the press, while the Portsmouth Naval Yard backdrop was mentioned in few news reports. Perhaps even more telling was the contrast between the two crowds. Obama drew an estimated 16,000 enthusiastic supporters—most were already working for the candidate and were mobilized for the event. The McCain team, on the other hand, relied on word of mouth, thus resulting in a modest crowd of people, many of whom were simply curious about what was happening—many were not even McCain supporters. Obama's spectacle suggested that he wanted to lead a movement that would begin in the heartland (Illinois) and sweep throughout the nation to change history, while McCain wanted to win the presidency, thus making his announcement in the state that held the first presidential primary. Obama invited citizens to become part of his crusade to change history, while McCain, the ultimate maverick, would fight alone, against all odds, to win.

Although it might be tempting to paint the contest as one between the old man who did not understand the new politics or the new digital technologies and the Web-savvy, BlackBerry-toting celebrity politician, in reality both campaigns developed postmodern strategies and both campaigns made use of digital technologies to the extent that they wanted and/or could. Perhaps more significant than the differences between the two camps was the fact that both employed postmodern strategies and tactics, the first time in electoral history that that had happened. In that sense, both contributed to the making of the postmodern presidency. Yet, at the same time, the structures of both campaigns were ultimately modern in their underlying assumptions about how campaigns should be run. Nevertheless, the electoral contest took place in a postmodern culture. Obama's advantage was that he employed new digital technologies that were more in tune with how citizens in that culture related to each other—horizontally—and was thus able to mobilize his supporters to a greater extent than McCain could mobilize his supporters.

Elections in the Modern Presidency Model

According to the modern presidency model, the significance of elections is based upon a realistic understanding of the nature of the electorate. Voters possess neither the knowledge nor commitments to democratic principles that would make them qualified to play active policy-related roles. Gerald Pomper (1968) puts it bluntly: "The voters are not prepared to exercise a sovereign control over policy" (244). According to this perspective, the sobering reality is that citizens are disconnected from politics (Teixeira 1992), dislike political conflict (Dionne 1991; Rosenthal et al. 2002), are distrustful of politicians (Cooper 1999), possess low levels of information about specific policies (Shenkman 2008), do not think ideologically (Converse 1964), are alienated and angry (Gilmour and Lamb 1975; Tolchin 1999), possess ambivalent attitudes about the role of government (Frankovic and McDermott 2001), and support basic democratic values only in the abstract (Prothro and Grigg 1960). In sum, the American people lack the kind of knowledge, dispositions, and interests required to be fully engaged citizens in a democracy.

Given this grim picture of the American electorate, how then does the system function as well as it does, and how, without a politically informed citizenry, can it be considered a democracy? The answer, according to the modern perspective, is that it is the few who are activists (i.e., the political elites) who assure that the political system functions in a democratic fashion. Compared with non-activists, activists are characterized by greater amounts of information, more knowledge about policies, and a tendency to think more ideologically (Campbell et al. 1960). They discuss politics with each other and occasionally with non-activists and, by doing so, they draw people into the political process. Furthermore, on most issues they possess stronger beliefs in fundamental democratic principles (e.g., freedom of speech). Ironically, then, it falls upon the elites to make the system function democratically for the many non-elites who possess attitudes at times hostile to democracy. Average citizens are not fools, however (Key 1966). They make decisions that adhere to what we may call "gut" rationality (Popkin 1991), but primarily their influence is indirect in that they select, through elections, the political leaders who, given fairly wide discretion, in turn, create policy. "The public's explicit task is to decide not what government shall do but rather who shall decide what government shall do" (Campbell et al. 1960, 541).

Taken as a whole, the complex, six-month nomination process, with its fifty-state mixture of caucuses; state conventions; open and closed primaries; advisory and loophole primaries; pledged, unpledged, and superdelegates; scripted national conventions; and three-month frenetic general election campaigns that strategically operate within the context of the antiquated electoral college, combines to produce a confusing political pastiche that appears to lack any internal logic. But according to the modern presidency model, what appears to be an irrational, disconnected selection process has an almost "hidden" logic to it. According to this model, the presidential nomination and election campaigns are tests of political character and leadership. Candidates must develop sophisticated organizations that control and moderate political conflict and channel political participation, providing healthy outlets whereby citizens can become a part of the political process, though admittedly most do so marginally.

The political elites are of critical importance to the viability of the electoral process—they develop the campaign organizations, set the issue agenda, recruit activists, create the campaign events, and develop the campaign strategies. Furthermore, because they are knowledgeable and interested in policy, they force the candidates to address issues. Thus, even though political participation is modest and the discussion of issues is limited, the interpretation is that "the electoral system works, but it does so imperfectly" (Wayne 2008, 25).

It is not my intent in this chapter to examine the entire presidential selection process. Instead, I will examine those aspects that are most relevant for assessing the status of postmodern presidential campaign politics, using the 2008 presidential contest as a way of gauging the extent to which campaign tactics and behaviors have come to shape presidential elections and contribute to the making of the postmodern presidency. The chapter will first examine the extent to which the campaigns of presidential candidates Barack Obama and John McCain relied upon modern and/or postmodern strategies, organizational structures, and tactics in their efforts to win the election. My second area of interest lies in assessing the nature of political participation in the campaigns. Was the involvement of the American electorate similar to that described by adherents of the modern presidency model, or has postmodernism opened the system to new forms of participation more consistent with the postmodern model?

The Postmodern Challenge

As mentioned in previous chapters, the postmodern approach places an emphasis on establishing emotional connections between the candidate and voters through the use of symbols that trigger feelings about fundamental American values and beliefs. This can be done in a number of ways: through the use of video images and sound, the creation of pseudo-events, or the staging of compelling spectacles. Whatever the specific format, the significant difference between the modern and the postmodern campaigns lies in the underlying strategies about how to obtain votes.

Ideally, the modern approach is based on the belief that voters make decisions, to some degree, through the use of rationality. While most voters use some types of "shortcuts" to reason about the candidates (e.g., party identification, endorsements), their decisions are, if not entirely rational, at least "reasonable" (Popkin 1991). In contrast, the postmodern approach places secondary emphasis on the rationality or the reasonableness of the voters, and primary emphasis on creating positive associations with one candidate and attaching negative associations to the opponent. As one political consultant says, "[T]he choice of words, images, sounds, music, backdrop, tone of voice, and a host of other factors is likely to be as significant to the electoral success of a campaign as its content" (Westen 2007, 87).

At the structural level, modern presidential campaigns are organized top-down—run by the candidates and their staffs and supported by the national, state, and sometimes local political parties. Years ago, campaigns were predominantly run by volunteers, but over the years a sophisticated campaign-management industry has developed, with professionals responsible for virtually all aspects of the campaign—fundraising, polling, focus groups, advertising, video production, issue research and development, opposition research, speech writing, strategizing, media communications, volunteer coordination, voter turnout, and the like. Although all campaigns take on a sense of the chaotic at times, professionally run campaigns attempt to control the process in some hierarchical fashion and control it as much as possible.

In contrast, postmodernism challenges the hierarchical order that characterizes the modern campaign structure. Because it emphasizes multiplicity and openness, postmodernism is skeptical of hierarchy, which is seen as marginalizing those persons, ideas, and interests which do not fit into predetermined, and needlessly narrow, structures. In place of the hierarchical control and coordination of participants, postmodernism is characterized by spontaneous, grassroots, horizontal politics. Simplistically overstated, modern campaigns are top-down while postmodern campaigns are bottom-up, side-to-side, and potentially chaotic.

Finally, postmodernism challenges assumptions about the motivation for participation as well as the forms that participation takes. Deeply embedded in the modern paradigm is the belief that people participate in politics for instrumental reasons, particularly in the pursuit of self interest (e.g., working or voting for the candidate who promises policies that will benefit—usually economically—the people the most). In doing so, one must accept a limiting structure: "Political participation means giving up the joys and pleasures of private life" (Kariel 1977, 8). In terms of electoral politics, those with campaign expertise (i.e., professionals) define the objectives (e.g., elect the candidate) and then create organizations and activities that are logically related to the accomplishment of that narrowly focused goal.

In contrast, postmodernism offers "play" as an alternative to instrumental behavior. Rather than focusing on some external objective, play is non–goal-oriented and is present-oriented. To play well is to be absorbed in playing the part that one is playing. At the same time, learning occurs through play. In adult play in particular, it is possible to learn about ourselves and about alternative possibilities: "[P]lay reveals the possibility inherent in the human capacity for change. In this sense, playing is a way we learn, not to recreate reality and the world, but to create it. Playing reveals the innate abilities of human beings to innovate and initiate action that was not there before" (Gorham 2000, 16).

Where instrumental behavior establishes boundaries, play challenges those boundaries. In doing so, it questions what is at the heart of any event and opens up structures that have been closed, encouraging interaction with new elements previously excluded. Allowing for more possibilities of expression, it invites others to participate and, in the process of participating, redefines the meaning and significance of events. "To survive and remain at play is to be engaged in the continuous experimental process of testing and changing the rules so as to extend the range of controlled experience. Extending consciousness entails a readiness to enact rules for including underprivileged elements within our play, rules that *legitimate* impulses identified as infantile or decadent or perverse" [emphasis in original] (Kariel 1989, 35).

As has been shown in previous chapters, the office of the presidency has changed so dramatically over the last three decades that we may conclude that a new presidential model, the postmodern presidency, now is the norm and that modern elements, although still present, are the exception. The behaviors that stem from that paradigmatic shift have altered the manner in which the president governs. The origins of many of those changes have, in fact, been adapted from tactics that had initially been used in campaigns, thus creating the permanent campaign. The permanent campaign makes it possible for the president to build public-opinion support for himself using many techniques used in the campaign, which, in turn, provides him with leeway to take unilateral action. In this chapter we will consider the 2008 presidential election, carefully examining it to identify modern and postmodern patterns.

Campaign Strategies

The 2008 presidential contest was commonly thought of as "one of the most remarkable in American history" (Abramowitz 2010, 91). Coming at the end of eight years of what many considered a failed Bush presidency, the country seemed ready for change. While that would seem to lead almost inevitably to a Democratic victory, the threat of terrorism and the wars in Iraq and Afghanistan made a candidate with a compelling military biography such as John McCain a viable option. On the Democratic side, the candidacies of both Barack Obama and Hillary Clinton symbolized change. After the early primary and caucus contests, it became clear that either a woman or an African-American would be the standard bearer for the Democratic Party and, if he or she won, would symbolize a significant step forward for members of groups previously excluded from serious consideration for the highest office of the land. But should either Obama or Clinton win the nomination, questions remained. Would Americans vote for a woman for president? Was America ready for an African-American president?

With the nominations of their parties in hand by the early summer of 2008, Senators John McCain and Barack Obama both enthusiastically set out to win the election. The contest would be unlike any that had preceded it. Both camps employed strategies, themes, and tactics drawn from a postmodern campaign playbook, but both tried to do so while maintaining modern campaign structures. Yet in many respects activities that took place during the campaign were beyond the control of either candidate's organizations and illustrate, to some extent, the limitations of postmodern politics.

The McCain Campaign Strategy

Senator John McCain employed a campaign strategy that dated back to the 1980 and 1984 campaigns of Ronald Reagan: deemphasize and talk vaguely about issues, emphasize a carefully edited biography, reveal a strong personality, attack the messenger, and smear your opponent. It was a campaign built on image and biography that emphasized McCain's military background and his character and deemphasized his over two decades of service in Congress.

In his failed run for the presidency in 2000, Senator McCain toured the country on his "Straight Talk Express" bus, where he instituted an open-door policy with the press. In fact, he established such a rapport with the press that he once referred to them as "our people." At his sixty-eighth-birthday party during the 2004 Republican National Convention in New York, he feted fifty network anchors and network executives at the La Goulue restaurant on Madison Avenue. Raising his glass, he toasted them, calling them "my base." But with the presidential nomination in hand McCain had to establish his credibility with the conservative base of the Republican Party, a base that was suspicious of, and even hostile to, the press. At the 2008 Republican convention McCain suddenly labeled the press "the enemy." They were now derisively referred to as the "eastern elite," the "establishment," the "left-wing media," the "liberal media," the "Washington insiders," or the legless, slithering "MEE-de-ah," as McCain's vice presidential nominee Sarah Palin put it. This was not a change of heart by McCain; it was a change of strategy.

Rick Davis, McCain's campaign manager, was surprisingly frank about the strategy in his discussion with the editorial board of *The Washington Post* on the eve of the national convention. Leaning back in his chair, Davis candidly summed up the McCain strategy: "This election is not about issues. This election is about a composite view of what people take away from these candidates—their values, their character, their opinions, their principles" (Davis 2008). The McCain strategy was to encourage voters to make decisions on the basis of the resumes of the candidates. McCain's biography would be conveyed through images and stories and would be subsumed under the theme of "Country First," a theme that never developed traction. Anticipating criticism from the media for avoiding issues, the second prong of the strategy was to defuse that criticism by attacking the media as being "the liberal media," inherently hostile to Republicans.

The McCain Biography. The modern presidency model was, to a large extent, based upon the behaviors of voters that occurred prior to the use of the kinds of sophisticated communication technologies that are omnipresent in American politics today. Beginning with the Reagan administration's use of television, presidential politics has been based on the assumption that images overwhelm issues. "While image making has always been important to the presidency ... the image making of the image-is-everything presidency has become preeminent among our most recent cohort of presidents" (Waterman et al. 1999, 160). When issues are addressed, they are done so in order to reveal something about the character of the candidate: "The issues then suggest adjectives and attributes. These ideas about their personality and character fix themselves in our minds. Then we forget about the issues and remember only the characteristics" (Morris 1999, 35). Some research has even concluded that the personal images of presidential candidates are so important to voters that they override issue positions (Emanuel 2009). What's more, as voters watch fewer major network news programs, and as they read fewer and fewer newspapers, the connections between opinion leaders and the average voter are undermined (Cohen 2008). With this crucial linkage between opinion leaders and voters eroded, images take on increasing importance.

Understanding this, the McCain campaign blatantly downplayed issues. For example, although 53 percent of McCain's television ads were about issues, this was significantly lower than the proportion of earlier presidential candidates (Kaid 2009). (In 2004, 79 percent of Kerry's ads were issue ads, while 85 percent of Bush's were). In place of issue ads, McCain tried to craft an attractive image. Initially it included three elements: McCain the experienced politician, McCain the war hero, and McCain the political maverick.

Paying close attention to the Democratic nomination battle between Obama and Clinton, McCain's advisors thought that they had identified a weakness in the Obama strategy. Obama, they believed, was vulnerable because of his lack of experience. This laid the groundwork for the McCain attack strategy that Obama was unproven and risky (Harwood 2008). Building on that, Obama was criticized for having little experience and being comparable to a rock star and a Paris Hilton–like "celebrity." That line of attack continued up until just before the Republican convention, when the McCain camp suddenly fell silent about the experience issue. Shortly thereafter, McCain announced that he had selected Sarah Palin as his vice presidential running mate, a person with an even thinner political resume than that of Obama. At that point, McCain ignored the experience issue and began to emphasize his war hero record and his reputation as a maverick. This strategy became problematic for two reasons: First, because McCain was never comfortable talking about his experience as a prisoner of war and, second, because voters in general have conflicting feelings about mavericks (Ditto and Mastronarde 2009). But, handicapped with issue positions that were unpopular (Kenski and Kenski 2009), the McCain campaign stuck with the candidate's biography and continued to deemphasize issues. Image, it was hoped, would prevail over substance. But, while McCain was rated higher than Obama on experience and the belief that he "shared my values," the candidate trait that drove the election was the trait "can bring change," and on that Obama possessed an overwhelming advantage.

The Palin Phenomenon.   The selection of Governor Sarah Palin as the Republican vice presidential running mate took almost all by surprise. A relatively unknown governor from Alaska, she was thrust into the political limelight and instantly became a national political phenomenon. Because she lacked any significant knowledge about national issues, as demonstrated in several disastrous television network interviews, the McCain campaign sought to limit her exposure to the media and emphasize her biography. But her biography was so thin that the McCain handlers were left with trying to make a virtue out of her inexperience and lack of political sophistication. She was presented as a gun-toting "hockey mom," who raised five children while taking on the "old boys' club" in Alaska. The image was repeated time and again: "[S]he's genuine. She's authentic. She's real. She's not somebody who scripted her life to be in a position of power and influence by age 30 or 40. She's just a woman from the nation's frontier state who lives among people who are open and honest, who don't know when not to talk to the media or how to speak in phrases empty and correct" (Wooten 2008, 14A).

In keeping with the postmodern emphasis on biography rather than issues, Palin was, in many ways, the ideal running mate. She was a woman and would, it was hoped, attract disaffected Hillary Clinton primary voters; she was an evangelical Christian and would mobilize the conservative base, which was never excited about McCain; and by taking on the "old boys' club" in Alaska, she forged her maverick credentials. "We're a team of mavericks," became her postmodern mantra at political rallies. Steve Schmidt, who had worked closely with Karl Rove and joined the McCain campaign in the middle of the summer, spun her credentials in the following manner: "[S]he fought the oil companies, she is building a huge natural gas pipeline. She is taking on the corrupt special interests. She is returning taxpayer money back to families in Alaska. She is the future of the Republican Party" (quoted in National Campaign News 2008).

Yet while Palin was presented as a politician who "told it like it was" and who was not overly scripted by political handlers, in truth her image was carefully crafted and tightly managed. For example, seeming to understand the importance of biography in the race, an anonymous Internet user with the name Young Trigg logged on to the Sarah Palin Wikipedia entry at 2 a.m. the morning before she was announced as McCain's running mate and made over 30 "edits" to the web entry, deleting critical material and adding flattering details. In fact, the careful crafting of her image extended right down to her clothes, where the campaign spent $150,000 for her designer wardrobe.

Palin's obvious lack of knowledge about policy and her ineffectiveness at handling the press led the McCain campaign to limit her access to reporters and to use her in controlled settings where she excelled, stirring up supporters by attacking the "liberal MEE-de-ah" and Barack Obama, who "pals around with terrorists." Her rallies generated enthusiasm that often bordered on fanaticism. Attacks on Obama regularly would stir chants of "Nobama" and "Socialist" at the mention of his name, and at one Florida rally an overly zealous rally-goer was heard yelling "Kill him!" after Palin mentioned Obama's name. As the campaign progressed, YouTube was showing videos of crowds shouting "Treason" and "Off with his head," while one man was taped calling Obama a "one-man terror cell." The Palin biography and stage presence, while initially exciting, wore off over time, particularly among those voters McCain was targeting—white independent women.

The Palin phenomenon illustrates both the possibilities and the limitations of postmodern campaigning. Many political pundits (and even many McCain campaign aides) concluded that Palin was ill-prepared for the rigors of the national campaign trail, let alone the vice presidency. She lacked basic knowledge about national issues, was undisciplined, was poorly prepared for many campaign events, and refused to take direction or advice. After the campaign had ended some of McCain's campaign staffers even admitted that the decision to select Palin made them question McCain's judgment (Purdum 2009).[1] Nevertheless, Palin's ability to emotionally connect with her audiences showed the power of image. Qualifications, temperament, and knowledge meant little to those who developed a deep, almost personal connection to her. And yet, even with the carefully crafted biography and the tight management and coaching she received, 60 percent of the voters did not think that she was qualified for the job (Kenski and Kenski 2009). Reality can be manipulated, but there are also limits on that manipulation.

The Obama Campaign Strategy

Learning from past elections where Democratic presidential candidates provided voters with well-researched, highly detailed policy initiatives designed to address problems, only to find voters responding to the simplistic emotional appeals of their opponents, the Obama team adopted a different approach. They developed a sophisticated strategy around a few simple ideas. First, they would establish Obama as the candidate of change and link McCain to the disastrous policies of the Bush administration. Second, they would use Obama in formats where he could inspire people. And third, Obama would appear presidential by remaining calm and appeal to people by linking his own biography to fundamental American values.

Although technically Barack Obama was running against John McCain, in reality he was running against someone whose name would not even appear on the ballot, George W. Bush. Because of the widely held belief that the Bush presidency had failed and was in disarray, the central strategy for the Obama campaign was to make the election a referendum on the Bush presidency and to link McCain to Bush. With Bush's approval rating at 29 percent at the time of the election, the candidate who was able to convince the electorate that he was the agent of change seemed certain to win. From the very first day of his campaign, Obama embraced the concept of change, turning it into the campaign theme "Change you can believe in," and inspiring crowds to chant "yes we can" in response to his cadenced oratory.

At the same time, while establishing Obama as the candidate of change, they sought to link McCain to George W. Bush.[2] Although McCain tried to distance himself from Bush by claiming he was a "maverick" and that he actually disagreed with Bush on a number of important issues, the Obama campaign countered with embarrassing Fox network videos of McCain saying that he supported Bush over 90 percent of the time, a charge driven home repeatedly at Democratic rallies where Obama would refer to him as "McSame."

Obama recognized that he would have to strike a delicate balance between remaining calm and collected in order to project a presidential demeanor, while appealing to the emotions of the voters. He did this by talking about fundamental American values and beliefs, something previous Democratic candidates (with the exception of Bill Clinton) were reluctant to do: "There are those who don't believe in talking about hope: they say, well, we want specifics, we want details, we want white papers, we want plans. We've had a lot of plans, Democrats. What we've had is a shortage of hope" (quoted in Nagourney and Zeleny 2007, 34). The message of hope and change continued throughout the campaign. In his final campaign stop in North Carolina, he talked about the heroic nature of his maternal grandmother, who had recently died, and linked her with his campaign theme:

> She was one of those quiet heroes that we have all across America, who—they're not famous, their names aren't in the newspapers, but each and every day they work hard. They look after families. They sacrifice for their children and their grandchildren. They aren't seeking the limelight. All they try to do is just do the right thing. North Carolina, in just one more day we have the opportunity to honor those quiet heroes all across America.... We can bring change to America to make sure their work and their sacrifice is honored. (quoted in Finnegan 2008, 13)

As he moved on to more familiar passages in his speech, he dabbed his tear-drenched cheeks with a white handkerchief, the most emotion he would publicly show in the entire campaign.

Because he had little national political experience and virtually no foreign policy experience, he took the unprecedented step of embarking on a trip to the Middle East and Europe in the late summer, about a month before the nominating convention. The trip contained virtually no substance (he was in no position to negotiate foreign policy), but the images that were created—Obama in shirtsleeves joking with the troops in Iraq, high-level meetings with foreign leaders, a speech in front of thousands of cheering Berliners reminiscent of JFK's "Ich bin ein Berliner" speech—sent the visual message that he could be envisioned as a commander-in-chief and a statesman who had worldwide respect.

In television ads, Obama, like McCain, ran far fewer issue ads than had previous candidates and, in fact, the percentage of such ads was statistically the same as McCain's percentage (Kaid 2009). But like Bill Clinton, Obama did take positions and made promises on a plethora of small-bore (as well as comprehensive) issues. By the time of the election, his website listed over 500 campaign promises. Most of these issues were peripheral to the race, but one issue emerged late in the campaign that proved decisive, and that issue took both campaigns by surprise. On Sunday, September 14, the news media was abuzz—Lehman Brothers, one of the largest and most prestigious investment banks, was going to file for bankruptcy. This was the beginning of the economic collapse that would assure that Barack Obama would be elected.

"It's the Stupid Economy"

In the 1992 presidential race, Bill Clinton's political advisor James Carville helped keep the campaign on message with a simple four-word phrase: "It's the economy, stupid." In 2008, although neither McCain nor Obama emphasized the issue as Clinton had done in 1992, the economy suddenly and surprisingly emerged as the single compelling issue that determined the outcome of the race. At the time of the election, 63 percent of the voters said it was the most important issue, while no other issue received more than 10 percent support (Kenski and Kenski 2009).

The bankruptcy of Lehman Brothers was followed closely by the sale of Merrill Lynch, both precipitated by massive losses in mortgage-related investments. On Monday, September 15, the Dow Jones Industrial Average lost more than 500 points. Only two days later, AIG declared a liquidity crisis and the Federal Reserve extended the insurance giant $85 billion in credit. On September 19, the Bush administration prepared a $77 billion bailout plan to inject capital into the banking system. The economy was in free-fall.

The economic collapse was not good news for McCain, and quotes he had made a few years earlier that he "still need[ed] to be educated" about economics and "the issue of economics is not something I've understood as well as I should" came back to haunt him. Sensing that a dramatic move might put him ahead in what, at the time, was a close race, McCain announced on September 24 that he was suspending his campaign to race back to Washington to participate in congressional negotiations about the Bush bailout proposal. He also asked that the first presidential debate scheduled for two days later be postponed (a proposal rejected by Obama, who said a president must be able to multi-task). This was a leadership spectacle on McCain's part, designed to show him as an experienced statesman taking charge of a crisis situation. Unfortunately for McCain, the spectacle flopped and he came out of it looking like a befuddled, feckless politician who was more a confused follower than a leader.

Although McCain said he was suspending his campaign, in fact, his campaign continued. He continued running television ads, his staff continued their normal operations, and, although he cancelled an appearance on David Letterman's show, he angered Letterman when it was discovered the he did not rush back to Washington and instead was taping an interview with Katie Couric and later appeared on the late-night Conan O'Brien show.

In an attempt to further play out the role of statesman, McCain pressured Bush to call a summit meeting at the White House of the congressional leadership of both parties and both presidential candidates to deal with the crisis. However, at the meeting it was Obama, not McCain, who presented himself as the statesman. President Bush opened the meeting by saying nothing more than they had a problem, and then he quickly turned the meeting over to Treasury Secretary Henry Paulson. In turn, Paulson briefly summarized the relief plan they were proposing (a three-page plan provided to everyone prior to the meeting) and then asked for input from the Democratic congressional leadership; House Speaker Nancy Pelosi and Senate Majority Leader Harry Reid. Following a decision agreed to earlier, they deferred to Obama, who then took control of the meeting, summarizing the problem, identifying critical sticking points, peppering staff aides from Treasury with questions, and finally sketching out the Democrats' position. He then quickly turned to McCain and asked for his input. Appearing confused, McCain deferred, saying, "I'll just listen." Throughout the meeting McCain added little of substance, was mostly mute, and when asked directly about Paulson's plan, admitted that he had not read the three-page memo.

McCain's attempt at statesmanship was a disaster. "The self-styled straight-talk maverick was reduced to a series of platitudes about how House Republicans had 'legitimate concerns' and everyone needed to 'work together' and 'move forward' until they reached an acceptable compromise" (Alter 2010, 11). When word got out about McCain's performance, his image as an experienced statesman crumbled. Perhaps even more devastating was Letterman's persistent criticism of him: "I don't know if we can trust him," "This doesn't smell right," "Somebody put something in his Metamucil," "Is he a man of his word, or not?" Letterman's harassment of McCain continued until he finally appeared on the show and issued a terse apology: "I screwed up," he admitted.

The damage had been done to the McCain campaign. The week before the economic collapse, national polls rated the race as a dead heat, with some polls giving a slight edge to McCain. Following McCain's erratic performance, doubts about his judgment and leadership ability arose, and by mid-October Obama experienced a 14-percentage-point lead (Pew Research 2008).

Spectacles are an important part of the postmodern presidency, but as the McCain experience shows, they must be conducted skillfully if they are to be effective. McCain made a number of crucial mistakes. First, he did not have complete control over the performance. The idea of suspending his campaign and rushing back to Washington to broker a deal was dependent on his ability to control, or at least influence, other political actors. This proved not to be possible. Although he was able to convince Bush to call a meeting of congressional leaders at the White House, he not only could not control the Democrats who controlled Congress, but he was even unable to control the congressional leaders in his own party.

Second, although the postmodern spectacle can be used to mask behavior that runs counter to the intended message of the spectacle, the images and behavior of the lead actor must consistently support that message. McCain undermined his own message several times. For example, when he cancelled on the Letterman show and was actually taping the interview with Couric, Letterman was able to broadcast the live taping and projected a video of McCain prepping for the interview. All the while Letterman sarcastically threw barbs at the image on the screen.

Third, McCain's staff failed to coordinate the supporting actors in the spectacle. Although McCain said he was suspending his campaign, the media quickly discovered that that had not occurred. What's more, the fact that his campaign was essentially continuing was widely reported and became a story in and of itself, thus producing a counter message that undermined the intended story.

Fourth, McCain's performance as the lead actor was poor. His actual behavior both in continuing to campaign when he said he was not going to and his disastrous performance in the White House meeting were behaviors inconsistent with the image of a statesman. People believe that leaders should be strong, decisive, persuasive, determined, and consistent. But McCain's behavior was seen as erratic, inconsistent, contradictory, confused, and ineffectual. Rather than having the effect of demonstrating his leadership skills, it raised questions about his age in the minds of voters.

While the economic collapse assured Obama of victory in November, it also would create challenges for Obama once he assumed office. As he confided to a senior staff aide just prior to the election: "[T]he good news is we're going to win, the bad news is the world's falling apart" (Alter 2010, 5). The economic crisis could not be ignored and would force Obama to spend far more time on it than he wanted, all the time running the risk of distracting his administration from its priorities.

Voter Mobilization

To a large extent, which candidate wins an election is dependent on two factors: who can control the issue agenda, and who can turn out the voters most likely to vote for them on election day. Although Obama had the issue agenda imposed on him, he nevertheless benefited by the economic crisis. Voter turnout, however, is a matter more directly under the control of the campaign. While attempts to turn out the vote are most visible on election day itself, in fact, voter mobilization starts months before, with canvassing efforts that identify voters who are most likely to vote for your candidate, somewhat likely, least likely, and certain to vote for your opponent. Volunteers spend countless hours identifying and categorizing voters and urging them to vote for their candidate.[3] In recent years the Republicans have out-mobilized the Democrats, but in 2008 the tide turned—the Democrats benefited from a larger than usual turnout in favor of their candidate while the Republican turnout effort sputtered.

The Republican Voter Vault

McCain ran an ill-conceived and poorly executed strategy that emphasized images over issues, but other aspects of the campaign were more traditional. In particular, the attempt to mobilize voters using the famous Republican Voter Vault was an approach embedded within a modern view of how to run a campaign. The Voter Vault is a massive computerized data bank that contains information on over 165 million Americans. The database is composed of psychographic information complied from public databases on voters, including information such as credit card reports; magazine subscriptions; the number of children people have and where they attend school; vehicle registration information; gym memberships; hunting and fishing licenses; interest group memberships; buying preferences; hobbies; professional associations; church memberships; and, of course, voter registration information, party identification, some attitudinal information, and voting habits. Coordinated with census information, the Voter Vault can identify a voter's income, the value of their home, how many TVs they own, and even how many bathrooms are in their house.

Based on these data, the Voter Vault software program is used to calculate an index that classifies people according to which party they are members of, how strongly they are attached to those parties, and how likely they are to actually vote in any particular election. The database is controlled at the national level, but is coordinated with local activists who are trained and directed in its use. In the hands of a skilled campaign worker, a voter can be micro-targeted and campaign workers can be sent out to his or her home to talk about issues important to that particular voter while ignoring less salient issues. In 2000 and 2004 the campaigns culminated with a 72-hour blitz (the 72-Hour Task Force) in which the candidates, staff, and local workers were put on "full-court press" to turn out their voters across the nation. Seven million workers scoured the country turning out the vote. In the hands of Karl Rove, who developed the Voter Vault, George W. Bush was able to easily out-mobilize his Democratic opponents, who relied upon more traditional turnout approaches in both 2000 and 2004. A superficial glance at the operation may lead one to believe it is a grassroots movement, but the manner in which the Voter Vault "micro-targets" voters is a top-down and, hence, modern approach to campaign management.

The McCain campaign had access to the Voter Vault; however, it failed to perform as it had done in the past because of the limited number of trained people available to use the data effectively, and because the data had not been updated and was therefore old and inaccurate. For example, in the critical state of Ohio on the Friday night before the Tuesday election, the McCain campaign had less than half the number of offices open compared to the Obama campaign, and virtually all offices were lacking in volunteers to man the phones (Drogin and Abcarian 2008). The final push to mobilize McCain voters fizzled because of a lack of enthusiastic, dedicated campaign workers.

The Long Tail: The Obama Organization

Much is made of the Obama campaign's use of cutting-edge technologies and, conversely, McCain's failure to use them. To a considerable extent this is a conclusion drawn from the two candidates' personal use of digital technologies rather than from the actual use of them by the campaign staffs. In fact, McCain's 2000 presidential campaign was praised by many for "taking a forward-thinking, Internet-driven approach to organizing, building support, and generating on-line donations" (Kaye 2009, 1). Although the campaigns differed substantially in their use of digital technologies to mobilize voters in 2008, those uses were driven more by the availability or lack of availability of resources (i.e., money and volunteers) than by anything else. McCain had fewer than 15 staff members whose primary responsibility was working with digital marketing, advertising, and mobilization, while the Obama campaign employed almost 100. With mostly young creative staffers feeding off of each other, the Obama digital team was seamlessly integrated into the entire campaign effort, as compared to McCain's limited use of the Internet—to raise money and send out massive, text-heavy, imageless messages (referred to by critics as "Tolstoy in my mailbox").

Modern political campaigns use mass marketing approaches to reach as many people as possible. In practice this means that in order to make the most efficient use of the campaign dollar, you would purchase advertising time in the places where you would reach the most people (taking into consideration the peculiarities of the Electoral College, of course). With a financial limit of $84 million because he accepted public funding for the general election, McCain wanted to make sure that every advertising dollar was wisely spent. Consequently, he advertised in large markets in states that were competitive.

Rather than accepting the assumptions of mass marketing, the Obama campaign employed the postmodern principle of the long tail. The concept of the long tail derives from a postmodern advertising strategy that has been made possible because of the Internet. It is based on a marketing curve that shifts marketing from mass markets to niche markets. The traditional way (the modern model) of marketing relied upon a few products to be sold to most consumers. The commonly accepted principle is that 20 percent of the products in a particular area account for 80 percent of the sales. The long tail (the postmodern model), on the other hand, promotes the idea of selling a large variety of different products to a wide variety of people with varying tastes and interests. The approach is viable if the manner in which the niche markets reached can be democratized and the costs of the tools of distribution can be reduced (Anderson 2006).

The principle of the long tail was, in effect, the organizational approach the Obama campaign used to mobilize its supporters. Through the use of the Internet, cell phones, text messaging, YouTube, Twitter, blogging, and even search engines, the campaign targeted niche audiences with messages tailored specifically to them. The Obama campaign was particularly creative at finding potential supporters in unorthodox places. For example, using behavioral targeting technology, they discovered that former Clinton supporters could be found at horror film sites and that ads lauding Obama's commitment to gender equality would be effective if placed on food recipe sites (Kaye 2009). Using tools available on the MyBO website, groups were organized with people who shared similar interests—Electricians for Obama, Somali-Americans for Obama, Women for Obama, Texans for Obama, Iron Range Voters for Obama, Macs for Barack, Students for Barack Obama, and the like. By the end of the campaign, over 35,000 niche groups had been created (Harfoush 2009). While on the one hand the niche groups were encouraged to be creative and innovative, at the same time they were controlled by integrating them into the campaign web.

For example, digital technology teams were integrated into the campaign by making sure that their activities had multiple purposes. Online ads were often designed to provide information about issues, provide access to where the users could find out about the latest campaign activities in their area, talk to other volunteers, make it easy for them to contribute money to the campaign (two-thirds of the $750 million raised for the campaign was raised online), and even provide them with tools they could download to help them create their own neighborhood organizations. Yet, in all activities the primary objective was to translate digital communications with on-the-ground activity (Kaye 2009). For example, cell-phone and computer-based networks were used to bring thousands of people to Obama rallies—23,000 in Des Moines, 50,000 in Manassas, 80,000 in Portland, and 100,000 in St. Louis (Gronbeck 2009). Once they were at the rallies, a campaign official would urge the audience members to pull out their cell phones and text friends and neighbors, thus exponentially spreading the effect of the rally.

But perhaps more significantly, the Obama team rejected the traditional Democratic approach of working through labor unions and relying on local party organizations. Instead, they trained their own "fellows" in a six-week long seminar and sent them across the country to build relationships in neighborhoods. "In addition to voter outreach, fellow responsibilities included writing letters to the editor, walking in parades, putting up lawn signs, representing the campaign at community gatherings, helping with Get Out the Vote (GOTV) initiatives, and various administrative tasks" (Harfoush 2009, 41).[4]

The use of digital technologies, even in the manner in which they were used in the Obama campaign, was not new. Indeed, the Howard Dean presidential campaign of 2004 used many of the same technologies and similar approaches. However, according to Dean's campaign manager Joe Trippi, there were some significant differences: "The Obama campaign, on the other hand, had taken a lesson from the flimsy-contraption days of the Dean campaign. They used the better tools they had and the much stronger organizational structure they were able to build. But they also learned to keep any walls they built low, and made sure the campaign's supporters knew their creative ideas were welcome" (2008, 264). To a large extent the organization was based on the belief that peer-to-peer (i.e., horizontal), local contact would increase voter turnout (Dreier 2008). The 2008 Obama campaign raises fundamental questions about the organization of politics itself: "[T]he evolution of oral to literate to electronic political cultures in fact has brought with it both shifting modes of doing politics and changing relationships between Leaders and the Led" [sic] (Gronbeck 2009, 240). The Obama campaign "understood the social dynamic at work in the netroots movement and gave supporters a platform, a set of tools upon which they could 'be their own generals'" (Germany 2009, 157).

The targeting of niche audiences, the horizontal communication networks, and the strategy of using the community organizing model as a way of mobilizing supporters in some respects are indicators of the Obama campaign staff recognizing and accommodating deeper political-cultural changes that became manifest by the time of the 2008 election. Two changes in particular made it possible to use the new digital technologies more effectively than they had ever been used before. First, the fragmentation of the American electorate enhanced the Obama campaign's attempts to mobilize niche audiences. For the last four decades, the Democratic Party has attempted to bring marginalized groups into politics. Encouraged to assert their rights on the basis of characteristics that define their identities, individuals have increasingly formed groups to support each other and to engage in political activity. Because of its extensive use of the Internet, the Obama campaign was able to identify and target these groups with messages that appealed to their concerns. While appealing to particular groups was important, at the same time the campaign maintained "message discipline" by maintaining a consistent look in its ads (a blue background with red accents and the message of hope, change, and action). One of the ways this was accomplished symbolically was through the use of the Obama "O" logo: "We decided early on that it would be great to design a logo mark for each constituency, while making it clear that each of them was part of a larger whole. . . . To keep identity yet create a distinctive image" (Harfoush 2009, 69).

The second change that was well under way at the time of the election was the increasing use of the Internet by Americans. Internet usage had grown from slightly over 10 percent of all Americans in 1995 to almost three-quarters at the time of the 2008 election. Of Internet users, 74 percent went online to either take part in or get news about the campaign. Furthermore, many users were not passive observers—38 percent actually talked about politics with other users at the same time over the course of the campaign. Although television remained the most popular medium used to obtain political information, the Internet is now on par with newspapers as the second most popular source. Not surprisingly, Obama's supporters used the Internet more than McCain's supporters, but, even more significantly, they used it not merely to obtain news and information, but to become actively engaged in the campaign itself (e.g., posting thoughts, donating money, volunteering for campaign work) (Smith 2009). The Internet provided the means by which citizens could connect with other citizens (horizontally) using the campaign organization merely as a conduit to find other citizens to talk to and work with. Interestingly, however, although the Obama campaign was successful at mobilizing supporters, there was no corresponding increase in the level or quality of their political knowledge as a result of that activity (Feezell et al. 2009).

There seems little doubt that the underlying changes that made it possible for Obama to effectively use a wide range of digital technologies were postmodern in character. But use of the technologies by itself was not an indication of postmodernism. In fact, the Obama campaign structure resembled the organizational structure of most modern campaigns. Strategic decisions were made by chief political strategist David Axelrod and campaign manager David Plouffe in consultation with Obama and implemented by aides beneath them. Technology, which was responsive to and capable of reaching a postmodern audience, was harnessed to a modern campaign structure for strategic purposes. But the power of the postmodern cultural changes was substantial, becoming most visible in areas beyond the control of the campaign.

Entertaining Politics

In the midst of the general election campaign, *Saturday Night Live* (SNL) brought back show veteran and former head writer Tina Fey to portray Republican vice presidential candidate Sarah Palin in a series of skits. Fey used many of the personal traits that defined Palin—her arrogance, provincialism, impulsiveness, lack of preparedness, and dismissiveness—to develop side-splitting satires. Often using Governor Palin's own words, Fey not only brilliantly imitated her accent and nasal voice inflections, but also captured the essence of the criticisms that had been leveled against her, all while portraying her in seemingly serious situations. The McCain campaign was so taken aback by these devastating satires that they believed the best way of dealing with them was to have the candidate herself appear on the show. Completing the postmodern blurring of entertainment and politics, Palin, wearing a red dress identical to Tina Fey's, whose red dress was identical to a red dress Palin had worn earlier in the campaign, could be seen by viewers awkwardly watching a monitor backstage as Fey imitated her. Later in the show, she half-heartedly participated in a rap skit satirizing herself, her husband, and the state of Alaska. SNL's TV ratings skyrocketed, a fact that prodded McCain to appear on the show alongside Palin/Fey the Saturday prior to the election, awkwardly participating in satiric humor directed at his own running mate.

Perhaps no aspect of the 2008 presidential campaign characterized the postmodern blending of fiction and reality as the YouTube video hit "Obama Girl." Early in the campaign season, BarelyPolitical.com's Amber Lee Ettinger introduced herself as "Obama Girl" and, in scantily clad outfits, performed her sensual music video "I Got a Crush . . . on Obama." During the campaign the video was viewed over 7 million times (twice as many views as any official campaign video) and was voted one of the top YouTube videos of all time. Perhaps even stranger was Obama Girl's video with Senator Mike Gravel, where they rapped and danced together as he tried to woo her to support his own presidential campaign. Not to be outdone, hip-hop musician will.i.am of the Black Eyed Peas wrote a song which was transformed into a popular music video entitled "Yes We Can" in support of the Obama campaign. The lyrics of the song were taken almost entirely from a speech Obama made following the New Hampshire presidential primary. It featured appearances from a host of celebrities, won numerous awards, and, similar to the Obama Girl video, was viewed by millions of people. Not to be outdone, celebrity extraordinaire Paris Hilton decided to enter the political campaign when John McCain used images of Britney Spears and her in an attack ad calling Obama the "biggest celebrity in the world" and implying that he was "not ready to lead." While the Obama campaign ignored these attacks, Paris Hilton saw her opportunity for even more attention and aired her own video where, lying on a chaise lounge in a leopard bikini, she called McCain "that wrinkly white-haired guy" and came out with her own energy plan.

These television skits and Internet videos were playful expressions and commentaries on the campaign. None were directly attached to either of the campaigns, but their effect was to increase the level of interest in the election by injecting a sense of playfulness. While some contained satirical commentary, none rose to the level of being considered advocacy or even serious political criticism. Other activities by celebrities, however, had more of a partisan flavor, some blatantly so. Entertainers such as Matt Damon, John Cleese, Betty White, Craig Ferguson, Natalie Portman, and Stevie Wonder all came out with videos attacking the McCain/Palin ticket or endorsing Obama, and Tom Hanks used his Facebook page to urge people to vote for Obama. From the celebrity right, country singer John Rich created a YouTube music video called "Raisin' McCain," which was viewed almost 100,000 times and, during the nomination phase of the campaign, Chuck Norris taped a video endorsing Governor Mike Huckabee. In one of the more popular videos (over 7 million views within the first two weeks of its release), comedian Sarah Silverman created a video funded by the Jewish Council for Education and Research called "The Great Schlep," in which she urged young Jews to travel to Florida where their grandparents lived and try to convince them to vote for Obama.

But perhaps even more representative of the postmodern cultural environment that has evolved was the spontaneous participation of average citizens across the country who produced mash-up videos and placed them on YouTube for all to see. Wanting to be an active part of the Obama campaign, thousands of people documented a wide variety of aspects of the campaign through photos they shared with others on Obama's Flickr.com page. The photos and videos went viral, and by the end of the campaign over 100,000 photos and videos had been posted by amateurs from throughout the world, all wanting to share their experience of the campaign with others, usually strangers. These ranged from the poorly produced and seldom viewed, such as a six-minute video monologue by Bob Kunst which was viewed only 340 times, to Phil de Vellis's mashing of Apple's famous Ridley Scott–directed 1984 Super Bowl ad featuring an Orwellian image of Hillary Clinton on a giant screen shattered by a sledgehammer thrown by an athletic dissident wearing a shirt with an Obama "O" on her chest. The ad was viewed almost 6 million times on YouTube and rebroadcast on CNN.[5]

The McCain campaign had its own spontaneous postmodern moments, although they were not nearly as supportive of his campaign. After the announcement of who his vice presidential running mate would be, the Internet was flooded with a picture of what appeared to be a young Sarah Palin wearing an American stars-and-stripes bikini, holding a rifle, and standing near what appeared to be a swimming hole. A few days later another picture was circulated, this time showing her standing at a bar dressed in a tight leather mini-skirt. Both pictures, of course, proved to be digitally manipulated creations cleverly pasted together. They were created not by the opposition campaign, but by individuals possessing the technological skills to produce such photos and videos.

None of the activities described were either endorsed by or linked in any direct fashion to the campaigns of either of the candidates. They represent a unique, horizontal aspect of postmodern campaigns not present in previous campaigns—the ability of citizens to relate directly to other citizens, often playfully and usually superficially. In the postmodern campaign, citizens spontaneously and playfully participate in ways neither coordinated nor sanctioned by the candidates' campaigns. While it is difficult to assess the effectiveness of such activities, they mark a shift in how average citizens can engage in the electoral process. This is the way one proponent of this trend puts it:

> In the past, we've thought of politics as something over there—isolated, separate from our daily lives, as if on a stage upon which journalists, consultants, pollsters and candidates spun and dictated and acted out the process. Now, because of technology in general and the Internet in particular, politics has become something tangible. Politics is right here. You touch it; it's in your laptop and on your cellphone. You control it, by forwarding an email about a candidate, donating money or creating a group. Politics is personal. Politics is viral. Politics is individual. (Vargas 2008, B1)

While modern presidential campaigns had certainly excited Americans and gotten them engaged in politics, those campaigns coordinated and controlled that enthusiasm by channeling it into traditional campaign activities. Activists worked phone banks, did door-to-door canvassing, stuffed and mailed envelopes, attended rallies, put up yard signs, and stood on corners dressed as human billboards. The postmodern campaign opens "spaces of appearance." While most activists participate in campaign-sanctioned activities, others have developed their own forms of participation quite independent of the officially sanctioned campaigns. Employing new digital technologies, amateur activists are spontaneously developing new forms of participation that blend the real with fiction—they are "playing" at politics.

At a deeper level, "playing" at politics may be seen as a form a postmodern participation that occurs in response to a system that creates oppression because of its unexamined institutional form (Kariel 1989; Hirschbein 1999; Gorham 2000). Institutional oppression is not intentional on the part of any particular actor; it is embedded within the nature of the culture that "breaks up, categorizes, and systemizes projects and people" (Kulynych 1997, 319). Thus, in political campaigns citizens are assigned particular roles which limit and control their participation. For example, the role of the citizen is that of spectator, an increasingly boring role. The postmodern response to this unseen and vaguely sensed oppression is "performative action." The performative actor does not argue against the system which narrowly defines his or her role, but instead mocks it. Performative action is theatrical, disruptive, unintentional, and sometimes irrational, and functions to broaden the range of political action. It "explodes the distinction between public and private, between the political and the apolitical" (Kulynych 1997, 337). It would be inaccurate to say that performative action characterized the 2008 election. But the excitement of the Obama candidacy combined with the capabilities of new "techno-personal systems" opened doors for those wanting to participate in politics but not in the traditional ways of doing so.

The Inauguration

On January 20, 2009, an estimated 1.8 million people converged on the National Mall in Washington, D.C., in frigid weather to be a part of history—the swearing in of Barack Obama, the first African-American president of the United States. Almost 46 years earlier, Martin Luther King, Jr. gave his historic "I Have a Dream" speech from the opposite end of the Mall on the steps of the Lincoln Memorial. With his hand on the same Bible Abraham Lincoln had used at his inauguration in 1861, Barack Obama awkwardly tried to follow Chief Justice John Roberts, who fumbled the constitutionally prescribed oath of office. Not far away, an African-American street vendor captured the significance of the moment, wearing a home-stenciled T-shirt that said "Mission Accomplished."

At the most obvious level, an inauguration is the replacing of one presidency with another. But, as is true of all rituals, there are additional symbolic meanings, and the 2009 inauguration was no exception. For many, the election of the first African-American president represented if not the end of blatant racism, at least the beginning of a post-racial or post-racist era. Indeed, Obama helped contribute to this perception by trying to avoid any overt discussion of race during the campaign. It was only when an embarrassing video of his pastor, Jeremiah Wright, emerged condemning America for its racism and violence that Obama addressed the issue of race. In what many considered a brilliant if not electrifying speech, Obama coolly and thoughtfully discussed the history and consequences of racism in America. The effect of the speech was to reassure many white Americans that he was not an angry black man and that he possessed the seriousness of character to be president.

But the reality is that race does matter and that racism still exists. While Obama's election was a significant achievement, it did not move American politics beyond racial divisions. In a sense, then, the spectacle of the Obama inauguration may be seen as a simulacrum, a representation of a post-racial America that does not exist (Friedman 2009).

In a like fashion 1.8 million people of different ages, races, and ethnic backgrounds who gathered on the mall symbolized unity among diversity. While, indeed, this may have been an accurate description of those who were in attendance, it did not represent a microcosm of America. The spectacle of unity is, of course, a powerful socialization message of any inauguration. With the chief justice of the Supreme Court swearing in a new president in front of congressional leaders in a public ceremony on the steps of the U.S. Capitol, it symbolizes the unity of the national government and links the national leaders with the people they are representing.

To be sure, any inauguration distorts the sense of unity that actually exists in the nation, especially in politics. Even then, the chasm between the sense of unity felt among those in attendance and others who were denying the legitimacy of Obama's qualifications (i.e., the "birthers"), or the leaders of the Republican Party who were plotting to oppose Obama on virtually every legislative proposal to assure that his presidency would fail was so vast that the inauguration, as a ritual exercise in unity, could be said to be a hyperreal event.

Obama ran for office on a vague promise to change the manner in which politics in Washington would be conducted. He wanted to bridge partisan divides and govern in a bipartisan fashion. Yet ironically, his campaign was organized on the basis of recognizing the fragmented nature of the electorate as he targeted niche audiences with focused messages. What he failed to appreciate was how deep and how intense the opposition was and would become—not just to his election but to his very legitimacy as president. Hence, the image of unity at the inauguration constituted a political simulacrum.

The 2008 Election Postmodern Legacy

Stephen Skowronek (1997) argued that a president's ability to act is significantly affected by the established commitments of the era he finds himself in when he enters office. The 2008 presidential election teaches us a different lesson. That election illustrates the veracity of Kenneth Gergen's (1991) argument that the postmodern condition is largely a product of communications-related technological changes.

To be sure, the Obama campaign, with its emphasis on images and its dramatic use of spectacles, possessed strong postmodern strategic dispositions. Although the marketing of the candidate employed postmodern techniques, the underlying assumptions of the organization were modern. Critical campaign strategies and decisions were made at the top to be implemented by those below. At the same time, however, the very types of technologies used to communicate and implement those decisions had the sometimes unintended consequence of creating new spaces of appearance where citizens might express themselves without the imprimatur of the campaign.

Citizens excited about the electoral campaign but who, for whatever reasons, were not able to work or were not interested in working through the traditional campaigns found an outlet for their desire to express themselves through the use of digital technologies. Still in their early stages of development, technologies such as Facebook, YouTube, blogging, social network sites, viral email, texting, MySpace, and LinkedIn could potentially alter campaigns, offering spaces for a rich form of horizontal postmodern politics.

Notes

1. Illustrative of the McCain campaign aides' disillusionment and frustration in trying to handle Palin was the nickname they gave her—"Little Shop of Horrors."

2. In fact, the Obama strategists had discovered the appeal of the premise of change from his involvement in the congressional races in 2006.

3. In some instances campaigns even try to discourage voting if they can identify who will vote for their opponent and if they can effectively employ tactics that will depress turnout.

4. Many of these tactics were similar to ones used by community organizers. Obama, of course, spent time in Chicago as a community organizer before entering politics, an experience he was derisively criticized for by Sarah Palin in her acceptance speech at the Republican National Convention.

5. De Vellis lost his job at Blue State Digital when it was revealed by the *The Huffington Post* blog that he had produced the video.

CHAPTER 7

THE JUXTAPOSED PRESIDENCY

BARACK OBAMA'S MODERN PRESIDENCY IN A POSTMODERN WORLD

[T]o become a trusted leader, one must be able to establish the reality of his or her identity. One must appear as an authentic being, whose persona is equivalent to his or her actual personality, who intrinsically possesses those qualities essential to superiority of position. Yet it is the achievement of authenticity that the technologies of social saturation serve to prevent.

Kenneth Gergen (1991, 203)

O n April 20, 2010, methane gas shot up a drill column on the oil rig Deepwater Horizon, 41 miles off the coast of Louisiana, creating a massive explosion that killed 11 oil rig workers and sent the drilling platform to the bottom of the Gulf of Mexico. The systems designed to shut down the oil flow from the damaged well failed, and the worst environmental disaster in the nation's history began. Other than the spectacular scenes of the fire and the reports of the deaths of the 11 workers, the accident attracted little media coverage until it was confirmed that oil was leaking from the wellhead at unprecedented rates. British Petroleum (BP) was leasing the rig and was the responsible party in charge of stopping the leak. After repeated attempts to stem the flow and a series of inaccurate estimates about how much oil was actually leaking into the Gulf, a gradual realization set in that the BP oil spill was not only an environmental disaster, but a potential political crisis as well.

Over the days, weeks, and months that followed, Americans watched reports of oil polluting the Gulf, killing wildlife, oozing into marshes, coating previously pristine beaches with tar balls, and destroying the livelihoods of people who depended on the water for their jobs. BP's inept attempts to stop the flow of oil—or at least capture most of it—combined with live online pictures of the wellhead gushing oil contributed to a growing frustration that gradually turned to anger as the disaster dragged on. As press coverage intensified, it was revealed that there was virtually no government regulation of deep water oil drilling and that BP's oil spill containment plans were woefully inadequate. (The clean-up plan referred to protecting walruses, none of which exist in the Gulf of Mexico, and involved contacting a professor who had been dead for years.) Contributing to the public anger were BP's bungled attempts to manage public relations surrounding the disaster. Sensing that it was important to have a high-ranking official at the scene, BP chief executive officer Tony Hayward temporarily moved to the Gulf area and became the image and voice of the oil conglomerate. But Hayward's numerous gaffes—the repeated underestimation of the extent of the environmental and economic devastation, the slow reimbursement of those whose businesses were being destroyed, and finally the video of Hayward's participation in a yacht race back in England while the oil continued gushing into the Gulf—pushed public anger into the danger zone and into the political arena.

Reflecting the anger were a number of Gulf-state politicians. One of the most visible was Louisiana Governor Bobby Jindal, who complained that not enough was being done by the federal government and, in fact, that the national government was preventing the state from implementing plans to prevent the oil from washing ashore. In the House of Representatives, Louisiana Democrat Charlie Melancon was so upset that he broke into tears at a hearing about the oil spill. But perhaps the most surprising and direct challenge to Obama came from ardent Democratic strategist and political pundit James Carville. Filmed from New Orleans with his wife Mary Matalin, who fought back tears, Carville pleaded with President Obama: "Man, you got to get down here and take control of this and put somebody in charge of this thing and get this thing moving. We're about to die down here."

Realizing that the frustration and anger that he believed should be directed at BP was now being directed at him, the president responded by holding a White House press conference. He awkwardly explained to the impatient reporters that although the spill and clean-up were the responsibility of BP, he took responsibility for trusting that BP knew what it was doing when he should not have done so. But more importantly, he tried to explain that he realized the spill was a major disaster and that he was directing the federal government to do what was necessary to solve the problem: "It is my job to make sure that everything is done to shut this down. That doesn't mean it's going to be easy. It doesn't mean it's going to happen right away or the way I'd like it to happen. It doesn't mean that we're not going to make mistakes. But there shouldn't be any confusion here. The federal government is fully engaged, and I'm fully engaged." Obama awkwardly tried to explain that he could be engaged with an issue without physically having to be on the scene (he had only visited the Gulf area once) and that there were limits on the president's power to solve problems. "The Gulf is going to be affected in a bad way. And so my job right now is just to make sure that everybody in the Gulf understands this is what I wake up to in the morning and this is what I go to bed at night thinking about."

The response of political commentators (especially those on television) was telling and revealed the essence of what, after more than a year in office, was emerging as the theme of the Obama presidency. President Obama was too cool and too analytical; they wanted him to feel and show the frustration and pain that Americans were feeling. While Obama was encouraging people not to panic, Republicans and Democrats alike were asking him to show emotion. At the daily White House press briefing the morning after the press conference, reporters continued with the same theme, asking Press Secretary Robert Gibbs if the president ever gets angry and, if so, how he shows it.

While, to some extent, Obama's cool analytical demeanor ("No Drama Obama" was the mantra of his campaign staff) was a reflection of his personality, his performance at that critical press conference also provides us with clues about his view of the presidency and his behavior as president. Although as of this writing the Obama presidency is less than two years old, his pattern of decision-making, the manner in which he engages in presidential politics, and his belief in the appropriate role of government all indicate that he is a modern president in a postmodern age—hence, a juxtaposed presidency. His use of analysis and the application of rationality to solve problems and to reason with the American people is a modern orientation, while the ability to connect with (i.e., manipulate) the American people through the use of emotion is an important characteristic of the postmodern presidency. The media, particularly television commentators, is imbedded in the postmodern culture (Baym 2010) and is expecting—even demanding—a show of emotion. But reflecting his belief that politics is too coarse and too irrational, and that Americans should be treated as adults, Obama is averse to the use of emotional appeals.

Perhaps ironically, the juxtaposed presidency of Barack Obama provides us with an opportunity to assess the extent and degree to which the postmodern presidency has become an enduring feature of American politics. If, as some might suggest, the postmodern presidency is specific to particular presidents (Clinton is often suggested as a case in point), then we should find little in the Obama presidency that we could identify as postmodern. If, on the other hand, we find Obama "slouching" toward postmodernism, the argument that we have entered a postmodern era—the argument of this book—is bolstered. Even more, the Obama presidency will allow us to identify specific areas where presidential behavior is more characteristic of postmodernism than modernism, thus allowing for an even more refined analysis of the making of the postmodern presidency.

Our examination of the making of the postmodern presidency covers three arenas of behavior—the electoral campaign, political strategies and behaviors of the president in office, and management of the executive branch. In the previous chapter, which examined the 2008 presidential election, we found that while many of the organizational assumptions of Obama's campaign were based on a modernist desire to control the chaos inherent in any campaign, Obama nevertheless adopted a postmodern strategy that downplayed issues and emphasized a non-political image that targeted niche audiences. In this chapter some of the major areas of presidential politics where we would expect postmodern characteristics to manifest themselves—presidential image-making, presidential communications, Obama's personality, and the use of spectacle—will be examined in light of Obama's juxtaposed presidency. Finally, we will examine Obama's executive branch management approach in light of the postmodern description of the neoadministrative state.

Presidential Politics

Although some angry critics have labeled Obama postmodern (see Tarpley et al. 2008), in fact, his personality and his belief about how presidential politics should be conducted are distinctively modern. While the White House makes use of some postmodern strategies and, at times, Obama behaves in a postmodern fashion, he does so reluctantly and grudgingly. Where he deviates from the modern model to adopt postmodern tactics will go a long way toward revealing the extent to which the presidency (as opposed to any particular president) has become postmodern. Our examination in this section takes us into four areas of presidential politics: Obama's personality, the White House's projection of the Obama image, the Obama administration's communications strategy, and the use of spectacle.

Personality

More than any other branch of government, the presidency is influenced by the character, style, and worldview of its occupant. How a person orients himself toward life, how he views human nature and social causality, and how he goes about making decisions, all contribute significantly to how a president organizes the executive office, how he engages in politics, and how he deals with the bureaucracy. In his classic book *The Presidential Character,* James David Barber (1992) argues that the best presidents are ones who are active and positive, who like making decisions, and who use rationality to make them. They do not use politics to compensate for their own psychological insecurities or inadequacies; instead, they are confident of who they are and engage in politics because of a sincere desire to improve society. Possessing high self-esteem, having an orientation toward productiveness, and being flexible and realistic, these presidents typify the personalities of the best modern presidents (e.g., Franklin Roosevelt, Harry Truman, and John Kennedy). By all indications Obama is such a person.

Despite a childhood which was absent of his natural father, Obama showed no psychological scars from the experience. Growing up in settings ranging from elementary schools in Indonesia to being raised by his maternal grandparents in Hawaii, he developed an ability to understand and appreciate the experiences of others, all while creating a firm sense of himself. While not getting into a deep psychological analysis of Obama, first-year chronicler Jonathan Alter (2010) characterizes him as possessing a "fully integrated personality" (210).

President Obama's leadership style can be called "deliberative conversationalist." It is a style of deliberation and conversation among all interested parties that emphasizes an inclusive community of equally valuable individuals, and that has as its goal building a consensus while allowing—indeed, encouraging—people to disagree (Lipkin 2008). Consensus occurs only after poking, prodding, and examining all positions and all advisors. Yet, although Obama is intensely engaged in decisions—often closely examining the details of a problem—he is not averse to delegating work to assistants. While doing that, however, he expects his aides to be competent and effective and, if they are not, he has little patience with them.

Above all, Obama relies on facts, rigorous analysis, and the application of logic to arrive at a decision. After interviewing numerous White House advisors who had worked with Obama, Alter (2010) observes that he "was a deductive thinker with a vertical mind. He thought deeply about a subject, organized it lucidly into point-by-point arguments for a set of policies or a speech, and then said, Here are my principles, and here are some suggestions for fleshing out the details.... He placed more faith in logic than imagination and insisted on a process that was tidy without being inflexible" (212).

The pragmatic approach of reserving judgment until all the data have been collected and analyzed may be seen by some as a reluctance to take positions. Indeed, a former colleague of Obama's at the University of Chicago Law School claimed as much: "His entire life, as best I can tell, is one in which he's always been a thoughtful listener and questioner, but he's never stepped up to the plate and taken full swings" (Kantor 2008, 1). Such a criticism, however, misses the mark. It is not that Obama has no beliefs or is not willing to stand up for what he believes, but rather he represents the ideal modern human in which reason and observation are the central elements for functioning in the world (Gergen 1991).

As noted, Obama's modern orientation has a significant influence on how he makes decisions and how he organizes the executive branch. However, the more relevant question for our purposes is how well-suited the modern presidential personality is to functioning in a postmodern age. The use of observation and logic are, no doubt, valuable tools, but at the same time, they restrict one's ability to understand the world and to act in it. For example, by relying heavily on detached reasoning to address the BP oil spill as a problem to be managed, he underestimated the emotional toll that the disaster was taking on people and was unable to publicly show empathy for those same people. Alter (2010) succinctly identifies this as one of his weaknesses in his first year as president: "Obama's unflappable nature may have hindered his ability to forge an emotional connection with the public" (142). As will be shown, this modern orientation influenced Obama's projection of his image, his communications strategy, and his postmodern use of spectacle.

Presidential Image

When Barack Obama announced that he was running for president he was virtu-ally unknown, and while that could be seen as a handicap for most politicians, for Obama it provided an opportunity to develop an image strategy based upon a postmodern view of the electorate. Obama would resist any definition of his "true character" and instead develop a style that allowed for multiple interpre-tations of who he was and what he stood for. In a candid interview with *Time* magazine conducted shortly before the Democratic National Convention, Obama said, "I serve as a blank screen on which people of vastly different political stripes project their own views" (quoted in Von Drehle 2008, 30). This phenomenon is referred to by postmodern cultural critic Marshall Blonsky as the "Vanna Factor." Coined by Ted Koppel in a graduation speech, it is a reference to the hostess of the game show *Wheel of Fortune,* who for years silently, but dutifully, turned letters and became a cultural phenomenon. Blonsky quotes Koppel on her: "Vanna leaves an intellectual vacuum, which can be filled by whatever the predisposition of the viewer happens to be. The viewer can make her whatever he wants" (quoted in Blonsky 1992, 301). Koppel, of course, was not as con-cerned about Vanna White as he was with what he saw as the "Vannafication" of American politics as it became increasingly viewed through the medium of television. Obama's "blank screen" was the postmodern political equivalent of Vannafication in the 2008 campaign.

In a fragmented, fluid environment typical of an electoral campaign, present-ing an image of a blank screen can be effective, but once in office postmodern presidents try to manage their image to obtain political advantage. At the same time, as the media environment has become increasingly fragmented and de-centered it has become more difficult to control the presidential image. In a centralized media atmosphere, Reagan's image team developed a sophisticated strategy to control the images they wished to project. After failing in the first few years, Clinton finally developed a clever shapeshifting strategy to respond to a more decentered environment. Not to be outdone, George W. Bush instituted a highly sophisticated strategy to produce desired images that involved hiring a professional media team.

In contrast, Barack Obama eschews image manipulation, to the extent that he refuses to allow "political" considerations to enter into policy discussions until after decisions have been arrived at. Instead, he embraces a modern belief that the way to protect his power prospects is to enhance his image by making wise choices (Neustadt 1980). He believes that if he makes wise decisions and clearly explains those decisions, he does not have to worry about image manipulation—politicians who deal with him and the political pundits who analyze presidential behavior will identify patterns of decision-making and by doing so will establish his reputation.

However, this modern approach is questionable given the postmodern media environment that now exists. Journalists no longer attempt to present reality or even to conduct analysis (journalists in the modern era claimed to do so). Instead, they attempt to patch together bits and pieces of visuals and sound bites to create narratives. Media critic Geoffrey Baym succinctly describes the process: "[T]he postmodern sound bite reduces the complexity of political discourse to informationally vacuous but easily packageable morsels of speech that the journalist in turn can assemble to illustrate the wider narrative frame" (2010, 37). Obama resisted providing the media with either compelling visuals or catchy sound bites, but instead of encouraging analysis on the part of journalists, this caused them to simply look elsewhere. Obama's critics were more than happy to oblige.

With a blank screen available to be written on and with no serious attempts to control the twenty-four-hour news cycle by the Obama administration, opponents vigorously attacked the president. Led by right-wing radio and talk-show commentators, Obama was labeled a socialist, a Muslim, an elitist, a radical, and a racist, and he was said to be pursuing the same policies that Adolf Hitler pursued. In an unprecedented attack on a president's very legitimacy, a group referred to as the "birthers" claimed that Obama's birth certificate was forged and that he was not an American citizen.

Lacking an effective counter image that the White House could, but did not, provide, the constant drumbeat of extremist rhetoric had the intended effect. A Harris poll conducted over a year after Obama had taken office revealed that 67 percent of Republicans believed Obama was a socialist, 57 percent believed he was a Muslim, and 24 percent believed that he might be the Anti-Christ (Hemmer 2010).

Obama did not want to manipulate the American people; he wanted to reason with them and, by doing so, change the political culture. Image creation and image manipulation were intentionally downplayed, and other avenues of communication with the American people were developed—particularly those that involved the use of new digital technologies that had been used so successfully in his campaign. This is consistent with the modern presidency.

Communications

On July 19, 2010, Shirley Sherrod, the Georgia State Director of Rural of Development and an African-American, was driving home after a speaking engagement when she received a series of urgent phone calls from Cheryl Cook, the undersecretary of the Department of Agriculture, demanding her resignation. Cook told her that a video of her making racist comments was circulating on the Internet and that she would be the subject of conservative commentator Glenn Beck's evening program. She was told that the administration wanted her out. Sherrod's explanation that her comments had been taken out of context fell on deaf ears and, after several heated conversations, she submitted her resignation.

That was just the beginning of a firestorm that was soon to follow. Conservative blogger Andrew Brietbart had started the controversy by putting a 2 minute and 38 second video of Sherrod addressing a National Association for the Advancement of Colored People (NAACP) meeting in Georgia in March, where she appeared to describe a situation where she had discriminated against a white farmer. But when one viewed the entire 43-minute video, it was clear that in fact, Sherrod was describing how she had overcome her initial feelings of racism to help someone in need, regardless of his race. Subsequent interviews with the farmer she talked about confirmed Sherrod's interpretation, as the farmer and his wife praised her for saving their farm. Administration officials scrambled to save face, issuing a spate of apologies from Secretary of Agriculture Tom Vilsack to Press Secretary Robert Gibbs to Barack Obama (who called Sherrod himself), and the administration offered her a new job in the Agriculture Department. The NAACP, which had also condemned her remarks, followed with its own apology. Absent from the list of apologies were Brietbart and Fox News, which had given time to commentators who had also condemned her comments and called for her resignation. Instead, both said it was a typical example of the Obama administration rushing to judgment.

This was the type of media environment that the Obama administration faced when it took office. News stories were increasingly originating less from the traditional media and more from the alternative media (e.g., blogs, postings on YouTube, political talk shows), with the emphasis more on speed than accuracy, sensationalism rather than analysis, and controversy over sober discussion. In this atmosphere the traditional media, with its professional norms of double-checking for accuracy, telling both sides of the story, and obtaining documentation from legitimate sources, has become quaint and obsolete.

To cope with this environment, the Obama administration developed a communications strategy that vacillated between ignoring the daily cable pundit spats, sporadically overwhelming media outlets with interviews on crucial topics, and communicating directly with people by using social networking and web-based tools. Obama believed that the cable news culture contributed to a "coarsening" of politics and that the preoccupation with compelling photo ops that previous presidents emphasized was superficial and manipulative. "He disdained efforts to win cable brawls or find the perfect pictures for the photo-ops or craft sound bites that cut through the clutter. He thought these staples of Washington politics were ephemeral" (Alter 2010, 26).

Obama did not ignore the traditional news media, but neither did he become obsessed with trying to control its coverage on a consistent basis. To be sure, the Obama administration conducted the daily media gaggles and briefings in the pressroom and responded to reporters' requests for background information in a timely manner, but their overall approach could more accurately be described as an occasional communications blitzkrieg followed by periods of normalcy. For example, in the first six months of his presidency, Obama hosted 15 town-hall meetings, posted more than 800 images on Flickr.com photo-stream, held four prime-time press conferences (the same number George W. Bush and Bill Clinton held in their entire terms in office), sent a video message to the people of Iran, gave a major address in Cairo on Mideast politics, appeared on numerous talk shows (including Leno's and Letterman's), made several appearances on *60 Minutes,* sat for scores of one-on-one interviews (152 in 2009 alone), and hosted a "day in the White House" interview with Brian Williams. On September 14, 2009, only days after his job approval ratings hit their lowest mark of his then-eight-month-old tenure, he became the first president in history to appear on five Sunday morning talk shows in the same day.

One of the dangers that presidents run in communications is overexposure. To avoid this, the communications blitzkrieg approach was used sparingly, only when the White House wanted to make sure that they obtained coverage on stories they deemed critical. But the real innovation of the Obama administration's communications strategy was the use of the Internet to communicate directly with the American people (and indirectly with the traditional media, which also monitors the Web).

Obama believed that if the American people were reasoned with and if policies were explained in greater detail, political dialogue would be improved. The issues that faced America were complex and could not be presented in a sound bite or a photo op; they required historical perspective, nuance, and detailed analysis—none of which would be provided by either the traditional media or the cable news crowd. To accomplish this, Obama turned to the Internet.

By placing material on the Internet, Obama was able to accomplish several of his goals simultaneously. He was able to go directly to the American people using rational arguments rather than talking points and images, and the Internet allowed people to access information whenever they liked. "[T]he web provides infinite space for both its own native forms (blogs, news aggregators, original YouTube posts) and old media (newspapers, TV clips), making it possible for us to watch a speech or read a story whenever we want, unconstrained by space and time. The resulting landscape is vast, diffuse, and multiplatform" (Senior 2009). There is no longer any need to focus on a single message of the day as there is no guarantee that the targeted audience will be watching; instead, the communications environment can be inundated with a wide variety of photos, videos, extended speeches, and stories, and it can be left to the viewers to select what they want at their convenience.

Thus, Obama's communications strategy is similar to his campaign strategy discussed in the previous chapter; his attempt to communicate with the American people is decidedly modern, but he uses technologies that are at least partially responsible for developing our postmodern culture to do so. Obama wants to explain and reason with the American people. Yet the technologies he employs to accomplish this are the very technologies that undermine thoughtfulness and reason. To be sure, Shirley Sherrod's entire 43-minute talk to the NAACP was online for people to view, but the reality is that most people—including people in Obama's own administration—watched only 2 minutes and 38 seconds taken out of context. Complex reasoning was discarded and knee-jerk emotions dominated.

Spectacle

All presidents—postmodern, modern, and even pre-modern—have staged spectacles. In particular, postmodern spectacles (1) are carefully and elaborately staged using attractive visuals; (2) are high on symbolism and mostly devoid of content; and (3) connect with the citizenry on the basis of emotion. From the Reagan administration to the George W. Bush years, we saw the addition to the White House staff of a coterie of professionals trained in the art of news management. Their sole responsibilities were to create attractive images and stage spectacles so visually appealing that they would be widely reported and reproduced by the media.

Obama mastered the art of the spectacle during the 2008 presidential campaign, and his campaign was checkered with them throughout the nineteen-month-long ordeal. One of the most dramatic spectacles was staged at the Democratic National Convention in Denver, when he accepted the presidential nomination of his party in front of 84,000 people who had crowded into Invesco Field (home of the Denver Broncos). With giant faux-Greek columns serving as a backdrop, flanked by JumboTron video screens, and framed by the Rocky Mountains in the distance, Obama accepted the nomination of his party in a forty-three-minute speech that attacked the Republicans even while it embraced his vision of change. The crowd was provided with mini American flags which were waved throughout the event, and flashing cell phones lit up the night. The platform from which Obama spoke was covered in a blue carpet with white stars and jutted out into the audience so that when he spoke it appeared on television as if he was surrounded by the American people. Perhaps most symbolic of all was the fact that the speech was delivered on the forty-fifth anniversary of Martin Luther King, Jr.'s "I Have a Dream" speech, a fact noted by a number of speakers and commentators. As illustrated by that event, the Obama campaign was certainly capable of producing dramatic spectacles that touched the emotions of the American people.

But, as a modern president, Obama has downplayed the use of emotionally laden spectacles. Instead, he prefers the presentation of extended, in-depth speeches on important topics, albeit sometimes in spectacle format. Such speeches have made minimal use of the symbols that trigger emotional associations and instead are more consistent with the recommendations of Richard Neustadt, who implored presidents to use the bully pulpit to educate the American people. President Obama has attempted to do just that with a fifty-five-minute speech in Cairo on the Mideast, a sixty-two-minute town-hall discussion in Green Bay on health care, a fifty-minute-long speech at the National Archives on torture, a thirty-five-minute speech at West Point explaining his Afghanistan troop deployment strategy, and a thirty-six-minute speech on just war theory at the Nobel Peace Prize ceremonies. Unlike his campaign speeches, however, these speeches were short on soaring rhetoric and were instead structured more like judicial opinions—stating and refuting counterarguments and using logic to methodically lead listeners to his positions. His goal was not to entice the media to latch onto sound bites or emotionally stir the citizenry, but rather it was to educate the American people about the major issues confronting them, discussing with them their own moral responsibility, and explaining what the legitimate role of government should be in addressing social problems (Senior 2009). Knowing that the traditional media would give them little coverage, all the speeches were posted on the Internet in their entirety. Yet the impact that they had on actually shaping public opinion is questionable because the key to persuasion is not merely rational argument; in the postmodern culture we live in, it is first to emotionally connect with the audience. As professor of psychology and political consultant Drew Westen explains, "A central aspect of the art of political persuasion is creating, solidifying, and activating networks that create primarily positive feelings" (2007, 85).

Obama believes, as modern presidents do, that elections settle, at least temporarily, political disputes. Once the election is over, it is the responsibility of those who won—Republicans and Democrats alike—to work together to make the best decisions possible, compromising their differences for the greater good. But the intensity and tenacity of the Republicans who refused to cooperate with virtually every major policy proposal put forward by the Obama administration caught almost all off guard. To break out of the political deadlock that this produced, Obama sometimes resorted to the use of spectacle. In what could prove to be his signature piece of legislation, health care reform, Obama exemplified how to use spectacle to obtain political advantage.

Believing that his election was due, at least in part, to his promise to reform health care, yet underestimating the intensity of the opposition, Obama hoped to pass a significant health care reform bill by fall 2009. But monolithic opposition from Republican senators, reluctance to support the legislation by a handful of Democratic senators, and the loss of the Massachusetts seat in the Senate in a special election (the late Ted Kennedy's seat) deprived the Democrats of a sixty-vote, filibuster-proof Senate, which meant that Obama entered 2010 with no bill and a growing feeling that reform was dead. The modern politics of behind-closed-doors bargaining, negotiation, and compromise had produced stalemate, and as that stalemate dragged on and as the economy continued to deteriorate, public opinion turned against the bill.

To break the deadlock, Obama resorted to the use of spectacle and, in this case, the spectacle played itself out in two acts. The opening performance occurred on January 29, 2010, shortly after he had delivered his State of the Union address. In that speech the president attempted to encourage lawmakers to break the impasse and, once again, he reached out to Republicans for their support in creating a bipartisan bill. Calling the president on what they believed to be an insincere offer, the House Republicans reciprocated by inviting him to their annual strategy retreat in Baltimore to discuss health care. Assuming he would decline, they believed they could then score political points and show that he was not serious about working with them. To their surprise the president accepted the invitation but insisted that the event be televised—a demand to which they acceded.

In a protracted ninety-minute nationally televised question-and-answer session, Obama stood on a stage looking down on the Republican representatives and delivered a masterful performance—lecturing them, correcting misstatements, mocking some of their more outrageous criticisms, occasionally lampooning them for hypocritical behavior, and even getting a few laughs. What emerged from the spectacle was an image of Obama behaving in a presidential manner—brave, decisive, articulate, knowledgeable, and determined, yet prudent and reasonable—amid a group of Republicans who appeared small-minded, petty, hypocritical, and poorly informed.

With the Republicans on their heels, Obama followed that performance with an invitation to congressional leaders of both parties to participate in a half-day health care summit to be broadcast live on television. Making the invitation during the Super Bowl pre-game show, he said, "I want to come back and have a large meeting, Republicans and Democrats, to go through systematically all the best ideas that are out there and move it forward" (quoted in Zeleny 2010, 1). Conscious of being out-maneuvered, the Republicans looked for any advantage they could get and ended up negotiating over the shape of the table, the seating arrangements, the total length of time of the summit, and the amount of time each side would be allocated. In late February at Blair House (across the street from the White House), the president masterfully presided over an extended seven-and-one-half-hour discussion in which both sides were given ample time to make their points. Although no breakthroughs emerged (none were expected) the effect was what Obama hoped for: Wavering Democrats vividly saw that they would get no help from Republicans to pass health care reform. Perhaps more significantly, the spectacle provided Democrats, who would have to justify their votes in the next election, with a defense that they had tried to listen to the opposition but that the Republicans were unwilling to seriously discuss the issue.

As president, Obama's use of spectacle was narrow and limited. In both health care performances the script was to listen to the opposition in a seemingly open and thoughtful manner. In reality, Obama had little hope that the Republicans would make any substantive compromises. But the image of the president, in a public forum, presiding over both meetings and masterfully controlling the agenda had the desired effect of mobilizing the Democratic majorities in both houses of Congress and breaking the deadlock.

Postmodern presidents form emotional links directly with the citizenry, often using spectacles to accomplish the effect. During his election campaign Obama clearly was capable of creating such spectacles, but as president his use of spectacle has been more limited. While the audience remained the passive citizenry, the goal of the spectacle was not primarily to build public-opinion support for the president by forging direct emotional linkages; it was to place Republicans in a politically precarious position and force wavering Democrats to act. This more limited use of spectacle—as a negotiating ploy—is more consistent with the modern than the postmodern presidency.

Governance

In the first two areas of presidential behavior examined—electoral campaigning (in Chapter 6) and presidential politics—a consistent pattern can be identified. Barack Obama's assumptions about politics and his preferred operating style are modern. Yet above all he is a pragmatist. When the occasion calls for it, he can skillfully use postmodern techniques to obtain political advantage, but he has only done so reluctantly. The third and final area to be examined is management of the executive branch—governance.

Unilateral Actions

When Obama won the presidential election, many critics of George W. Bush who believed that he had violated the Constitution breathed a sigh of relief. Statements made by Obama during the campaign and early in the transition period by members of his administration stated that the president would respect and adhere to constitutional boundaries. Specifically, the Obama administration did not assert a belief in the legitimacy of the unitary theory of the presidency when such an opportunity arose. During Attorney General Eric Holder's confirmation hearings, Holder stated his belief that no one, including the president, was above the law. Likewise, other administration officials publicly indicated their willingness and desire to work with Congress. One area where postmodern presidents have aggressively used unilateral power is in the use of signing statements. While not categorically rejecting the use of them, the administration posted a policy position on the presidential website indicating a hesitancy to use them and expressed a desire to work with Congress to iron out disagreements before bills were passed.

Yet the record of the use of unilateral action on the part of the Obama administration over the first eighteen months is a mixed bag. In some areas, particularly in domestic policy, Obama has pursued large, controversial issues but has allowed Congress to take the initiative while participating in bargaining and negotiation with congressional leaders—behavioral hallmarks of the modern presidency. In other areas, especially in counterterrorism and foreign policy, Obama has maintained some policies of his predecessor (e.g., in counterterrorism) and changed other policies (e.g., working cooperatively with other nations). In both areas, though, he has done so unilaterally. Yet the overall pattern of working with Congress on domestic matters and acting unilaterally in foreign policy is consistent with the modern presidency.

In fact, several unilateral actions by Obama have raised concerns about his commitment to voluntarily limit the use of unilateral presidential actions. While Obama issued fewer signing statements in his eighteen months as president than did George W. Bush during a comparable time (eleven for Obama compared to thirty-four for Bush), his use of other unilateral actions (e.g., memoranda, directives, executive orders, and proclamations) exceeded the number of such actions of any other president in history during the first year in office.

Perhaps even more unsettling for those hoping that the Obama administration would voluntarily "roll back" many of the actions taken by previous presidents are the Obama administration's arguments involving national security in court cases begun during the Bush administration. Disappointing many constitutional scholars, the Obama administration has taken virtually identical positions as the Bush administration took, arguing that the cases should be dismissed because allowing them to continue would result in revealing "state secrets." Interestingly, these were positions that Obama as a presidential candidate criticized. Comparing the Bush and Obama administrations on the issue of unilateral action, one scholar concluded that "while there is no doubt that the rhetoric of the two administrations is markedly different, particularly if the baseline is the first term of the Bush administration, it is not clear that a similarly dramatic shift in actual behavior has occurred" (Desch 2010, 425).

An issue of lesser significance was the administration's response to a congressional committee's request for testimony from the White House social secretary regarding the crashing of a state dinner by Tareq and Michaele Salahi. Although he pledged to create "an unprecedented level of openness in government" (quoted in Shear 2009, C7) in a public statement on the second day after taking office, less than a year later, he refused to allow his social secretary to testify on even this trivial matter, claiming that to do so would violate the separation of powers provision in the Constitution. While that justification appears patently absurd, it is not inconsistent with the pattern of secrecy established by postmodern presidents and is a chilling reminder that the precedents set by one president can easily be used by another.

For the most part Obama's behavior as president has returned the presidency to its more restricted constitutional boundaries. But it remains to be seen if those changes will be lasting. During his first two years he has enjoyed substantial Democratic majorities in both houses of Congress. Consequently, the pragmatic strategy is to work with Congress, and even defer to congressional leadership, to achieve policy successes. But if the Democrats lose control of either branch of Congress in the mid-term elections, or even if their majorities are reduced significantly (as often occurs for the party in power), Obama may feel compelled to resort to a more expanded use of unilateral action. Certainly, precedents have been set by previous postmodern presidents for just such a possibility.

Management of the Executive Branch

The BP oil spill is an excellent example of a "wicked problem." As discussed in earlier chapters, a wicked problem is a problem that not only eludes solutions, but it is difficult to define exactly what the problem actually is, and thus it becomes difficult to determine what resources to employ and how to direct the resources to solve the problem. In the case of the BP oil spill, it was obviously an ecological disaster of unprecedented proportions that threatened the Gulf habitat of birds, mammals, fish, and plant life. But at the same time, it was an economic disaster that threatened the livelihood of millions of residents of the Gulf Coast who relied, either directly or indirectly, on fishing, tourism, and, ironically, even the oil industry for jobs. From a broader perspective, the spill illustrated the difficulty of coordinating new complex technologies with outdated regulatory procedures. Even further, the problem could be seen as one of coordinating and establishing clear lines of responsibility: There were thousands of BP employees, federal government bureaucrats, state and local government leaders, Coast Guard men and women, mobilized national guard members of the affected states, and local fishermen hired to clean up the spill. For engineers the problem was one of attempting to create new, untried systems to stop a leak in waters deeper than they had ever worked in before. Stepping back further from the particulars of the spill, the problem became one of too heavy a reliance on fossil fuels, which forced energy companies to take on risky projects. For many Americans not directly affected by the spill, but who watched as attempt after attempt to plug the leak failed, it became a gut-wrenching national nightmare. Indeed, the myriad of ways the problem could be described defied the imagination.

Obama believes in the use of rationality to organize people and resources to address problems. It is this belief that provides the basis for deploying resources through government bureaucracies. It assumes that those closest to a problem make accurate observations, collect unbiased data, and make appropriate recommendations, all of which are passed up the chain of command to decision-makers. Once decisions are made at the higher levels of the bureaucracy, the directives are passed down the line to be implemented.

While this is an entirely rational process, it fails to deal with the complexity of postmodern wicked problems. The rational regulatory process relies on the validity of the observations of those closest to the problem as well as the particular perspectives and responsibilities of the decision-makers higher in the bureaucracy. But these observations and decisions are restricted and colored by the vision and interests of each bureaucrat. Put bluntly, "where you stand depends upon where you sit." Thus, in the instance of the oil spill, a bureaucrat from the Environmental Protection Agency will view the spill as an environmental issue, while someone who works for the Occupational Safety and Health Administration will be concerned about the health of the workers charged with cleaning up the beaches, the National Oceanic and Atmospheric Administration is concerned about the long-term effects of the oil and oil dispersion chemicals on the Gulf's fisheries, and on and on. All bureaucrats are working within a rational regulatory framework, but the effect is often confusion, conflict, and sometimes contradictory decisions, all because the definition of what the problem is and who should take responsibility cannot be agreed upon. While postmodern scholars of bureaucracy have made recommendations about how to address wicked problems (e.g., Durant 1998), the Obama administration instead relies upon fairly traditional management approaches, grounded in public administration modern assumptions.

The entirely rational regulatory process directed by the Minerals Management Service (MMS) illustrated common bureaucratic problems as it attempted to regulate deep water drilling for oil. It developed too cozy a relationship with the industry it was regulating, its regulations failed to keep pace with changes in technology, it granted exceptions to rules (hoping to avoid lawsuits), and its bureaucrats in the agency were overwhelmed by the workload (DeParle 2010). Yet none of these problems are unusual in the regulatory environment, and each response is entirely rational given what bureaucrats believe is their function. But for our purposes, Obama's response to the problem can be used to reveal his management perspective.

Believing that the oil spill was a result of deregulation, the administration abolished the MMS in an effort to separate its function of promotion of energy from its charge to regulate energy resources. Such an approach still operates from within the modern management framework of regulation. The underlying assumption is that regulation, usually top-down, is still the best possible way of addressing the problem; the regulatory method merely needs to be separated from the promotion function to respond to the problem more effectively.

Obama's second approach to executive branch management includes innovations that have at least the possibility of being consistent with postmodern administration (i.e., the neoadministrative state). This initiative is referred to as Open Government. In his Open Government Directive, issued in late 2009, President Obama directed government agencies to enhance transparency by making data more readily available to citizens and creating new avenues for citizen input and collaboration. Following his campaign model, the primary method of achieving these objectives was to be through enhanced use of the Internet. Each agency was encouraged (not directed) to work with Chief Technology Officer Aneesh Chopra to develop plans on how specifically to accomplish those goals, but clearly they were to be accomplished through technology.

The objective was to structure and cultivate two-way exchanges so that the public would not only be able to have access to decisions that were made, but also to allow the public to have input into making the decisions in the first place (Jacobs 2010). If implemented effectively, this approach would move the bureaucracy further in the direction of a postmodern administrative model that emphasizes collaboration with stakeholders. Still, early indications are that although some agencies have made information more accessible, realistic input via the Internet continues to be an objective rather than a reality.

Obama in Postmodern Perspective

Ironically, the juxtaposed presidency of Barack Obama allows us to assess the extent to which the postmodern presidency has become an institutionalized feature of American politics. Obama's political assumptions and his preferred way of behaving are based on the modern presidency paradigm. Yet he occupies the presidency in a time when postmodernity is a powerful force shaping American politics. Following a line of presidents who have moved the presidency in a postmodern direction, Obama's presidency represents resistance. At the same time, he has demonstrated a willingness to employ tactics more comfortably used by postmodern presidents should the occasion demand it.

Far from demonstrating the demise of the postmodern presidency, the juxtaposed modern presidency of Obama is illustrating the extent to which the postmodern presidency has become the norm. When the media calls for the president to show emotion, it is an indictor of the extent to which postmodern tactics have become accepted; when biographers criticize the president for failing to control the message of the administration, it is a sign of the extent to which postmodern manipulation has been not only accepted, but anticipated and even desired. When stalled policy initiatives are given new life through the use of spectacle, it demonstrates the need for the president to use postmodern tactics to govern. Obama will continue to try to govern as a modern president, but as the political environment becomes less favorable, as it inevitably will, he will embrace elements of the postmodern presidency to a greater extent or run the risk of a failed presidency.

CONCLUSION

Normatively speaking, no clear boundary can be drawn that provides
the nation with the potential benefit that it requires from a strong
presidency while also protecting the nation from the risks presented by
presidential power.

Rockman and Waterman (2008, 344)

Throughout this book I have tried to convince the reader that a new paradigm
is needed in order to understand contemporary presidential behavior—the postmodern presidency has replaced the modern presidency. Beginning with Ronald
Reagan, presidents of both parties and all ideological persuasions, through times
of war and times of peace, during economic prosperity and times of recession, have
all contributed in some fashion to the making of the postmodern presidency.

If this paradigmatic shift has indeed occurred—and I believe it has—there
are consequences for scholars and political pundits who study the institution,
for political actors such as members of Congress, for the American people, for
our constitutional system, and for democracy itself. The postmodern presidency
is a change in the way we view presidential behavior, but it is more than just an
academic re-conceptualization. Its ability to more accurately explain presidential
behavior occurs because the actual behavior of presidents has changed.

The postmodern presidency paradigm does not ask scholars to search for new
patterns of behavior, but rather it invites academics to look at behaviors already
observed using a lens different than the one they have used in the past—the
modern presidency model. For example, one behavior that all presidents have
participated in is to issue commands—unambiguous directives from the president

that rely upon his accepted authority for enforcement. When viewing such actions through the lens of the modern presidency, those actions are seen as indicators not of power, but of weakness. Neustadt says that instances of command are "a painful last resort, a forced response to the exhaustion of all other remedies, suggestive less of mastery than failure" (1980, 21).

But if we adopt the postmodern presidency lens, we see instances of unilateral actions in a different light. Directives are a significant part of the postmodern president's arsenal of available resources to control the policy agenda. They force action, and they are difficult for other political actors to counteract. Once policies are changed through the use of command, it becomes easier to block changes advocated by those wishing to overturn the commands.

For scholars, they can more accurately describe and explain presidential behavior by adopting the new paradigm. But it should also be noted that presidential behavior has changed. Once again, the example of command illustrates the point. Now more than ever, presidents make a greater use of command. Using the modern paradigm, we would be faced with a paradox. Why would presidents increasingly use actions that are indicators of failure when other "softer" options are still available? The modern presidency has no satisfactory answer for that question and other similar questions.

The Founding Fathers, in particular James Madison, feared tyranny, and to prevent it they devised a system of government that pitted ambition against ambition through a system of checks and balances. The interests of each branch of government were to be pitted against the interests of others, thus preventing any single branch from obtaining a disproportionate amount of power. The modern president, although acting to expand his power, still operated within Madison's clever system. Presidents were supposed to initiate action, but were supposed to do so through the political means of persuasion. In order for a president to succeed, he had to engage in a democratic discourse with other political actors. This did not negate the use of bargaining, negotiation, and compromise—indeed, it encouraged it—but it did mean that ultimately decisions that were made were based on appeals to reason. This occurred while operating within the constitutional frame devised by the founding fathers.

However, the propensity of the postmodern president to use unilateral actions undermines the Madisonian design of the Constitution. Such actions weaken the checks on the president at the expense of the other branches of government. In dealing with Congress, for example, the postmodern president can directly challenge Congress by issuing signing statements which can nullify any laws passed, can simply bypass Congress by issuing executive orders or memoranda, or can manipulate Congress by playing factions off against other factions (referred to as "triangulation" by Clinton). In any case, the consequence is to make the president the preeminent branch of government, so much so that it undermines Madisonian checks. Given that laws, the Constitution, and other political actors are ineffectual at curbing executive abuse of power, the single remaining check is that which was initially designed to be furthest from the presidency—the people.

One could make the case that the postmodern presidency, although violating constitutional checks, is nevertheless consistent with democracy because the ultimate check is the people. The modern president is primarily concerned about public opinion as the time for reelection approaches. But the postmodern president is continually concerned about what Americans think and feel. Presidents spend considerable time, energy, and money polling the public to determine which policies to promote, which policies to oppose, and which policies to ignore. On its face it could be argued that the postmodern presidency is consistent with a popular democratic model.

When we examined postmodern presidents, we found that they, indeed, had established a direct personal relationship with the American people. As even the modern presidency model has noted, presidents now "go public" far more than they did in the past. They hold town-hall meetings across the country, meet with local media, and give talks to a variety of groups on a regular basis. But if we examine these interactions more closely, we can see their postmodern characteristics.

The president's use of spectacle and traditional American symbols that emotionally link citizens to them can be seen more as attempts to manipulate than to inform or listen. The primary avenue used to communicate is not reasoned discussion, but rather it is the sophisticated use of images. In such an environment, rationality takes a back seat to emotion.

One of the consequences of this is that the media reports not on the substance of the communications (there is little of substance to report), but reports instead on the political strategizing and staging that was behind the creation of the images. The effect of this type of reporting is not to inform the citizenry and aid in encouraging dialogue, but instead to breed cynicism (Cappella and Jamieson 1997).

When the presidency is loosened of many of the constitutional shackles designed to check presidential power, we might expect such power to run rampant. But not surprisingly, the very postmodern political environment that has allowed recent presidents to construct the postmodern presidency has also spawned counter groups that use similar, if not even more aggressive, tactics to counteract presidential initiatives. Often with little regard for the truth, these groups have conducted vicious campaigns that exploit people's worse fears. The result is a toxic political environment filled with anger, lies, half-truths, and petty squabbles.

The trend toward postmodern politics, especially a postmodern presidency, shows no signs of abating, no matter how much particular presidents may want to stem the tide. All indications are that the postmodern presidency will continue to be constructed by future presidents and will become an enduring feature of the political scene. Our challenge is not to resist the trend, but rather it is to point it in a direction that enhances and enlivens democracy. In theory, postmodernism offers liberatory possibilities; it gives voice to those who have been previously excluded, it offers the possibility of creating new spaces of appearance in which people can act politically, and it reveals the artificial nature of barriers to political engagement.

The challenge facing citizens today, then, is to find ways to participate in the political process in ways that are meaningful to them. For presidents, the challenge is to make a postmodern presidency that enhances rather than undermines democracy.

BIBLIOGRAPHY

Aberbach, Joel D. 2000. "A Reinvented Government, Or the Same Old Government?" in *The Clinton Legacy,* eds. Colin Campbell and Bert A. Rockman. New York, NY: Chatham House Publishers, pp. 118–139.

Abramowitz, Alan I. 2010. "How Obama Won and What It Means," in *The Year of Obama: How Barack Obama Won the White House,* ed. Larry J. Sabato. New York, NY: Longman, pp. 91–114.

Adler, David Gray. 2006a. "The Law: George Bush as Commander in Chief: Toward the Nether World of Constitutionalism," *Presidential Studies Quarterly* 36: 525–540.

———. 2006b. "The President as King: The Usurpation of War and Foreign Affairs Powers in the Modern Age," in *The Presidency and the Challenge of Democracy,* eds. Michael A. Genovese and Lori Cox Han. New York, NY: Palgrave Macmillan, pp. 93–117.

Alford, C. Fred. 1988. "Mastery and Retreat: Psychological Sources of the Appeal of Ronald Reagan," *Political Psychology* 9: 571–589.

Alter, Jonathan. 2010. *The Promise: President Obama, Year One.* New York, NY: Simon & Schuster.

Anderson, Chris. 2006. *The Long Tail: Why the Future of Business Is Selling Less of More.* New York, NY: Hyperion.

Apple, R. W., Jr. 1989. "Capital," *The New York Times* (September 6): 5.

Aronowitz, Stanley. 1988. "Postmodernism and Politics," in *Universal Abandon? The Politics of Postmodernism,* ed. Andrew Ross. Minneapolis, MN: University of Minnesota Press, pp. 46–62.

Auletta, Ken. 2004. "Fortress Bush: Annals of Communications," *The New Yorker* 79: 53–65

Bahl, Roy. 1984. *Financing State and Local Government in the 1980s*. New York, NY: Oxford University Press.

Bai, Matt. 2002. "Rove's Way," *The New York Times* (October 20): 56+.

Balazs, Bela. 2004. "The Close-Up," in *Film Theory and Criticism: Introductory Readings*. 9th ed., eds. Leo Braudy and Marshall Cohen. New York, NY: Oxford University Press, p. 314.

Barber, James David. 1992. *The Presidential Character: Predicting Performance in the White House*. 4th ed. Englewood Cliffs, NJ: Prentice Hall.

Barilleaux, Ryan J. 1988. *The Post-Modern Presidency: The Office After Ronald Reagan*. New York, NY: Praeger.

Barilleaux, Ryan J. and Mark J. Rozell. 2004. *Power and Prudence: The Presidency of George H. W. Bush*. College Station, TX: Texas A&M University Press.

Barnes, Fred. 1993. "Gored," *The New Republic* 209 (September 20): 11–13.

Barnhurst, Kevin G. and Catherine A. Steele. 1997. "Image-Bite News: The Visual Coverage of Elections on U.S. Television, 1968–1988," *Critical Studies in Mass Communication* 13: 187–209.

Baum, Matthew A. 2003. *Soft News Goes to War: Public Opinion and American Foreign Policy in the New Media Age*. Princeton, NJ: Princeton University Press.

Baym, Geoffrey. 2010. *From Cronkite to Colbert: The Evolution of Broadcast News*. Boulder, CO: Paradigm Publishers.

Beal, Richard S. and Ronald H. Hinckley. 1984. "Presidential Decision Making and Opinion Polls," *Annals of the American Academy of Political and Social Science* 472: 72–84.

Bell, Cora. 1989. *The Reagan Paradox: U.S. Foreign Policy in the 1980s*. New Brunswick, NJ: Rutgers University Press.

Bennett, William J. 1998. *The Death of Outrage: Bill Clinton and the Assault on American Ideals*. New York, NY: The Free Press.

Benoit, William L. 2001. "Framing Through Temporal Metaphor: The 'Bridges' of Bob Dole and Bill Clinton in Their 1996 Acceptance Addresses," *Communication Studies* 52: 70–84.

Berke, Richard L. and Frank Bruni. 2001. "Architect of Bush Presidency Still Builds Bridges of Power," *The New York Times* (February 18): 1, 22.

Berry, Michael J. 2009. "Controversially Executing the Law: George W. Bush and the Constitutional Signing Statement," paper presented at the 2009 American Political Science Association Conference, Toronto, Canada.

Black, Ryan C., Anthony J. Madonna, Ryan J. Owens, and Michael S. Lynch. 2007. "Adding Recess Appointments to the President's 'Tool Chest' of Unilateral Powers," *Political Research Quarterly* 60: 645–654.

Blonsky, Marshall. 1992. *American Mythologies*. New York, NY: Oxford University Press.

Blumenthal, Sidney. 1980. *The Permanent Campaign: Inside the World of Elite Political Operatives*. Boston, MA: Beacon Press.

Boorstin, Daniel J. 1962. *The Image: Or What Happened to the American Dream*. New York, NY: Atheneum.

Brady, John. 1997. *Bad Boy: The Life and Politics of Lee Atwater*. Reading, MA: Addison Wesley Publishing.

Bumgarner, John. 2007. "The Administrative, Politicized, and Unitary Presidency in the Neoadministrative State: A Fish Out of Water?" paper presented at the 2007 Midwest Political Science Association Conference, Chicago, IL.

Bumiller, Elisabeth. 2002. "Bush's Pilgrimage Ends With Vow to Prevail Over 'Terrorist or Tyrant,'" *The New York Times* (September 12): 8.

Burke, John P. 1992. *The Institutional Presidency*. Baltimore, MD: Johns Hopkins University Press.

Bush, George. 1988. "Text of Republican Presidential Nominee George Bush's Acceptance Speech," *The Washington Post* (August 19): A28.

———. 1992. "Remarks at Dedication Ceremony of the Social Sciences Complex at Princeton University in Princeton, New Jersey," *Public Papers of the Presidents of the United States: George Bush*, Vol. 1. Washington, DC: United States Government Printing Office, pp. 496–499.

Butler, Christopher. 2002. *Postmodernism: A Very Short Introduction*. Oxford: Oxford University Press.

Cameron, Charles M. 2002. "Studying the Polarized Presidency," *Presidential Studies Quarterly* 32: 647–663.

Cammarano, Joe. 2009. "From Substance to Symbol: Head Start and the Change From Modern to Postmodern Presidents," paper presented at the 2009 American Political Science Association Conference, Toronto, Canada.

Campbell, Angus, Philip E. Converse, Warren E. Miller, and Donald E. Stokes. 1960. *The American Voter*. New York, NY: John Wiley & Sons.

Canes-Wrone, Brandice. 2001. "The President's Legislative Influence From Public Appeals," *American Journal of Political Science* 45: 313–329.

Canes-Wrone, Brandice, Michael C. Herron, and Kenneth W. Shotts. 2001. "Leadership and Pandering: A Theory of Executive Policymaking," *American Journal of Political Science* 45: 532–550.

Cannon, Lou. 2000. *President Reagan: The Role of a Lifetime*. New York, NY: Public Affairs.

Canon, David T. and Kenneth R. Mayer. 2001. "Everything You Thought You Knew about Impeachment Is Wrong," in *Aftermath: The Clinton Impeachment and the Presidency in the Age of Political Spectacle*, eds. Leonard V.

Kaplan and Beverly Moran. New York, NY: New York University Press, pp. 47–62.

Cappella, Joseph N. and Kathleen H. Jamieson. 1997. *Spiral of Cynicism: The Press and the Public Good*. New York, NY: Oxford University Press.

CBS Evening News. 1988. "George Bush Dan Rather Showdown," *YouTube* (January 25) (www.youtube.com/watch?v=xy45grGpB6o). Retrieved October 31, 2010.

Clines, Francis X. 2003. "Karl Rove's Campaign Strategy Seems Evident: It's Terror, Stupid," *The New York Times* (May 10): 20.

Clinton, William J. 1996. "Remarks Accepting the Presidential Nomination at the Democratic National Convention in Chicago" (August 29). The American Presidency Project. University of California–Santa Barbara. (www.presidency.ucsb.edu). Retrieved September 23, 2009.

———. 1998. "The President's Testimony: Part Four of Eight," *The New York Times* (September 22): B3.

Clymer, Adam. 1982. "Poll Finds Reagan Popularity Rating Misleads," *The New York Times* (January 31): A22.

Cohen, Florette, Daniel M. Ogilvie, Sheldon Solomon, Jeff Greenberg, and Tom Pyszczynski. 2005. "American Roulette: The Effect of Reminders of Death on Support for George W. Bush in the 2004 Presidential Election," *Analysis of Social Issues and Public Policy* 5: 177–187.

Cohen, Jeffrey E. 2008. "Presidential Leadership in an Age of New Media," in *Presidential Leadership: The Vortex of Power*, eds. Bert A. Rockman and Richard W. Waterman. New York, NY: Oxford University Press, pp. 171–190.

Combs, James. 1989. "The Post-Modern Presidency: The Office After Ronald Reagan by Ryan J. Barilleaux," *Annals of the American Academy of Political and Social Science* 503: 165–166.

Conklin, Jeff. 2005. *Dialogue Mapping: Building Shared Understanding of Wicked Problems*. West Sussex, UK: John Wiley & Sons.

Converse, Philip E. 1964. "The Nature of Belief Systems in Mass Publics," in *Ideology and Discontent*, ed. David Apter. New York, NY: The Free Press, pp. 206–261.

Coontz, Stephanie. 1992. *The Way We Never Were: American Families and the Nostalgia Trap*. New York, NY: Basic Books.

Cooper, Joseph. 1999. "The Puzzle of Distrust," in *Congress and the Decline of Public Trust*, ed. Joseph Cooper. Boulder, CO: Westview Press, pp. 1–26.

Cooper, Phillip J. 1997. "Power Tools and an Effective and Responsible Presidency," *Administration & Society* 29: 529–556.

———. 2001. "The Law: Presidential Memoranda and Executive Orders: Of

Patchwork Quilts, Trump Cards, and Shell Games," *Presidential Studies Quarterly* 31: 126–141.

Cronin, Thomas E. 1979. "Presidential Power Revised and Reappraised," *The Western Political Quarterly* Vol. 32: 381–395.

Crotty, James. 2009. "Structural Causes of the Global Financial Crisis: A Critical Assessment of the 'New Financial Architecture,'" *Cambridge Journal of Economics* 33: 563–580.

Dasgupta, Gautam. 1988. "The Theatricks of Politics," *Performing Arts Journal* 11: 77–83.

Davidson, Roger H. 1999. "Congress and the Public Trust: Is Congress Its Own Worst Enemy?" in *Congress and the Decline of Public Trust*, ed. Joseph Cooper. Boulder, CO: Westview Press, pp. 65–78.

Davis, James W. 2005. *Terms of Inquiry: On the Theory and Practice of Political Science*. Baltimore, MD: Johns Hopkins Press.

Davis, Richard and Diana Owen. 1998. *New Media and American Politics*. New York, NY: Oxford University Press.

Davis, Rick. 2008. "McCain Campaign Manager: 'Election Not About Issues'" (September 2). (www.washingtonpost.com/wp-dyn/content/video/2008/09/02/VI2008090201523.html). Retrieved October 31, 2010.

DeMott, Benjamin. 2003. "Junk Politics: A Voter's Guide to the Post-literate Election," *Harper's Magazine* 307: 35–41.

Denton, Robert E., Jr. 1988. *The Primetime Presidency of Ronald Reagan: The Era of the Television Presidency*. New York, NY: Praeger.

Denton, Robert E., Jr., and Rachel L. Holloway. 1996. "Clinton and the Town Hall Meetings: Mediated Conversation and the Risk of Being 'In Touch,'" in *The Clinton Presidency: Images, Issues, and Communications Strategies*, eds. Robert E. Denton, Jr. and Rachel L. Holloway. Westport, CT: Praeger, pp. 17–42.

DeParle, Jason. 2010. "Leading the Way Into Deep Water," *The New York Times* (August 8): 1+.

Desch, Michael C. 2010. "The More Things Change, the More They Stay the Same: The Liberal Tradition and Obama's Counterterrorism Policy," *PS: Political Science and Politics* 43: 425–429.

DiIulio, John, Jr. 1999. "The Political Theory of Compassionate Conservatism," *The Weekly Standard* (August 23): 10.

Dionne, E. J. 1991. *Why Americans Hate Politics*. New York, NY: Simon & Schuster.

Ditto, Peter H. and Andrew J. Mastronarde. 2009. "The Paradox of the Political Maverick," *Journal of Experimental Social Psychology* 45: 295–298.

Dole, Robert. 1996. "Address Accepting the Presidential Nomination at the Republican National Convention in San Diego" (August 15). The American Presidency Project. University of California–Santa Barbara. (www.presidency .ucsb.edu). Retrieved September 23, 2009.

Dreier, Peter. 2008. "Obama's Youth Movement," *The Nation* (September 15). (www.thenation/doc/20080929/dreier). Retrieved September 30, 2008.

Drew, Elizabeth. 1994. *On the Edge: The Clinton Presidency*. New York, NY: Simon & Schuster.

Drogin, Bob and Robin Abcarian. 2008. "Election 2008: Swing State," *Los Angeles Times* (November 3): A1.

Duffy, Michael and Dan Goodgame. 1992. *Marching in Place: The Status Quo Presidency of George Bush*. New York, NY: Simon & Schuster.

Durant, Robert F. 1998. "Agenda Setting: The 'Third Wave,' and the Administrative State," *Administration & Society* 30: 211–247.

Durant, Robert F. and Adam L. Warber. 2001. "Networking in the Shadow of Hierarchy: Public Policy, the Administrative Presidency, and the Neoadministrative State," *Presidential Studies Quarterly* 31: 221–244.

Edwards, George C., III. 2000. "Campaigning Is Not Governing: Bill Clinton's Rhetorical Presidency," in *The Clinton Legacy,* eds. Colin Campbell and Bert A. Rockman. New York, NY: Chatham House Publishers, pp. 33–47.

———. 2008. "Impediments to Presidential Leadership: The Limitations of the Permanent Campaign and Going Public Strategies," in *Presidential Leadership: The Vortex of Power,* eds. Bert A. Rockman and Richard W. Waterman. New York, NY: Oxford University Press, pp. 145–169.

Emanuel, Richard C. 2009. "Picking a President: Candidate Over Content; Personality Over Platform," *Journal of College & Character* 10: 1–7.

Feezell, Jessica T., Meredith Conroy, and Mario Guerrero. 2009. "Facebook Is.... Fostering Political Engagement: A Study of Online Social Networking Groups and Offline Participation," paper presented at the 2009 American Political Science Association Conference, Toronto, Canada.

Finnegan, Michael. 2008. "Election 2008: The Democrats; Obama Tears Up in a Tribute to His 'Hero,'" *Los Angeles Times* (November 4): 13.

Fitzwater, Marlin. 1995. *Call the Briefing!* New York, NY: Random House.

Fontaine, Juston K. 2003. "Beyond the Modern Era? An Analysis of the Concept of the Postmodern Presidency." Master's thesis at the Virginia Polytechnic Institute and State University.

Fox, Charles F. and Hugh T. Miller. 1994. *Postmodern Public Administration: Toward Discourse*. Thousand Oaks, CA: Sage Publications.

Frankovic, Kathleen A. and Monika L. McDermott. 2001. "Public Opinion in the 2000 Election: The Ambivalent Electorate," in *The Election of 2000*, ed. Gerald M. Pomper. New York, NY: Chatham House, pp. 73–91.

Frederickson, H. George. 1994. "The Seven Principles of Total Quality Politics," *Public Administration Times* 17: 9.

Friedman, Max Paul. 2009. "Simulacrobama: The Mediated Election of 2008," *Journal of American Studies* 43: 341–356.

Gardner, Dan. 2008. *Risk: The Science and Politics of Fear.* Toronto: McClelland & Stewart Ltd.

Genovese, Michael A. and Lori Cox Han. 2006. "Preface," in *The Presidency and the Challenge of Democracy*, eds. Michael A. Genovese and Lori Cox Han. New York, NY: Palgrave Macmillan, pp. vii–x.

Gergen, Kenneth J. 1991. *The Saturated Self: Dilemmas of Identity in Contemporary Life.* New York, NY: Basic Books.

Germany, Julie Barko. 2009. "The Online Revolution," in *Campaigning for President 2008: Strategy and Tactics, New Voices and New Techniques*, ed. Dennis W. Johnson. New York, NY: Routledge, pp. 147–159.

Gilmour, Robert S. and Robert B. Lamb. 1975. *Political Alienation in Contemporary America.* New York, NY: St. Martin's Press.

Ginsberg, Benjamin and Martin Shefter. 1999. *Politics by Other Means: Politicians, Prosecutors, and the Press From Watergate to Whitewater.* New York, NY: W. W. Norton & Company.

Goffman, Erving. 1959. *The Presentation of Self in Everyday Life.* New York, NY: Doubleday Anchor Books.

Gorham, Eric B. 2000. *The Theater of Politics: Hannah Arendt, Political Science, and Higher Education.* Lanham, MD: Lexington Books.

Graber, Doris A. 1996. "Say It With Pictures," *Annals of the American Academy of Political and Social Science* 546: 85–96.

Greene, John Robert. 2000. *The Presidency of George Bush.* Lawrence, KN: University Press of Kansas.

Greenstein, Fred I. 1998. "There He Goes Again: The Alternating Political Style of Bill Clinton," *PS: Political Science and Politics* 31: 178–181.

Gregg, Gary L., II. 2004. "Dignified Authenticity: George W. Bush and the Symbolic Presidency," in *Considering the Bush Presidency*, eds. Gary L. Gregg II and Mark J. Rozell. New York, NY: Oxford University Press, pp. 88–106.

Greider, William. 1981. "The Education of David Stockman," *The Atlantic Monthly* 248: 27–54.

Gronbeck, Bruce E. 2009. "The Web, Campaign 07–08, and Engaged Citizens: Political, Social, and Moral Consequences," in *The 2008 Presidential Campaign: A Communication Perspective*, ed. Robert E. Denton, Jr. Lanham, MD: Rowman & Littlefield, pp. 228–243.

Hahn, Dan F. 1987. "The Media and the Presidency: Ten Propositions," *Communication Quarterly* 35: 254–266.

Halstead, T. J. 2007. "Presidential Signing Statements: Constitutional and Institutional Implications," *CRS Report for Congress.* Washington, DC: Congressional Research Service.

Hamilton, James T. 2003. *All the News That's Fit to Sell: How the Market Transformed Information Into News.* Princeton, NJ: Princeton University Press.

Harfoush, Rahaf. 2009. *Yes We Did: An Inside Look at How Social Media Built the Obama Brand.* Berkeley, CA: New Riders.

Hargrove, Erwin C. 2001. "Presidential Power and Political Science," *Presidential Studies Quarterly* 31: 245–263.

———. 2008. *The Effective Presidency: Lessons on Leadership from John F. Kennedy to George W. Bush.* Boulder, CO: Paradigm Publishers.

Harvey, Diane Hollern. 2000. "The Public's View of Clinton," in *The Postmodern Presidency: Bill Clinton's Legacy in U.S. Politics,* ed. Steven E. Schier. Pittsburgh, PA: University of Pittsburgh Press, pp. 124–142.

Harwood, John. 2008. "McCain Takes a Page From Clinton's Playbook," *The New York Times* (August 4): 12.

Havel, Vaclav. 1994. "The Need for Transcendence in the Postmodern World," speech given in Independence Hall (July 4). (www.worldtrans.org/whole/havelspeech.html). Retrieved January 23, 2010.

Helman, Scott. 2007. "McCain Aims to Turn His Age to Advantage: Cites Experience in Launching Run," *The Boston Globe* (April 26): A1.

Helmore, Edward. 2003. "Private Jessica Says President Is Misusing Her 'Heroism,'" *The Guardian* (November 9). (www.guardian.co.uk/world/2003/nov/09/usa.politicsphilosophyandsociety). Retrieved September 14, 2009.

Hemmer, Nicole. 2010. "Shock Poll: Why Do So Many Republicans Think Obama Is a Socialist, a Muslim, or Even the Anti-Christ?" *The Christian Science Monitor* (March 25). (www.csmonitor.com/Commentary/Opinion/2010/0325/Shock-poll-Why-do-so-many-Republicans-think-Obama-is-a-socialist-a-Muslim-or-even-the-anti-Christ). Retrieved August 1, 2010.

Hershey, Marjorie Randon. 1989. "The Campaign and the Media," in *The Election of 1988: Reports and Interpretations,* ed. Gerald M. Pomper. Chatham, NJ: Chatham House Publishers, pp. 73–102.

Hertsgaard, Mark. 1989. *On Bended Knee: The Press and the Reagan Presidency.* New York, NY: Schoken Books.

Hirschbein, Ron. 1999. *Voting Rites: The Devolution of American Politics.* Westport, CT: Praeger.

Hoffman, Donna R. and Alison D. Howard. 2003. "Ask and Ye Shall Receive?

Policy Requests in State of the Union Addresses," paper presented at the 2003 American Political Science Association Conference, Philadelphia, PA.

Howell, William G. 2005. "Unilateral Powers: A Brief Overview," *Presidential Studies Quarterly* 35: 417–439.

Howell, William and Douglas Kriner. 2008. "Power Without Persuasion: Identifying Executive Influence," in *Presidential Leadership: The Vortex of Power,* eds. Bert A. Rockman and Richard W. Waterman. New York, NY: Oxford University Press, pp. 105–144.

Hutcheon, Linda. 1993. "Beginning to Theorize Postmodernism," in *A Postmodern Reader,* eds. Joseph Natoli and Linda Hutcheon. Albany, NY: State University of New York Press, pp. 243–272.

Ifill, Gwen. 1993. "Federal Cutbacks Proposed by Gore in 5-Year Program," *The New York Times* (September 8): A1.

Ignatius, David. 1989. "Press Corps to Bush: Manipulate Us!" *The Washington Post* (May 7): B1.

Ingraham, Patricia W., James R. Thompson, and Elliot F. Eisenberg. 1995. "Political Management Strategies and Political/Career Relationships: Where Are We Now in the Federal Government?" *Public Administration Review* 55: 263–272.

Jacobs, Lawrence R. 2010. "The Presidency and the Press: The Paradox of the White House Communications War," in *The Presidency and the Political System.* 9th ed., ed. Michael Nelson. Washington, DC: CQ Press, pp. 236–263.

Jones, Charles O. 2000. "Nonstop!" *The Brookings Review* 18: 12–15.

Kaid, Lynda Lee. 2009. "Videostyle in the 2008 Presidential Advertising," in *The 2008 Presidential Campaign: A Communication Perspective,* ed. Robert E. Denton, Jr. Lanham, MD: Rowman & Littlefield, pp. 209–227.

Kampfner, John. 2003. "The Truth About Jessica," *The Guardian* (May 15). (www.guardian.co.uk/world/2003/may/15/iraq.usa2/print). Retrieved September 14, 2009.

Kantor, Jodi. 2008. "Teaching Law, Testing Ideas, Obama Stood Slightly Apart," *The New York Times* (July 30): 1+.

Kariel, Henry S. 1961. *The Decline of American Pluralism.* Stanford, CA: Stanford University Press.

———. 1977. *Beyond Liberalism, Where Relations Grow.* San Francisco, CA: Chandler & Sharp Publishers.

———. 1989. *The Desperate Politics of Postmodernism.* Amherst, MA: The University of Massachusetts Press.

Kaye, Kate. 2009. *Campaign '08: A Turning Point for Digital Media.* Lexington, KY: CreateSpace.

Kelley, Christopher S. 2002. "'Faithfully Executing' and 'Taking Care'—The Unitary Executive and the Presidential Signing Statement," paper delivered at the 2002 American Political Science Association Conference, Boston, MA.

———. 2003. "The Unitary Executive and the Presidential Signing Statement." Unpublished dissertation at Miami University. (www.ohiolink.edu/etd/view.cgi?miami1057716977.) Retrieved January 8, 2009.

Kenski, Henry C. and Kate M. Kenski. 2009. "Explaining the Vote in the Election of 2008: The Democratic Revival," in *The 2008 Presidential Campaign: A Communication Perspective*, ed. Robert E. Denton, Jr. Lanham, MD: Rowman & Littlefield, pp. 244–290.

Kernell, Samuel. 2007. *Going Public: New Strategies of Presidential Leadership*. 4th ed. Washington, DC: CQ Press.

Kettl, Donald F. 1995. "Building Lasting Reform: Enduring Questions, Missing Answers," in *Inside the Reinvention Machine: Appraising Governmental Reform,* eds. Donald F. Kettl and John J. DiIulio. Washington, DC: The Brookings Institution, pp. 9–83.

Key, V. O., Jr. 1966. *The Responsible Electorate: Rationality in Presidential Voting, 1936–1960*. Cambridge, MA: The Belknap Press.

Klein, Joe. 2006. *Politics Lost: How American Democracy Was Trivialized by People Who Think You're Stupid*. New York, NY: Doubleday.

Kohut, Andrew, Kimberly Parker, Gregory Flemming, Molly Sonner, and Beth Donovan. 1998. "Deconstructing Distrust: How Americans View Government," paper presented to the Pew Research Center for the People and the Press.

Krutz, Glen S. and Jeffrey S. Peake. 2006. "The Changing Nature of Presidential Policy Making on International Agreements," *Presidential Studies Quarterly* 36: 391–409.

Kuhn, Thomas S. 1970. *The Structure of Scientific Revolutions*. 2nd ed. Chicago, IL: The University of Chicago Press.

Kulynych, Jessica J. 1997. "Performing Politics: Foucault, Habermas, and Postmodern Participation," *Polity* 30: 315–346.

Kumar, Martha Joynt. 2007. *Managing the President's Message: The White House Communications Operation*. Baltimore, MD: The Johns Hopkins University Press.

Kuo, David. 2006. *Tempting Faith: An Inside Story of Political Seduction*. New York, NY: Free Press.

Levine, Charles H. 1986. "The Federal Government in the Year 2000: Administrative Legacies of the Reagan Years," *Public Administration Review* 46: 195–206.

Lifton, Robert Jay. 1968. "Protean Man," *Partisan Review* 35: 13–27.

————. 1970. *Boundaries*. New York, NY: Random House.

Lipkin, Robert Justin. 2008. "The Obama Phenomenon: Deliberative Conversationalism & the Pursuit of Community Through Presidential Politics." Widener Law School Legal Studies Research Paper.

Livingston, Steven. 1997. *Clarifying the CNN Effect: An Examination of Media Effects According to Type of Military Intervention*. Boston: The Joan Shorenstein Center. Research Paper R-18.

Maisel, L. Sandy and Mark D. Brewer. 2008. *Parties and Elections in America: The Electoral Process*. 5th ed. Lanham, MD: Rowman and Littlefield Publishers.

Maxwell, Mackenzie. 2009. "Where Bush Went Wrong," *Daily Toreador* (January 13). (www.dailytoreador.com/2.13411/where-bush-went-wrong-1.1826129.) Retrieved May 18, 2009.

Mayer, Kenneth R. 1999. "Executive Orders and Presidential Power," *The Journal of Politics* 61: 445–466.

Mayer, Kenneth R. and Kevin Price. 2002. "Unilateral Presidential Powers: Significant Executive Orders, 1949–99," *Presidential Studies Quarterly* 32: 367–386.

McAvoy, Gregory E. 2003. "Substance vs. Style: Distinguishing Presidential Job Performance from Personal Approval," paper presented at the 2003 American Political Science Association Conference, Philadelphia, PA.

McClellan, Scott. 2008. *What Happened: Inside the Bush White House and Washington's Culture of Deception*. New York, NY: PublicAffairs.

Meyrowitz, Joshua. 1995. "New Sense of Politics: How Television Changes the Political Drama," *Research in Political Sociology* 7: 117–138.

Milbank, Dana. 2004. "In Cheney's Shadow, Counsel Pushes the Conservative Cause," *The Washington Post* (October 22): A21.

Miroff, Bruce. 2000. "Courting the Public: Bill Clinton's Postmodern Education," in *The Postmodern Presidency: Bill Clinton's Legacy in U.S. Politics,* ed. Steven E. Schier. Pittsburgh, PA: University of Pittsburgh Press, pp. 106–123.

————. 2006. "The Presidential Spectacle," in *The Presidency and the Political System*. 8th ed., ed. Michael Nelson. Washington, DC: CQ Press, pp. 255–282.

Moe, Ronald. C. 1994. "The 'Reinventing Government' Exercise: Misinterpreting the Problem, Misjudging the Consequences," *Public Administration Review* 54: 111–122.

Moe, Terry and William Howell. 1999. "Unilateral Action and Presidential Power: A Theory," *Presidential Studies Quarterly* 29: 850–872.

Moore, David W. 2008. *The Opinion Makers: An Insider Exposes the Truth Behind the Polls*. Boston, MA: Beacon Press.

Morris, Dick. 1999. *The New Prince.* Los Angeles, CA: Renaissance Books.

Mucciaroni, Gary and Paul J. Quirk. 2004. "Deliberations of a 'Compassionate Conservative': George W. Bush's Domestic Presidency," in *The George W. Bush Presidency: Appraisals and Prospects,* eds. Colin Campbell and Bert A. Rockman. Washington, DC: CQ Press, pp. 158–190.

Naftali, Timothy. 2007. *George H. W. Bush.* New York, NY: Times Books.

Nagourney, Adam and Jeff Zeleny. 2007. "Obama Formally Enters Presidential Race With Calls for Generational Change," *The New York Times* (February 11): 34.

National Campaign News. 2008. "Schmidt: Palin an 'Exceptional' Reform Governor." *Newswire.*

Nelson, Lars-Erik. 1983. "Ron Flies by Seat of Pants?" *New York Daily News* (December 18).

Neustadt, Richard E. 1955. "Presidency and Legislation: Planning the President's Program," *American Political Science Review* 59: 980–1021.

———. 1980. *Presidential Power: The Politics of Leadership from FDR to Carter.* New York, NY: John Wiley & Sons.

Parmet, Herbert S. 1997. *George Bush: The Life of a Lone Star Yankee.* New York, NY: Scribner.

Parry-Giles, Shawn J. and Trevor Parry-Giles. 2002. *Constructing Clinton: Hyperreality & Presidential Image-Making in Postmodern Politics.* New York, NY: Peter Lang.

Parry-Giles, Trevor and Shawn J. Parry-Giles. 1996. "Political Scopophilia, Presidential Campaigning, and the Intimacy of American Politics," *Communication Studies* 47: 191–205.

Perry, James M. 1979. "To George Bush, Seeking Presidency Seems Almost a Duty," *Wall Street Journal* (July 6): 1.

Petrocik, John R. 1996. "Issue Ownership in Presidential Elections, With a 1980 Case Study," *American Journal of Political Science* 40: 825–850.

Pew Research Center for the People and the Press. 2008. "Growing Doubts About McCain's Judgment, Age and Campaign Conduct." October 21. Pew Research Center. (http://people-press.org/report/?pageid=1408). Retrieved June 29, 2010.

Phillips, Donald T. 2007. *The Clinton Charisma: A Legacy of Leadership.* New York, NY: Palgrave Macmillan.

Pika, Joseph A. and Norman C. Thomas. 1992. "The Presidency Since Mid-Century," *Congress and the Presidency* 19: 33–46.

Pious, Richard M. 1979. *The American Presidency.* New York, NY: Basic Books.

———. 2002. "Why Do Presidents Fail?" *Presidential Studies Quarterly* 32: 724–742.

Polsby, Nelson W. and Aaron Wildavsky. 2008. *Presidential Elections: Strategies and Structures of American Politics.* 12th ed. Lanham, MD: Rowman & Littlefield Publishers.

Pomper, Gerald M. 1968. *Elections in America: Control and Influence in Democratic Politics.* New York, NY: Dodd, Mead & Company.

———. 1975. *Voters' Choice: Varieties of American Electoral Behavior.* New York, NY: Harper & Row.

Popkin, Samuel L. 1991. *The Reasoning Voter: Communication and Persuasion in Presidential Campaigns.* Chicago, IL: The University of Chicago Press.

Prothro, James W. and Charles M. Grigg. 1960. "Fundamental Principles of Democracy: Bases of Agreement and Disagreement," *Journal of Politics* 22: 276–294.

Purdum, Todd S. 2009. "It Came From Wasilla," *Vanity Fair* 51: 92+.

Pyszczynski, Tom, Sheldon Solomon, and Jeff Greenberg. 2003. *In the Wake of 9/11: The Psychology of Terror.* Washington, DC: American Psychological Association.

Rector, Robert and Michael Sanera. 1987. *Steering the Elephant: How Washington Works.* New York, NY: Universe Books.

Renshon, Stanley A. 1995. "Character, Judgment, and Political Leadership: Promise, Problems, and Prospects of the Clinton Presidency," in *The Clinton Presidency: Campaigning, Governing, and the Psychology of Leadership,* ed. Stanley A. Renshon. Boulder, CO: Westview Press, pp. 57–87.

Rich, Frank. 2006. *The Greatest Story Ever Sold: The Decline and Fall of Truth in Bush's America.* New York, NY: Penguin Books.

Ridge, Tom. 2009. *The Test of Our Times: America Under Siege... And How We Can Be Safe Again.* New York, NY: Thomas Dunne Books.

Rimmerman, Craig A. 1993. *Presidency by Plebiscite: The Reagan-Bush Era in Institutional Perspective.* Boulder, CO: Westview Press.

Rittel, Horst J. W. and Mekin M. Webber. 1973. "Dilemmas in a General Theory of Planning," *Policy Sciences* 4: 155–169.

Roberts, Nancy. 2000. "Wicked Problems and Network Approaches to Resolution," *International Public Management Review* 1: 1–19.

Rockman, Bert A. 1988. "The Style and Organization of the Reagan Presidency," in *The Reagan Legacy,* ed. Charles O. Jones. Chatham, NJ: Chatham House, pp. 3–29.

Rockman, Bert A. and Richard W. Waterman. 2008. "Two Normative Models of Presidential Leadership," in *Presidential Leadership: The Vortex of Power,* eds. Bert A. Rockman and Richard W. Waterman. New York, NY: Oxford University Press, pp. 331–347.

Rockwell, Llewellyn. 2003. "George W. Bush," The Free Market 23. (mises.org/freemarket_detail.aspx?control=463). Retrieved October 12, 2009.

Rose, Richard. 1991. *The Postmodern President.* 2nd ed. Chatham, NJ: Chatham House.

Rosenthal, Alan, Burdett A. Loomis, John R. Hibbing, and Karl T. Kurtz. 2002. *Republic on Trial: The Case for Representative Democracy.* Washington, DC: CQ Press.

Rubenstein, Diane. 2008. *This Is Not a President: Sense, Nonsense, and the American Political Imaginary.* New York, NY: New York University Press.

Savage, Charlie. 2006. "Bush Challenges Hundreds of Laws: President Cites Powers of His Office," *Boston Globe* (April 30): A1+.

———. 2007. *Takeover: The Return of the Imperial Presidency and the Subversion of American Democracy.* New York, NY: Little, Brown.

Schachter, Hindy Lauer. 1995. "Reinventing Government or Reinventing Ourselves: Two Models for Improving Government Performance," *Public Administration Review* 55: 530–537.

Scheer, Robert. 1996. "Clinton's the One: There's Already a Republican in the White House," *Pittsburgh Post-Gazette* (August 9): A13.

Schmitt, Eric. 2003. "Rumsfeld Says Dozens of Important Targets Have Been Avoided," *The New York Times* (March 24): 12.

Scully, Sean. 2001. "Bush Embraces Faith-Based Help to Ease Social Ills," *The Washington Times* (January 30): A1.

Senior, Jennifer. 2009. "The Message Is the Message," *New York* 42 (August 10–17). (www.nymag.com/news/politics/58199.) Retrieved January 1, 2010.

Shear, Michael D. 2009. "Government Openness Is Tested by Salahi Case," *The Washington Post* (December 4): C7.

Shenkman, Rick. 2008. *Just How Stupid Are We?: Facing the Truth About the American Voter.* New York, NY: Basic Books.

Sidey, Hugh. 1983. "The Presidency by Hugh Sidey: School Days, Then and Now," *Time* (July 11): 16.

Skowronek, Stephen. 1997. *The Politics Presidents Make: Leadership from John Adams to Bill Clinton.* Cambridge, MA: The Belknap Press of Harvard University Press.

Sloboda, John and Hamit Dardagan. 2004. "Civilian Deaths in 'Noble' Iraq Mission Pass 10,000," Iraq Body Count (February 7). (www.iraqbodycount.org/analysis/beyond/ten-thousand/8). Retrieved October 31, 2010.

Smith, Aaron. 2009. "The Internet's Roles in Campaign 2008," *Pew Internet.* Washington, DC: Pew Internet & American Life Project.

Smith, Fred L., Jr. 1987. "Privatization at the Federal Level," *Proceedings of the Academy of Political Science* 36: 179–189.

Smith, Sam. 1994. *Shadows of Hope: A Freethinker's Guide to Politics in the Time of Clinton.* Bloomington, IN: Indiana University Press.

Spitzer, Robert J. 2006. "The Commander in Chief: Power and Constitutional Invention in the Bush Administration," in *The Presidency and the Challenge of Democracy,* eds. Michael A. Genovese and Lori Cox Han. New York, NY: Palgrave Macmillan, pp. 93–117.

———. 2009. "Bush, the Post-Bush Presidency, and the Constitutional Order," paper presented at the 2009 American Political Science Association Conference, Toronto, Canada.

Stephanopoulos, George. 1999. *All Too Human: A Political Education.* Boston, MA: Little Brown.

Stuckey, Mary E. and Richard Morris. 1998. "The Other Side of Power: Who Is Left Out of Presidential Rhetoric?" in *Presidential Frontiers: Underexplored Issues in White House Politics,* ed. Ryan J. Barilleaux. Westport, CT: Praeger, pp. 179–193.

Sullivan, John L., Amy Fried, and Mary G. Dietz. 1992. "Patriotism, Politics, and the Presidential Election of 1988," *American Journal of Political Science* 36: 200–234.

Suskind, Ron. 2003. "Why Are These Men Laughing?" *Esquire* 139: 96–105.

———. 2004. "Faith, Certainty and the Presidency of George W. Bush," *The New York Times* (October 17): 44.

Susman, Warren I. 1984. *Culture as History: The Transformation of American Society in the Twentieth Century.* New York, NY: Pantheon Books.

Tarpley, Webster Griffin, Bruce Marshall, and Jonathan Mowat. 2008. *Obama: The Postmodern Coup: Making of a Manchurian Candidate.* Joshua Tree, CA: Progressive Press.

Taylor, Ronald A. 1993. "Clinton Hails Plan to 'Fix' Bureaucracy," *The Washington Times* (September 8): A1.

Teixeira, Ruy A. 1992. *The Disappearing American Voter.* Washington, DC: The Brookings Institution.

Thomas, Dan B. and Larry R. Baas. 1982. "Presidential Identification and Mass-Public Compliance with Official Policy: The Case of the Carter Energy Program," *Policy Studies Journal* 10: 448–464.

Thomas, Dan B. and Lee Sigelman. 1984. "Presidential Identification and Policy Leadership," *Policy Studies Journal* 12: 663–675.

Thomas, Dan B., Lee Sigelman, and Larry R. Baas. 1984. "Public Evaluations of the President: Policy, Partisan, and 'Personal' Determinants," *Political Psychology* 5: 531–542.

Tiefer, Charles. 1994. *The Semi-Sovereign Presidency: The Bush Administration's Strategy for Governing Without Congress.* Boulder, CO: Westview Press.

Toffler, Alvin. 1980. *The Third Wave*. New York, NY: Bantam Books.

Tolchin, Susan J. 1999. *The Angry American: How Voter Rage Is Changing the Nation*. 2nd ed. Boulder, CO: Westview Press.

Trippi, Joe. 2008. *The Revolution Will Not Be Televised: Democracy, the Internet, and the Overthrow of Everything*. Rev. ed. New York, NY: Harper.

Van Natta, Don, Jr. 2008. "They Got Game. It Just May Be the Wrong Game," *The New York Times* (April 6): 3.

Vargas, Jose Antonio. 2008. "Politics Is No Longer Local. It's Viral," *The Washington Post* (December 28): B1+.

Von Drehle, David. 2008. "The Five Faces of Barack Obama," *Time* 172 (September 1): 28–34.

Waterman, Richard W., Robert Wright, and Gilbert St. Clair. 1999. *The Image-Is-Everything Presidency: Dilemmas in American Leadership*. Boulder, CO: Westview Press.

Wayne, Stephen J. 1978. *The Legislative Presidency*. New York, NY: Harper & Row.

———. 2008. *The Road to the White House 2008*. 8th ed. Boston, MA: Thomson Wadsworth.

Weaver, William G. and Robert M. Pallitto. 2005. "State Secrets and Executive Power," *Political Science Quarterly* 120: 85–112.

———. 2006. "The Law: 'Extraordinary Rendition' and Presidential Fiat," *Presidential Studies Quarterly* 36: 102–116.

Weisberg, Jacob. 1999. "The Governor-President," *New York Times Magazine* (January 19): 30–35, 41, 52, 65.

Weisman, Steven R. 1981. "President Proposes 83 Major Program Cuts: Tells Congress U.S. Faces Day of Reckoning," *The New York Times* (February 19): A1.

Westen, Drew. 2007. *The Political Brain: The Role of Emotion in Deciding the Fate of the Nation*. New York, NY: Public Affairs.

White, Theodore H. 1961. *The Making of the President 1960*. New York, NY: Atheneum Publishers.

Will, George F. 1990. "It's Not Modesty, It's Arrogance," *The Washington Post* (October 12): A21.

Williams, Walter. 2003. *Reaganism and the Death of Representative Democracy*. Washington, DC: Georgetown University Press.

Wooten, Jim. 2008. "Our Values Reflected in Those of Palin," *The Atlanta Journal-Constitution* (September 7): 14A.

Wrabley, Raymond B. 2008. "Cowboy Capitalism or Welfare Ranching? The Public Lands Grazing Policies of the Bush Administration," *Public Land & Resources Law Review* 29: 85–122.

Yoo, John C. 2003. "Memorandum for William J. Haynes II, General Counsel of the Department of Defense," secret memorandum, declassified March 31, 2008.

Zeleny, Jeff. 2010. "Obama Plans a Joint Summit on Health Care," *The New York Times* (February 8): 1+.

Index

About the Author

John F. Freie is professor of political science at Le Moyne College in Syracuse, New York. He has written a variety of articles in the areas of civic education, technology, education, and electoral behavior that are linked by his concern about democracy. He is author of *Counterfeit Community: The Exploitation of Our Longings for Community*. An optimist, he believes that this is the year the Cubs will win it all.

DATE DUE